80

To Larry
with gratitude and
affection.

JEWISH LAW
IN AMERICAN
TRIBUNALS

JEWISH LAW IN AMERICAN TRIBUNALS

by Bernard J. Meislin

KTAV PUBLISHING HOUSE, INC.

1976

Library of Congress Cataloging in Publication Data

Meislin, Bernard J
    Jewish law in American tribunals.

    Includes bibliographical references and index.
    1. Law—United States—History and criticism.
2. Jewish law. I. Title.
KF358.M44   340'.0973   75-25587
ISBN 0-87068-460-4

To my uncle, Dr. Solomon Grayzel,
who gave me the good fortune to grow
up in the presence of a man to revere.

TABLE OF CONTENTS

PREFACE

JEWISH LAW came to America aboard the Mayflower and the Arbella and struck deep roots in rocky New England. It was the law of the Old Testament, unvarnished and barely changed to fit a "State planted, and growne up . . . like Israel in the wilderness." Colonial Massachusetts was the original American Bible belt.

With the coming of independence and church-state separation, controversy, which still smolders, was sparked over the extent of religious impregnation of law. Can blasphemy be constitutionally prosecuted? Is Sunday a day of rest at common law? To what extent may Jewish observances be protected civilly?

The end of the Colonial period, a decline in Old Testament identification, the new United States and the First Amendment principle of separation led to a dispersal of Jewish law references from the commanding infallibility they had once exercised, graven in stone as they were to the Pilgrims, to a random and desultory presence under the influence of Jeffersonian democracy.

This volume seeks no more than to gather some of those scattered Jewish law references which may be found in American legal writings and introduce a degree of coherence by topic to a number of their American appearances. They have often been cited by bewildered judges following conflicting rabbinic testimony in acrimonious litigations. Their precise role in American law, United States and Canadian, has never been judicially delineated. There is an unease about these references, deriving from their undoubted rightful place, historically and culturally, along with their Puritan sponsors, on the American scene at the same time that they stir considerations of constitutional separation. There is an accompanying uncertainty whether Jewish law is religious law or cognizable as foreign law, puzzlement over great issues of relations between law and morality, between legal writs and Holy Writ, and, as no judge likes to admit, Jewish law references are often simply not understood.

IX

Those Jewish law references in their American legal appearance which have been collected in this volume by no means are intended as an exhaustive, definitive *corpus juris*. They have been assembled by general topic as loose groupings of related subjects. But many promising lines of investigation were dropped when a Jewish law reference did not fit into a readily expandable category. Other leads were intriguing but legal tracking lost the spoor before successful focus could be fixed on the quarry. Stray references were noted "subject to being connected up," such as a quotation from Isaiah in Control Data Corporation's brief in its suit against IBM when settlement was reached between them,[1] but no Jewish "connection" was made. Similarly, a court's resort to the Bible piques interest in a trademark infringement case concerning the exclusive use of the Hebrew word, "Hadar,"[2] and a judge's reliance on Genesis to define the scope of sodomy in a criminal prosecution[3] also fascinates, but no direct Jewish law applications are involved. Perhaps, a future volume will tie together such loose ends and more. Some of the omitted Jewish law references appear in articles previously published.

I cannot adequately express my indebtedness to my uncle, Dr. Solomon Grayzel, whose encouragement and invaluable suggestions guided the course of my research and whose editorial comments shaped its content. From the first article, written in collaboration with Professor Morris Cohen, Law Librarian of the Harvard Law School, on a Jewish law theme ("Backgrounds of the Biblical Law Against Usury," published in *Comparative Studies in Society and History*, Vol. VI, No. 3) over ten years ago, Dr. Grayzel's assistance has been invigorating and supportive.

To Professor Edward M. Gershfield of the Jewish Theological Seminary, I owe the suggestion to combine and revise various published and unpublished studies in book form under the KTAV Publishing House imprint. To Stewart Wahrsager, Esq., I am indebted for his suggestions in connection with the chapter on Kashruth. Particularly, he recommended areas of investigation and expanded footnote material. The Master's project of Isaac Nathan Tuchman on *Jewish Law and Custom and The Courts of New York State*, submitted in 1971 to the Bernard Revel Graduate School, also provided valuable source material and for this assistance, I am grateful to the author.

For access to unpublished legal material relating to cases concerning Jewish law in which the late Louis Gribetz, Esq. participated, I am deeply in debt to Lester Lyons, Esq., who acted "of counsel" to him in his active and committed legal career.

Of all the varied sources of Jewish law references in American proceedings, the work of Professors Daniel J. Elazar and Stephen R. Goldstein which appears in Volume 73 of the *American Jewish Year Book 1972*, published by the Jewish Publication Society, entitled "The Legal Status of the American Jewish Community," has been frequently drawn upon and proved especially valuable.

Grateful acknowledgement is made to the several publications from which material originally published in article form has been adapted for inclusion in this book: To Cambridge University Press, publisher of *Comparative Studies in Society and History* and to the Society for the Comparative Study of Society and History for permission to reprint from my article, "Parallels Between Talmudic and New York Usury Laws," Vol. IX, No. 1 (October, 1966); to the Editorial Board of the *Israel Law Review*, for permission to republish excerpts from my article, "Jewish Law in American Tribunals," *Israel Law Review*, Vol. 7, No. 3 (July, 1972); and to the *Journal of Family Law* and Fred B. Rothman & Co. for permission to reprint from my article, "Jewish Law of Marriage in American Courts," *Journal of Family Law*, Vol. 11, No. 2 (1971). To all three publications and their publishers, I express my thanks.

Thankful appreciation is also extended to the Jewish Community Center of Summit, New Jersey and Rabbi William Horn, its leader, for providing a forum and environment in which the pleasant exchange of useful ideas was vigorously pursued. My deepest thanks are also extended to my Canadian legal researcher, Eric Gross, and my research assistants, Amy Pollack and Nancy Siegel. My copy editor, Ruth Stein, has been patient, meticulous, unflagging and gracious throughout an exacting assignment. My publisher has been extremely indulgent in holding proof open to the very last moment to allow the reporting of the most curent judicial developments. Above all, my wife, Zelda, has been an unfailing source of encouragement and assistance during the book's progress.

June 30, 1975

NOTES TO PREFACE

1. In an outbreak of unrestrained conciliation the brief submitting the settlement recites in full Isaiah, Chapter 2, Verse 4. *New York Times*, Feb. 1, 1973, 49, col. 2.

2. *Erba Food Products v. Rokeach & Son, N.Y.L.J.* Jan. 13, 1975, 15, col. 1. The plaintiff, a distributor of various food items under the "Haddar" label, was not entitled to an injunction to prevent defendant from marketing a line of imported baked goods under the "Hadar" label. The court held the term to be of general description. "Despite plaintiff's unexplained insistence before the Patent Office that 'Haddar' is the Hebrew word of 'the generation' (see, Trial Transcript, p. 314), both parties agree that both 'Hadar' and 'Haddar' are transliterations of the Hebrew word meaning 'beauty' or 'quality' (Trial transcript, pp. 168-9, 174, 184, 205, 252). The word appears in the Bible with such meaning in Leviticus, 23:40 ('On the first day you shall take the fruit of goodly trees'), Isaiah, 53:2 ('He had no form nor comeliness that we should look upon him'), Psalms, 96:6 ('Strength and beauty are in His sanctuary') and Proverbs, 20:29 ('The beauty of old men is the grey head') (see, also, Ben Yehuda, Thesaurus of the Hebrew Language, Vol. II, p. 1046)."

3. People *ex rel* Farr v. Mancusi, 335 N.Y.S. 2d. 161, 163. (1972).

1·

THE COLONIAL PERIOD

Thy statutes have been my songs
in the house of my pilgrimage

Psalms: 119:54

WITH THE DEVOUT resolution of the zealots they were, the Puritan settlers of Massachusetts, both in Plymouth and Massachusetts Bay Colonies, deliberately chose as their governing legal systems the laws of the ancient Hebrews. Not since the Second Temple's destruction more than fifteen hundred years before, save in their spiritual forerunner, Calvin's Geneva,[1] had there existed a political state whose everyday laws derived from Old Testament codes and whose internal government was theocratic. Any examination of Jewish law's influence on American society is drawn inevitably to the colonizers of Plymouth and Massachusetts Bay. For them, as for the Sadducees,[2] the unalloyed "sermones" and teachings of Moses were the regulators of conduct. They sought to strip from the basic law those "wicked and profane Incroachments" which gather about "even lawes themselves by long tract of time" [3]

1

and to purify society through return to Scripture. The incubator
of Puritanism was the England of the Reformation's aftermath
and the Puritans were the radicals of reform seeking a return to
unadulterated Holy Writ.

During the century preceding the Puritan Revolution, and
before the readmission of Jews to its shores, agitation for law
reform marked England's history. At the start of the seventeenth
century the complexities of English law are reflected in Lord
Edward Coke's works.[4] In *Coke on Littleton,*[5] the author described
fifteen separate "divers lawes within the realme of England," including "the law of the crowne," the law of parliament, the law of
nature, "customes reasonable," the law of "armes, war, and chival-
rie," ecclesiastical or canon law, civil law "in the courts of the
constable and marshall, and of the admiraltie," forest law, "the
law of marque or reprisal," "lex mercatoria, merchant, etc." Although Coke saw "admirable benefit, beauty and delectable variety"[6] in the law's diversity, proposals for reform came from
lawyers as close to King James as Francis Bacon and as celebrated
as Matthew Hale, as well as from radical Puritan reformers. The
influence of the latter directly affected Colonial America, especially
the Puritan settlements of New England.

The radical Puritans based their proposals for model legal
systems directly on Scripture, particularly the Old Testament.
Observable correspondences between Puritan codes and Jewish
law interpretations are all the more striking for the absence of
any direct personal Jewish participation. Not a single Jew had
resided openly in England from the time of exile in 1290.[7] Prior
to banishment, Jewish law influences on many aspects of common
law, particularly commercial transactions, were considerable. Mort-
gages, recognizances, general releases, and certain warranties had
their origin in Jewish law sources.[8] But after 1290 these influences
subsided to the point where major legal historians could express
honest doubt

> Whether the sojourn of the Jews in England left any
> permanent marks upon the body of our law . . . we can hardly
> suppose that from Lex Judaica, the Hebrew Law which the
> Jews administered among themselves, anything passed into
> the code of the contemptuous Christians. But that the in-

ternational Lex Judaismi perished in 1290 without leaving any memorial of itself, is by no means so certain.[9]

But there can be no question of the exalted status of the Old Testament to Puritanism. It stood sublime and nonpareil, inviting the believer to invoke its codes as correctives for the abuses of an age awash in religious dissensions. *Examen Legum Angliae,*[10] attributed to A. Booth, published in 1656, makes proposals representative of the Puritan mind which held intellectual sway over the New England Colonies of the same period. After criticizing Coke's reverence for Littleton and his praise of "Fifteen sorts of Laws, which, he saith, are in force in England," the author reflects "then is the Law such an *Individuum vagum,* as no man living knows what it is, in respect of the variance and alteration thereof, from what it was in former times . . . the Judges themselves (who are said to be the speaking Law) in many cases are divided, and Truth itself is oft-times set upon the Tenters, for want of a standing Rule, and because the Law lies merely in Opinion, without other Foundation. . . ."[11] This uncertainty may be cured, according to *Examen Legum Angliae,* by a return to "the Law of God contained in the Holy Scriptures." Claimed as authority for its beneficent practical impact is King Alfred's allegedly successful secular imposition of Mosaic law, late in the ninth century. Alfred's laws purportedly begin with an acknowledgment of the divine nature of Moses'

> sermones . . . and so recites the Decalogue, and then proceeds to mention the most material Laws set down in the 20, 21, 22 and 23 Chapters of Exodus, which he affirms to be the most apt and compatible for the Government of his Kingdome: and according to his Laws, his Government was blessed with universal Peace and Quiet, above other Kings of this Nation: There being neither Thieves nor Robbers to molest the People.

This rosy vision of an idealized past recommended to the author of *Examen Legum Angliae* the wisdom of expanding the application of Biblical Law to the polity of the England of his own day:

> Now not only the Decalogue, but also the Judicial Laws of Moses, are an eminent Foundation of Politick Laws, holding

forth plainly the Reason of Commanding and Prohibiting. Of these Judicial Laws, some belonged to the Jews properly, as being appendent to the ceremonial Law, as the punishment of him that touched a dead body; others concerned the Jews Commonwealth in their own Land, as that concerning the year of Jubilee, etc. The rest are Laws of Common Justice and Equity, belonging to the Moral Law, as Expositions thereof, as the punishment of Murther, and Adultery, etc. with death. These, as many others . . . were given to the Jews as men, and did not only bind the Conscience of the Jews, but also of the Gentiles: and as the Morall Law is principally grounded upon the Law of Nature; so these Judicial Laws (called by Moses Judgements) flowed from the same Fountain, and necessarily declared the punishments for the breach of the Moral Law, which are not therein expressed.[12]

In comparison to the Laws of Moses, which the author owns to have been the original source of the laws of the Saxons, Danes and Normans, the laws of contemporary England had become polluted by accretions from "the Roman Clergie, or rather Idolatrous Priests, being Chancellors, Judges, Reporters, Scribes and Compilers of our Laws." These interlopers added many "Heathenish, Impious, Superstitions, and wicked Customes, and imposed the same upon the poor conquered and enslaved People, for Laws." Their additions are "like the Statutes of Omri and Ahab," [13] idolatrous abominations superimposed on the pure laws of Moses.

Accommodating the Law of Moses through Legislation

What is the proper accommodation of Mosaic law and contemporary society? This was the issue the seventeenth-century Puritan law reformers faced, both in England and in the American Colonies. The Massachusetts colonists saw themselves as spiritual heirs to the Israelites and favored a close correspondence between those laws adaptable for their governance and those of the Pentateuch. Sir Matthew Hale, the Lord Chief Justice of England, on the other hand, reflected conservative episcopal opinion in his "Considerations Touching the Amendment or Alteration of Lawes" when he wrote,[14]

Since all human laws are imperfect, and only the counsells and determinations of Almighty God are perfect, why then may we not take a short compendious course, and take in the judicials given by God by the hand of Moses, and so avoid that inconvenience of the imperfections of human lawes, the positive judicial law of Almighty God being substituted in the place of all other human lawes, and all human lawes abrogated and exterminated? . . . Although the moral law, or the law of the two tables, were materially universal both in respect of extent and duration . . . yet the judicial lawes, as likewise the ritual or ceremonial, were never in the design of Almighty God intended farther than that people to whom they were given, and no longer possibly to that people than the state of that republic continued . . . Let any man but consider the judicials given to the Hebrews, he will find them in a special manner accommodated and attempered to the state of that people, which would not be apposite to the state of another people; as some of their judicials, that referred to the distributions of their possessions, to their discrimination from the rest of mankind, to the redemption of their possessions and keeping them within their tribes, to their late state of captivity amongst the Egyptians, and the extermination of their practices used in Egypt.

The Pilgrims, however, identified closely with the Hebrews of Exodus. They were akin to a people lately released from captivity, discriminated from the rest of mankind and anxious to extirpate certain practices acquired from those among whom they had recently dwelt. They thought of Massachusetts Bay as "this our Israel." [15] The Priestly Code[16] was "in a special manner accommodated and attempered to the state of that people." Thus the author of *Examen Legum Angliae* could seriously propose for a seventeenth-century state a series of laws based on Scripture, with no hesitancy whatever:

A Post-Script

Containing sundry Positions, founded upon the holy Scriptures, serving for principal grounds of Laws amongst Christians

Many things are to be judged according to the discretion
of the judges with reference to the Law of God, and such
Judgments not to be accounted Arbitrary, much less to favour
of tyrannical Government, Exod. 21, 22, 30, 35. Numb. 27.8
I Kings 2.44. and 3.16, 25, 27. . . .

That for felonies of Goods, or Cattle stollen, the Thief
not to suffer death, but to make restitution, according to Gods
Law, as the case shall be, and be bounden to serve in case
he cannot satisfie. Prov. 6.30.31. Exo. 22. 1.7.4.7. Job 20. 15. 18.
2 Sam. 12.6. Luk. 19.8. . . .

That no man to be convicted in any case Capital, but by
the Testimony of two witnesses at least. Deut. 17.6. 2 Cor. 13.1.
Heb. 10.28. Numb. 35.30.

That a single witness shall convict no man, in any case
without other proof, or evincing circumstances, Deut. 19. 15.
18. John 8.17. and 5.31. Math. 18.16. 2 Cor. 13.1.

That a perjured, or malitious false witnesse shall suffer
the same punishment, or losse, which his false Testimony regu-
larly should cause another to suffer, and the suborner of
Perjury in like manner, Dan. 6.24 Deut. 19.18. 19.21. Prov.
19.5. . . .

All estates of inheritance, are to be Estates in Fee simple,
and no Intails upon the Heirs Males, Numb. 27. 7.8. I Tim. 5.8.
Gen. 23. 11, 17.20.

All estates with the Owners Pedegree, are to be Inrolled
in some convenient known place, for avoiding strife and
contention, Jer. 32.11.12. Josh. 14.14.15. Josh. 18.8.9. Ezra
2.62. . . .

The eldest Son not being guilty of any Notorious offence,
ought to have a double portion,[17] Deut. 21. 17. I Kings 2.15.
Gen. 25.33. and 48.22.

All younger children to have parts of their Parents
Estates, according to their deserts, and as the Estate will bear,
Gen. 25.6. Luke 15.12. Josh. 14.14.15. . . .

Schooles of learning are to be maintained, and godly
learned men to be countenanced and encouraged, Acts 19.9.
I Kings 18.4. I Sam. 19.20. . . .

That such as run in Debt, shall have their estates sold,
to pay their Debts, he that hath nothing to pay, not to be

imprisoned for Debt, 2 Kings 4.7. Exo. 22.26, 27. Luke 6.35. and 7.42. Math. 18. 25, 27, 33, 34. . . .

That no Counsel be retained for any Suters, but that the Pleaders be rewarded by the State, and be sworn as assistants to the Judges, as indifferent men to endeavour to finde out the truth, and not to obscure, or overthrow it, Exo. 23.2 Lam. 3.35, 36. Judges 19.30 and Judges 20.7, 8 Numb. 22.7, 17.2 2 Pet. 2.15. Acts 24.5. . . .

That the circumstances and equity of every Cause be weighed together with the Justice, and matter of fact, and Judgement to be given accordingly, Isa. 59.13, 14, 15. 2 Sam. 8, 15. Josh. 7. 11, 25. . . .

That the Oaths of two, or more witnesses may be a sufficient conviction in Law, without any Indictment, Deut. 17.6. and 19.15. Math. 18.16. 2 Cor. 13.1. . . .

That all Suits and controversies, although popular, or Criminal, be determined, upon hearing witnesses sworn, and giving evidence on both parts as well as for the party accused, as the Commonwealth, and in cases where there are no witnesses, that the accused's own voluntary Oath be taken for his discharge, Exod. 22.9.10,11. 1 Kings 8.31. Job 29.16. Acts 26.5. Isa. 43. 9,10.

That there be Judicatories, and Courts established in every Citie and County, where the Judges may sit constantly in open places to hear, and determine all controversies, Exod. 18.13,25,26. Deut. 21.19. Prov. 31,23. and 25.7. Ruth. 4, 1, 2, 9. . . .

That the Process in all Cases of Suite, be onely a Summons, which being duely served, if the Defendant refuse to appear, or shew not sufficient cause to the contrary, the Plaintiff may proceed to his proof, and so to hearing, or trial, as if the Defendant had appeared, Numb. 16.11.14.28.32. Deut. 25.8. Hest. I. 10.11.19.21.

That no man have final judgment against him by default without proof in any Case, be it never so small, unless the party accused do at the time of the Judgement openly confess the fact, Numb. 35.30. Deut. 17.6. I Kings 8.31. . . .

That the body of the Law may be collected into a volume, that it may be known to the Supream Magistrate, and to

the Judges, and the people, I Sam. 10.25. Deut. 17.18.19. Exod.
20. from verse 3 to the 9. verse of Chap. 23. Hester 1.19.

What is of greater surprise, and of lasting imprint on American history, is the adoption of many of the projected reforms as
practical Colonial legislation. The Puritans in Plymouth counted
among their number many Separatists from the Anglican church
who took literally Calvin's injunction that Mosaic law should govern
political society.[18] They adopted the first Colonial code in 1636.
Their neighbors in Massachusetts Bay Colony followed them in
congregationalism as well as in favoring codification,[19] and in Puritan piety yielded to no man. A tracing of the law's development
in Massachusetts Bay Colony typifies the high-water marks and
subsequent receding of Old Testament law influences in both
Colonies. In 1641 the Body of Liberties was officially adopted by the
General Court as a set of fundamental propositions in the manner
of a constitution for Massachusetts Bay Colony. Its predecessor,
and competitor for official recognition, had been a draft law code
prepared by John Cotton, a Puritan minister. The General Court in
1636 named Cotton, together with two other ministers, to a
commission "to make a draught of laws agreeable to the word
of God, which may be the fundamentals of this Commonwealth, and
to present the same to the next General Court." [20] It is likely
Cotton was influenced by the Plymouth Laws codified contempo-
raneously in that neighboring Colony. But the overriding influence
in both compendia was the conviction of Calvin that the Pentateuch
was the true source of law for the regulation of mankind.

The records of the General Court fail to show that the commission's labors resulted in a draft code; however John Cotton
presented the fruit of his sole labors, "a copy of Moses his judicials,
compiled in an exact method." [21] This draft code, together with one
by Nathaniel Warde, was circulated in every town. Eventually in
1641, Warde's work, the Body of Liberties, was officially accepted.

Both *Moses his Judicials* and the Body of Liberties "put the
law of God into a statutory form." [22] Typical are the following selec-
tions from the former work: [23]

All magistrates are to be chosen. Deut. I. 13,17,15.
First, By the free burgesses

Secondly, Out of the free burgesses

Thirdly, Out of the ablest men and most approved
amonst them. Ex. 18,21.

Fourthly, Out of the rank of noblemen or gentlemen among
them, the best that God shall send into the country; if
they be qualified with gifts fit for government, either
eminent above others, or not inferior to others. Eccle.
10.17. Jer. 30.21. . . .

And because these great affairs of state cannot be attended or
administered, if they be after changed; therefore the counsel-
lors are to be chosen for life, unless they give just cause of
removal, which if they do, then they are to be removed by the
general court. Kings 2.4.

Of Crimes. And first, of such as deserve capital punishment, or cutting off from a man's people, whether by
death or banishment.

First, blasphemy, which is a cursing of God by atheism or the
like, to be punished with death . . . To worship God in a
molten or graven image, to be punished with death . . .

Murder, which is wilful man-slaughter, not in a man's just
defense, nor casually committed, but out of hatred or cruelty,
to be punished with death. Ex. 21, 12, 13, Num. 35.16, 17, 18,
to 33. Gen. 9.6. . . .

Of other crimes less heinous, such as are to be punished
with some corporal punishment or fine . . .

Drunkeness, as transforming God's image into a beast, is to
be punished with the punishment of beasts: a whip for the
horse, a rod for the fool's back . . .

If any man steal a beast, if it be found in his hand he shall
make restitution two for one; if it be killed and sold, restitution is to be made of five oxen for one; if the thief be not able
to make restitution, then he is to be sold by the magistrate
for a slave, till by his labour he may make due restitution. Ex.
22. 1, 4 . . .

The Body of Liberties reduced John Cotton's list of capital
crimes from seventeen to twelve, but this represented no fundamental change, the principal cause of the reduction stemming from
Warde's exclusion from capital offenses those punishable by banish-

ment. Warde included provisions granting individual rights, and attempted to soften some harsher provisions of "God's law." For example; "No man shall be beaten with about 40 stripes, nor shall any true gentleman, nor any man equal to a gentleman be punished with whipping, unless his crime be very shameful, and his course of life vicious and profligate." [24] But, essentially, the Body of Liberties incorporated Old Testament laws into a code which regulated justice for a functioning seventeenth-century New England society.

Hebrew Authority Applied to Disputes

The laws of the Hebrews were not only codified but Old Testament citations and examples were the ultimate authority for the settlement of every vexing issue from petty litigation to political quandaries. *Sherman v. Keayne*, as reported in Governor John Winthrop's summary,[25] is a case law example. The case was important historically for it led to legislation establishing once and for all a bicameral legislature for Massachusetts; which in turn served as a model for later widespread imitation. But the litigation itself concerned the attempted recovery of damages for a lost pig. The plaintiff's wife and attorney, Goody Sherman, "pursued the alleged converter through all but one of the principal courts of the Colony of Massachusetts Bay," [26] and while successful in persuading a majority of the General Court and of the Deputies (being one of the representative bodies comprising the General Court), she failed to win over the other representative body, the Magistrates. Her case was lost when the General Court dissolved without a conclusive decision. This led to clarifying legislation and "it is as the mother of Senates that Goody Sherman's sow has achieved immortality." [27]

Winthrop's summary of the General Court proceedings weighed the testimony pro and con, and while finding "probable evidence" in plaintiff's favor, concluded, on balance, that if all the testimony be true "It is not possible the defendant should be guiltye or anye of these Sowes the plaintiffs." In support of the conclusion reached that "probable evidence" may turn out to be at odds with the facts, Winthrop turns to Genesis: [28]

For Instance

Joseph wanders alone in the wilderness his coate is found
torne and bloudie, he is never heard off for manye yeares: upon
this probable evidence, Jacob concludes that Joseph was de-
vowred of a wilde beast: But when evidence of a certaintye
comes out of Aegipt that he was then alive, and Lord of Egypt
the former evidence was invailed and the Spirit of Jacob re-
vived, and now he concludes he was living: though he knewe
not how he should come thither, or how he should be soe
advansed there. Now lett anye impartiall hande hold the Scales
while Religion and sound reason give Judgment in the case.

Thorny political issues also yield to skillful application of Old
Testament remedial examples. Following Goody Sherman's defeat
the thwarted Deputies raised a clamor "for such a body of laws,
with prescript penalties in all cases, as nothing might be left to
the discretion of the magistrates . . ." [29] Governor Winthrop opposed
the notion of fixed and arbitrary remedies to cover every contin-
gency and in a tract entitled "Arbitrary Government" [30] he undertook to adduce scriptural authority in support of magisterial
discretion. He cites example upon example of Old Testament
flexibility in the administration of justice as his answer to the
Deputies call for "prescript and certain penalties": [31]

. . . in prescript penalties authority shoots at adventure: if
the same penalty hits a rich man, it pains him not, it is not
affliction to him, but if it lights upon a poor man, it breakes his
back.
　　Every law must be just in every part of it, but if the
penalty annexed be unjust, how can it be held forth as a just
law? To prescribe a penalty, must be by some rule, otherwise, it
is an usurpation of Gods prerogative: but where the law
makers, or declarers cannot find a rule for prescribing a
penalty, if it come before the judges *pro re nata*, there it is
determinable by a certain rule, viz: by an ordinance set up of
God for that purpose, which hath a sure promise of divine
assistance, Exo: 21: 22, Deut: 16: 18: Judges and officers
shalt those make etc. and they shall judge the people with just

judgment: Deut: 25: 1: 2: and 17: 9: 10: 11. If a law were
made that if any man were found drunken he should be
punished by the judges according to the merit of his offence:
this is a just law, because it is warranted by a rule: but if
a certain penalty were prescribed, this would not be just,
because it wants a rule, but when such a case is brought before
the judges and the quality of the person and other circumstances considered, they shall find a rule to judge by; as if
Naball, and Uriah and one of the strong drunkards of Ephraim
were all 3 together accused before the judges for drunkenness,
they could so proportion their several sentences, according to
the several natures and degrees of their offences, as a just and
divine sentence might appear in them all: for a divine sentence is in the lips of the King his mouth transgresseth not in
judgment Pro: 16: 10: but no such promise was ever made to
a paper sentence of human authority or invention. . . .

Prescript penalties take away the use of admonition,
which is also a divine sentence and an ordinance of God,
warranted by Scripture: as appears in Solomons Admonition
to Adonijah and Nehemiahs to those that brake the Sabbath:
Eccl: 12: 11: 12: The Words of the wise are as goads, and
as nailes fastened by the masters of Assembly—by these (my
son) be admonished, Pro: 19: 1: Isay. 11: 4: Pro. 17: 10:
A Reproofe entereth more into a wise man, then 100 stripes
into a foole.

Judges are Gods upon earth: [32] therefore, in their admini-
strations, they are to hold forth the wisdom and mercy of God,
(which are his attributes) as well as his justice: as occasion
shall require, either in respect of the quality of the person or
for a more general good; or evident repentance, in some
cases of less public consequence, or avoiding imminent danger
to the state, and such like prevalent considerations. Exo: 22:
8:9: for theft and other like trespasses, double restitution was
appointed by the law: but Lev: 6: 2: 5: in such cases, if the
party confessed his sin, and brought his offering, he should
only restore the principal, and add a fifth part thereto. Adultery
and incest deserved death, by the law, in Jacobs time (as
appears by Juda his sentence, in the case of Thamar): yet
Ruben was punished only with loss of his birthright, because

he was a Patriot. David his life was not taken away for his adultery and murder, (but he was otherwise punished) in respect of public interest and advantage, he was valued at 10,000 common men: Bathsheba was not put to death for her adultery, because the kings desire, had with her, the force of a law. Abiathar was not put to death for his treason, because of his former good service and faithfulness. Shemei was reprived for a time, and had his pardon in his own power, because of his profession of repentence in such a season. Those which brake the Sabbath in Nehemiah his time, were not put to death but first admonished, because the state was not settled etc. Joab was not put to death for his murders, in David's time, for avoiding imminent public danger, the sons of Zeruiah had the advantage of David, by their interest in the men of War: and the Commonwealth could not spare them. But if judges be tied to a prescript punishment, and no liberty left for dispensation or mitigation in any case, here is no place left for wisdom or mercy: whereas Solomon saith Pro: 20: 28: mercy and truth preserve the King; and his throne is upholden by mercy.

I would know by what rule we may take upon us, to prescribe penalties, where God prescribes none.

The Body of Liberties of 1641 gave way to the Laws and Liberties of 1648, a more sophisticated code which introduced a greater number of common law procedures than were found in the earlier compendium. This reconciliation with the laws of England marked a shift away from efforts at almost exclusive reliance on scripture, but the change was gradual and justified in Old Testament terms.

Puritan Laws and English Authority

Although the original charter of incorporation of Massachusetts Bay Colony provided that the Great and General Court was empowered from time to time "to make, ordain, and establish all manner of wholesome orders, laws, statutes and ordinances, directions and instructions not contrary to the laws of this our realm of England," and, in another passage, "so such laws and ordinances be not contrary or repugnant to the laws and statutes of our realm of England," [33] the Puritans laid great stress on a significant omission from their charter which was present in those issued to other groups of overseas settlers. The difference lay in the absence of those customary clauses indicating that the governing authority of the corporation was to remain in England.[34] The omission has been deemed intentional by historians, for if the clauses reserving England's authority had been included in the Massachusetts charter a number of leaders of the venture would never have set sail.[35]

At any rate, the Massachusetts settlers took full advantage of their independence, and were strengthened in their resolve to cut away those "abuses and corruptions, and wens and excrescences, and delays and formalities and exactions" [36] which much of the common law represented to them. Adding to their free rein was the decision of the Commissioners for Plantations that they would not hear appeals from the Colonial courts. One commentator [37] has written:

> It would probably be an exaggeration to suggest that it was a central purpose of the Massachusetts Puritans to abandon the whole of the common law, but certainly it was their intention to let their own law develop without special regard to the technicalities of the law of England.

The introductory Epistle to the Laws and Liberties of 1648 still retains the Old Testament flavor of the earlier Body of Liberties, even as the substantive provisions of the code itself borrow increasingly from the common law. The Epistle begins: [38]

> To our Beloved Brethren and Neighbours the Inhabitants of the Massachusetts, the Governour, Assistants and Deputies assembled in the General Court of that Jurisdiction with grace and peace in our Lord Jesus Christ: So soon as God had set up Politicall Government among his people Israel hee gave them a body of lawes for judgment both in civil and criminal causes. These were brief and fundamental principles, yet withall so full and comprehensive as out of them clear deductions were to be drawne to all particular cases in future

times. For a Commonwealth without lawes is like a Ship without rigging and steeradge. Nor is it sufficient to have principales or fundamentalls, but these are to be drawn out into so many of their deductions as the time and condition of that people may have use of. And it is very unsafe & injurious to the body of the people to put them to learn their duty and libertie from generall rules, nor is it enough to have lawes except they be also just. Therefore among other priviledges which the Lord bestowed upon his peculiar people, these he calls them specially to consider of, that God was nearer to them and their lawes were more righteous than other nations, God was sayd to be amongst them or near to them because of his Ordnances established by himselfe, and their lawes righteous because himselfe was their Law-giver; . . . But the nations corrupting his Ordinances (both of Religion, and Justice) God withdrew his presence from them proportionably whereby they were given up to abominable lusts. Rom. 2.21. Whereas if they had walked according to that light & law of nature they might have been preserved from such moral evils and might have injoyed a common blessing in all their natural and civil Ordinances; now, if it might have been so with the nations who were so much strangers to the Covenant of Grace, what advantage have they who have interest in this Covenant, and may injoye the special presence of God in the puritie and native simplicitie of all his Ordinances by which he is so near to his owne people. This hath been no small priviledge, and advantage to us in New England that our Churches, and civil State have been planted, and growne up (like two twinnes) together like that of Israel in the wildernes by which wee were put in minde (and had opportunitie put into our hands) not only to gather our Churches, . . . but also withall to frame our civil Politie, and lawes according to the rules of his most holy word whereby each do help and strengthen the other (the Churches the civil Authoritie, and the Civil Authoritie the Churches) and so both prosper the better without such aemulation, and contention for priviledges or priority as have proved the misery (if not ruine) of both in some other places.

The Epistle reviews the legal history of the Colony, recalling Cotton's "modell of the Judiciall Lawes of Moses," the subsequent Body of Liberties which "after three years experience & generall approbation" required amendment, and continues somewhat defensively,[39]

> For if it be no disparagement to the wisedome of that High Court of Parliament in England that in four hundred years they could not so compile their lawes, and regulate proceedings in Courts of justice &c: but that they had still new work to do of the same kinde almost every Parliament: there can be no just cause to blame a poor Colonie (being unfurnished of Lawyers and Statesmen) that in eighteen years hath produced no more, nor better rules for a good, and settled Government then this Book holds forth:

Doubts about the practicability of an exclusive resort to Biblicism had begun to creep into Puritan thinking. The substantive provisions of the 1648 code contained many more common law provisions and procedures than the Body of Liberties.[40]

Toward the latter part of the seventeenth century, there was a noticeable cooling of Puritan ardor and the influence of Biblical law had gone into decline. More and more cases leaned toward the common law for guidance. The Restoration in England, the influence of great common law judges like Matthew Hale, internal dissensions, and, above all, a growing adaptation to peculiarly local conditions, all served to temper the ideal vision of directly transplanting ancient Hebrew law in virgin purity to New England.

But in their ascendance, the Massachusetts Colonies, seeking to apply and execute Biblical law, wrestled with many of the same issues that rabbis and scholars had disputed for centuries.

Analogies between Puritan and Hebrew Legal Attitudes

Governor Winthrop's disagreement with the Deputies who sought prescribed penalties and a limitation on magisterial discretion is a paradigm of the same division between liberal and strict constructionists, between equity and law, between reform and orthodoxy, between the schools of Hillel and Shammai that has characterized law from antiquity.[41]

Hebrew and Puritan alike claimed a special relationship to the Old Testament. Both exercised an ingrained familiarity with, and stood in awe of, the Pentateuch. Certain legal questions, peculiar to Puritan radical reform, have their counterparts in Talmudic deliberations and debates. A particular sensitivity marked any allusion to "law." John Cotton called his draft code, "Moses his Judicials" and the Massachusetts Bay Colony's first official code was called "The Body of Liberties." The word "law" was assiduously avoided, except with regard to crimes extracted in definition and penalty almost verbatim from the Bible. "Laws" without Scriptural pedigree are not really laws. As the author of the preface to a 1655 legal compendium wrote,[42]

> And if thou possibly meetest with some rules, to which no scriptures are annexed for proof (as in the 2d and 3d chapters, and some sections in the 4th, 5th and 9th chapters) consider, that these are not properly laws, but prudential rules, which he (the compiler) commended to that colony, to be ratified with the common assent of the freemen in each town, or by their representatives in the general court, as public contracts. Which being once made and assented to for their own convenience, do bind as covenants do, until by like public consent they be abrogated and made void. For though the author attribute the word (law) into some of them; yet, that it was not his meaning they should be enacted as laws (if you take the word *law* in a proper sense) appears by his conclusion, taken out of Isaiah 33. 22. The Lord is our Judge, the Lord is our Law giver, the Lord is our King, he will save us.

We may compare this attitude with the "Interdict on Writing Down,"[43] the opinion that it was forbidden to commit to writing the Jewish oral law, the rabbinic Biblical commentaries. The Palestinian Amora (Expositor) Johanan bar Nappaha in the third century wrote "he who writes down Halakoth is as one who commits the Torah to flames."[44] In a version presented by an Amora of the fifth century,[45]

> Moses was desirous that the Mishna should be written down likewise. God, however, foresaw that the nations would in

time translate the Torah into Greek and read it in Greek and
then say: "We are Israel." Therefore God said to him: "Were
I to write for them (the Israelites) the whole abundance of
My law, they would be accounted as the strangers." Now,
however, the Mishna is the secret of God, and the Lord makes
His secret known only to them that fear Him (Ps. 25.14).

The impulse to keep the Bible pure for His People is recurrent.
In another formulation,

> God gave them (Israel) the oral law, that by this they might
> be distinguished from the other nations. Hence it was not
> given in writing, or else the other nations would falsify it,
> as they have dealt with the written Torah, and then say that
> they were Israel.

The distinction between Puritan shying from "law" and early
rabbinic reluctance to commit post-Biblical law to writing is that
whereas the Puritans so revered Scripture they would not dignify
any variance from it with the word "law," Jewish motives may be
variously ascribed to reverence for the divinity of the commentary
itself, and a concern that its reduction to writing for public use
would endanger the unity of Judaism.[46] Written commentary was
likely to preserve contradictory opinion and to freeze for all time
rules applicable to a particular day and age.[47]

Similarity of outlook also marked Puritan and Jewish attitudes
toward a favorite legal subject, the division of law and equity.
In England, principles of equity and the system of equity courts
sprang from a need to supplement common law inadequacies. The
authority appealed to for redress was the conscience of the King,
initially the line of ecclesiastical chancellors who acted as con-
fessors to the King, the keepers of the conscience of England.[48]
It was the chancellor, and later the chancery courts which were
charged with the duty of remedying the shortcomings of "an age
when the common law developed strong liking for technicality for
its own sake."[49] The Puritans found the separation of law and
equity particularly galling, "conscience" to them being the heart
of the law. *Examen Legum Angliae*[50] devotes a chapter to the
proposition

That there ought not to be a Court of Law or Justice, and another of Equity (Such as now are in England) maintained or suffered in any Nation professing the Gospel.

This Position is so clear, that the contrary hath no manner of Foundation of Truth, either in the Law of Nature, Right Reason, or the Word of God: For that Justice is but one, as Truth is but one, and simply one; and Justice and Injustice are opposites. . . . These two Courts can no more consist with Justice, then two Weights or Measures of different bigness or length. I use this familiar Comparison, because it pleaseth the Holy Ghost to make use thereof to this very purpose, Prov. 20. 10. Diverse weights and diverse measures, word for word out of the Original, are a stone and a stone, that is different Weights and Measures, of several sizes, one bigger, another less: and this is expounded by that in Deut. 25. 13, 14. *Thou shalt not have in thy bagge diverse Weights, a great and a small: Thou shalt not have in thy house diverse Measures, a great and a small.* These words by a Synecdoche speciei, forbid all unjust and unequal dealing and commerce amongst men, and all injustice and Iniquity, and the instruments, tools, and means thereof; and implicitely, the same Law commends, all Justice and Equity; and directly forbids two Courts, having contrary Powers and Jurisdictions, and executing things Repugnant and contrary one to another: If the one proceed justly, the other must needs be unjust. Neither do the Scriptures anywhere mention Justice and Equity as two several things, to be distributed in one Case; as if that might be done by the one, which might not be done by the other; nor that ever any good Judges gave any such Judgments; but rather, when they are said to do Justice, it's intended, That they did justly and equally. It's true, that the Judicial Laws are called Judgements, and the execution of the Moral Law, is called Justice. And so David is said, to execute Judgement and Justice; that is, to judge justly and righteously both in respect of the Moral and Judicial Laws. . . . To conclude this point: If the Law were just and equal, as it ought to be, there were no need of any Court of Equity; and the Law, as now it is, having need of such Courts of Equity as there are, is an Oppression of the People, and so clearly against the Law of God. . . .

Jewish law has also struggled with inequitable features. Its
ideal is to make law and justice synonymous and inextricable; [51]
its practice has been a series of unending efforts to attain the
ideal. Where common law judges, faced with a claimant seeking
relief, were impotent to help unless the grievance fell within the
scope of an existing writ, [52] the rabbi was admonished "so long as a
matter is not settled in the codes, you may build or demolish as
you think fit, even contrary to the precedents set by the great
ancients." [53]

The nature of Jewish law is pervasive to a degree approach-
ing undifferentiation. [54] Religion, law and morals are equally touched
by "law."

> Thus, in Jewish law it is very difficult to mark the border
> between the utilitarian and the moral considerations of the
> legislator and determine the nature of the *res* which a certain
> provision of the law seeks to protect. [55]

The Puritans were in agreement. Equity, ethics, morality, if
lacking, were the court's obligation to provide. Jewish law was
often quite precise and particular in direct consequence of its
emphasis on explicating duties through rules to a conscientious
inquiring citizenry, [56] as opposed to the common law's formulation
of standards against which the facts of a case are measured. Such
Jewish law rules invited Jewish "equity" when inflexible rule
application courted injustice. In this way the sages of the Talmud
developed a concept of court "expropriation" to achieve results
the rules foreclosed. For example, [57]

> by the process of purporting to expropriate the amount of
> damages or of a penalty from a defendant and vesting that
> amount in the plaintiff, the court exercised a jurisdiction
> based on law, even though there was no law in existence by
> virtue of which that plaintiff could recover from the defendant.
> Or, where existing law gave the plaintiff a cause for action,
> but because of some formal defect in the pleadings or in the
> evidence that action would have to fail, the court would, in
> the exercise of this peculiar jurisdiction, be entitled to award
> the plaintiff the amount due to him by expropriating it from
> the defendant (Kiddushin 74a).

When law dictated the septennial release of debts,[58] but the economic consequence was the decline of commerce as lenders in the period of the Second Temple became discouraged from making loans, Hillel introduced the legal device known as the "prosbol" to make credit available.[59] It was a fiction by which the creditor assigned his claim to the court prior to the Sabbatical year. That assigned debt was deemed secured by any land in which the debtor had an interest. Secured debts were not released septennially and hence the debt survived and commerce was encouraged. The *prosbol* has been justified legally as the merger of the creditor's claim in a judgment prior to the year of release, enforceable by court officers and not the creditor himself, and in this manner not violative of release year prohibitions.[60] Other equitable fictions circumvented rules against usury, against burials of heathens and pagans under certain conditions, extended Poor Law benefits and made testamentary provisions accord with a broader donative intent than was originally authorized.[61] Equity was the essence of law. It did not have a reluctant piecemeal growth through a separate court system, but was the reflexive response of "the will to do justice" which distinguished Jewish law.[62] In the later periods of dispersion, religious and national survival dictated hedging the faith behind a rigid legal fence, a precaution necessitated by the absence of any political or quasi-political means of Jewish law enforcement.[63] The law's appeal went directly to the people's sense of duty and will to live; its restrictions born of necessity. But equity lived within that hardened shell.

> The exiled people willingly confined itself within the four corners of the Halacha—ritual law, civil law, and criminal law—knowing that only in the protected zone would it be able to retain its national character until it returned to the land of the fathers, until the day of redemption.[64]

Within that protected zone, the rabbi was "speaking Law" in the Puritan phrase. His discretion and creative interpretation were the sources of Jewish law suffused, as it was, with equity. Thus the concern for judicial independence, for community autonomy and deemphasis of precedent. The lacunae were vast within which the rabbi legislated; making laws "within the interstices"[65] was a common law, not a Jewish law, conception. Judicial free rein was congenial to Puritan thought as well.

Winthrop's defense of magisterial discretion, the proposed abolition of any distinction between law and equity in *Examen Legum Angliae* and the image of judges as "speaking Law," taken together, acted to promote an infusion of equity and a departure from technical restraints on judicial law-making. There was a practical objective in Winthrop's plea as well. At the time he wrote, Massachusetts Bay Colony was seeking the broadest latitude for its General Court. The Court had named Edward Winslow as its agent to argue before the Commissioners for Plantations in England, which eventually declared it had no intention

> to encourage any appeals from your justice, not to restrain the bounds of your jurisdiction to a narrower compass than is held forth by your letters patent, but to leave you with all the freedom and latitude that may, in any respect, be duly claimed by you . . .[66]

Winslow's successful arguments were particularly directed against any imposition of Establishment doctrine upon the Colony and pointed out as gently as possible the supremacy of "the laws of God and right reason." [67]

Jewish communities, too, especially during and since the Middle Ages, had fought continually to maintain a delicate balance between obedience to state authority and the active functioning of their own religiously based legal system. The Jews, like the Puritans, were religious separatists with legal and patriotic ties to a governing authority at odds with their interpretation of the source and nature of legal obligation. The object of Jew and Puritan was to keep this disagreement philosophical and avoid confrontation. Accommodation was sought through reduction of points of contact. Quarantining disputes within the separatist community was the aim of both groups. The holding of the Commissioners for Plantations, discouraging appeals from Colonial decisions, a result forcefully argued by the Colony's English agent, was an important step in this direction. Correspondingly, the ghetto communities actively sought to discourage their residents from resorting to Gentile courts in disputes between Jews.[68] The first verse of Chapter 21 of Exodus[69] was interpreted to forbid a Jew from seeking relief in a non-Jewish court. Rabbinic legislation of the twelfth century put under a *herem,* or ban, any Jew who sued a fellow Jew civilly. In Germany of the thirteenth century a Jew who sued a fellow Jew in a Gentile court was to be publicly flogged unless he had received Bet Din or community permission. In the seventeenth century, German Jewry threatened a Gentile court litigator with deprivation of such customary honors as being called to the Torah.

At any rate the serious concern of Puritan and Jew was to avoid the toils of secular authority while maintaining adherence to basic religious precepts framed in their own legal terms. The Puritans were very much aware of their Charter's admonitions against "laws, statutes, and ordinances, directions, and instructions" contrary to the "laws of this our realm of England." [70] A contributing factor in denominating their codification the Body of Liberties rather than "laws" has been attributed to "the fear that if they were so described their repugnancy to the laws of England would have brought the charter in jeopardy." [71]

The Jews sought to reconcile subjection to civil authority with perpetuation of religious precepts through a principle credited to a Babylonian sage of the third century. Mar Samuel's opinion was: the law of the Kingdom is the law, *Dina D'Malkhuta Dina,* and it applied to civil matters only. [72] Making this distinction work through the centuries in a society whose every law was infused with religious obligation was a demanding labor. But the incentive was group survival; legal confrontation being a ready pretext for expulsion or captivity. [73]

The Puritan and Jewish societies shared a common subject status and "an inherent, if hidden clash in rivaling doctrines of sovereignty" vis-à-vis the Establishment. [74] The Puritans would see themselves as Jews and would substitute "English" for "Christian" in a characterization of the contemporaneous Jewish predicament:

> the church and the state viewed all rights of Jews in the Christian world as derived from the privileges issued in their behalf by their rulers, whereas from the rabbinic standpoint regulations enacted by Kings regarding their Jewish

subjects also had to meet the criteria of the truly sovereign, because divinely ordained, Jewish Law.[75]

Both Crown and Separatist, however, in theory acknowledged the same ultimate divine source of law and neither Puritan nor Jew would allow the pre-eminence of this source to be obscured. Charles Chauncey for example, one of the Plymouth Elders, and later President of Harvard College, had decided a legal question on Old Testament authority and briefly justified resort to it,[76] "the judicials of Moyses . . . are appendances to the morall law, and grounded on the law of nature, or the decalogue, are immutable and perpetuall . . ." Again, when remonstrance was made by several disaffected colonists to the Commissioners for Plantations that the Colony was disregarding English law, Governor Winthrop argued in reply that, since the remonstrants did

> seem to admit of laws not repugnant, they mean, as the word truly imports, and as by the charter must needs be intended, they have no cause to complain, for we have no lawes diametrically opposite to those of England, for then they must be contrary to the laws of God and of right reason . . .[77]

The self determination of Massachusetts Bay Colony ended with the withdrawal of its privileges in 1684. Ironically, the charter of the Massachusetts Bay Company was annulled in *scire facias* proceedings in Chancery, the English Court of Equity. The English government in the successor Provincial Charter, finally issued in 1691, put the Colony on a much shorter leash. The mother country had learned from experience "that effective controls over the legislative and judicial processes of law-making were essential if conformity to the law of England was to be a reality." [78] The Provincial Charter contained provisions for the royal examination of all legislation and for appeals to the King in Council. The heyday of Biblical law in America was over.

Is Scriptural Law Part of Common Law?

Opposition to Biblicism had always run as an undercurrent through anti-Puritan Christian thought. Anne Hutchinson, banished from the Colony in 1637 for favoring salvation through works rather than grace and other theological transgressions, including "traducing the ministers and their ministry in this country," expressed the conventional Christian wisdom on Puritan absorption in the Pentateuch: "A company of legall professors lie poring on the law which Christ hath abolished." [79]

But the assumption that the decalogue at least, and probably the entire "lex scripta" were incorporated in the common law died hard. It remained for eighteenth-century rationalism to pursue the process of extrication and present to the newly formed United States of America a constitution which, as amended in 1789, provided "Congress shall make no law respecting an establishment of religion, or prohibiting the free exercise thereof." The wall of separation between church and state had replaced the Puritan "priviledge and advantage to us in New England that our Churches and civil state have been planted and growne up like two twinnes together like that of Israel in the wildernesse . . ." [80]

Some eighty years after the annullment of the Massachusetts Bay Colony charter a young Thomas Jefferson, the architect of American church-state separation, undertook to demolish the proposition, then widely held, that "to such laws of the church as have warrant in holy scripture, our law giveth credence." [81] He traces this and similar statements to a common Norman French source which had made a passing reference to "ancien scripture" in referring to early church writings. Jefferson alludes to the cited quotation disparagingly and notes:

> Justice Fortescue Aland, who possessed more Saxon learning than all the judges and writers before mentioned put together, places this subject on more limited ground. Speaking of the laws of the Saxon Kings, he says, "the ten commandments were made part of their law, and consequently were once part of the law of England; so that to break any of the ten commandments, was then esteemed a breach of the common law of England; and why it is not so now, perhaps, it may be difficult to give a good reason." The good reason is found in the denial of the fact. [82]

Jefferson then proceeds to expose "the falsification of the

laws of Alfred, by prefixing to them four chapters of the Jewish law, to wit, the 20th, 21st, 22nd and 23rd chapters of Exodus." These citations by the Puritan author of *Examen Legum Angliae* had been adduced as the strongest possible proof of the practicability of regulating society through Holy Writ. Jefferson summons history and internal evidence to confute assertions of the legitimacy of the preface to Alfred's laws: [83]

> And the very words of Alfred himself prove the fraud; for he declares in that preface, that he has collected these laws from those of Ina, of Offa, Aethelbert and his ancestors, saying nothing of any of them being taken from the scripture. It is still more certainly proved by the inconsistencies it occasions. For example, the Jewish legislator, Exodus, xxi. 12, 13, 14 (copied by the Pseudo Alfred sec. 13) makes murder, with the Jews, death. But Alfred himself LI. xxvi. punishes it by a fine only, called a weregild, proportioned to the condition of the person killed. It is remarkable that Hume (Append. I. to his History) examining this article of the laws of Alfred, without perceiving the fraud, puzzles himself with accounting for the inconsistency it had introduced. To strike a pregnant woman, so that she die, is death by Exod. xxi. 22, 23, and Pseudo Alfred sec. 19, 20, if of a servant by his master, is freedom to the servant; in every other case, retaliation. But by Alfred LI. xi. a fixed indemnification is paid. Theft of an ox or a sheep, by the Jewish law Exod. xxii. 1, was repaid five fold for the ox, and four fold for the sheep; by the Pseudograph sec. 24, double for the ox, and four fold for the sheep. But by Alfred LI. xvi he who stole a cow and a calf, was to repay the worth of the cow and 40s. for the calf. Goring by an ox, was the death of the ox, and the flesh not to be eaten; Exod. xxi. 28. Pseud. Alfr. sec. 21. By LI. Alfr. xxiv. the wounded person had the ox. This Pseudograph makes municipal laws of the ten commandements: sec. 1-10, regulate concubinage; sec. 12, makes it death to strike, or to curse father or mother; sec. 14, 15, gives an eye for an eye, tooth for tooth, hand for hand, foot for foot, burning for burning, wound for wound, stripe for stripe; sec. 19, sells the thief to repay his theft; sec. 24, obliges the fornicator to marry the woman he

has lain with; sec. 29, forbids interest on money; sec. 28, 35, makes the laws of bailment and very different from what Lord Holt delivers in *Coggs* v. *Bernard*, and what Sir William Jones tells us they were; and punished witchcraft with death, sec. 30, which Sir Matthew Hale 1. P.C. ch. 33, declares was not a felony before the stat. 1. Jac. c. 12. . . . Now all men of reading know that these pretended laws of homicide, concubinage, theft, retaliation, compulsory marriage, usury, bailment and others which might have been cited from this Pseudograph, were never the laws of England, not even in Alfred's time; and of course, that it is a forgery. Yet, palpable as it must be to a lawyer, our judges have piously avoided lifting the veil under which it was shrouded. In truth, the alliance between church and state in England, has ever made their judges accomplices in the frauds of the clergy; and even bolder than they are; for instead of being contented with the surreptitious introduction of these four chapters of Exodus, they have taken the whole leap, and declared at once that the whole Bible and Testament, in a lump, make a part of the common law of the land; the first judicial declaration of which was by this Sir Matthew Hale, And thus they incorporate into the English code, laws made for the Jews alone . . .

The conventional Anglican viewpoint had come to prevail. Old Testament laws were consigned no "farther than (to) that people to whom they were given . . ."[84] But it was easier for Jefferson to order "dismissed" by paper command than to enforce such uprooting in fact. American judges found scriptural influence deep dyed in the warp and woof of the young country's society and were reluctant to allow its disappearance from America's *corpus juris*.

Chancellor Kent, one of the new nation's leading jurists,[85] gave voice to a continuing concern for scripture in deciding a prosecution for blasphemy.[86] The defendant had been convicted of declaring in public, "Jesus Christ was a bastard, and his mother must be a whore."[87] In affirming conviction, Chancellor Kent noted that "such words, uttered with a disposition," constituted an offense at common law. The anti-establishment clause of the New York constitution was "never meant to withdraw religion in general, and with it the best sanctions of moral and social obligation, from all consideration and notice of the law." [88] The common law was still construed to preserve and protect scripture. "The authorities show," according to Kent "that blasphemy against God, and contumelious reproaches and profane ridicule of Christ or the holy scriptures (which are equally treated as blasphemy) are offenses punishable at common law . . ." [89]

Separation of church and state, in its Jeffersonian ideal, was not going to be a simple matter. The legacy of Hebrew laws, nourished by the Massachusetts Puritans, was to remain part of the American heritage.

NOTES TO CHAPTER 1

1. John Calvin conceived the Bible as a manifestation of how the Christian community should be organized to do God's work on earth and he found in the Pentateuch the law for effecting this achievement. Troeltsch, *Die Soziallehren der Christlichen Kirchen* (1912) 620; Calvin, *The Commentaries on the Four Last Books of Moses* (Bingham ed., 1844). The "perfect school of Christ" instituted by Calvin in Geneva is entertainingly described in *The Horizon Book of the Elizabethan World* (New York, 1967) 113-117.

2. The Sadducees in the last two centuries of the Second Jewish Commonwealth were Torah literalists, in opposition to the Oral Law. The Karaites, founded in 760, claim descent from the Sadducees. The majority of present-day Orthodox Rabbis consider the Karaites as Jewish but do not approve of intermarriage with them. The Karaites do not allow their members to intermarry with other Jews. The Rabbinical Court of Haifa had occasion to declare, reluctantly, as legal a marriage between a Karaite and a Jew who accepts the Rabbinic tradition (Case 1293/5726, reported in *Mahlekhim* I, 1969, 16).

3. Matthew Hale, "Considerations Touching the Amendment or Alterations of Lawes" (date unknown—before 1690), *Hargrave Tracts*, 260.

4. Sir Edward Coke, the first Lord Chief Justice of England (1552-1634) was one of the most illustrious judges in English history. He overshadowed his predecessors, Fitzherbert, Dyer and Plowden, in establishing the authority of precedent. They were called eminent "rabbins of the law" by a Puritan writer. Max Radin, *Handbook of Anglo-American Legal History* (St. Paul, Minn., 1936) 354. See also Theodore Plucknett, *A Concise History of the Common Law* 4th ed. (London, 1948) 265.

5. Edward Coke, on Littleton. *Coke's Institutes* (London, 1628) I, 11b.

6. Proeme to *Coke's Fourth Institute* (London, 1628).

7. Cecil Roth, *History of the Jews in England* (Oxford, 1941) 137 ff.

8. Jacob J. Rabinowitz, *Jewish Law* (New York, 1956) 250 *et seq.* Also credited to Jewish law sources are principles of inchoate dower and suretyship. Prior to 1290 the Jews lived in England merely by the tolerance of the King, "squeezed out of the frame of the system." The right of protecting and exploiting this excluded class was a royal prerogative. "Nobody might 'have Jews' but the King." Between the Norman Conquest and 1290 they played a large part in the economy of the Kingdom. Radin, *op. cit.* 462-463.

9. Frederick Pollack and Frederic Maitland, *History of English Laws,* 2d ed. (1891) I, 475.

10. *Examen Legum Angliae: On the Laws of England Examined by Scripture, Antiquity and Reason* (1656), reprinted in part in Mark DeWolfe Howe, *Readings in American Legal History* (Cambridge, 1949) 86 *et seq.*

11. *Ibid.,* 87.

12. *Ibid.,* 87-88.

13. The reference is not to any particular laws or codices, but to idolatrous practices introduced from Tyre in Phoenicia during the politically successful Omriad dynasty. Omri and his son Ahab (and the latter's infamous wife Jezebel) were idolators who introduced "the cult of the great Tyrian divinities Baal Melcarth and Asherah" to the Northern Kingdom of Israel in the ninth century B.C., incurring the wrath of the prophet, Elijah. William F. Albright, *The Biblical Period from Abraham to Ezra* (New York, 1962) 65 *et seq.*; Harry M. Orlinsky, *Ancient Israel* (Ithaca, N.Y. 1960) 81 *et seq.*

14. Hale, *op. cit.*, 249.

Matthew Hale's decisions were highly respected repositories of the common law. John Greenleaf Whittier, nineteenth-century abolitionist and heir to Puritan thought, alludes in verse to the judge of the Salem witchcraft trials, Samuel Sewall, and his dual reliance on Jewish and common law sources

> "When he sat on the bench of the witchcraft courts,
> With the laws of Moses and Hale's Reports
> And spake, in the name of both, the word
> That gave the witch's neck to the cord."

Whittier, "The Prophecy of Samuel Sewall," *The Poetical Works of John Greenleaf Whittier* (Boston and New York, 1891), 223.

15. Opinion of Samuel Symonds, Assistant, in *Giddings v. Brown,* County Court, Essex County, 1657; 2 *Hutchinson Papers* 1. The Assistant (a judicial and legislative officer) had written at the conclusion of his opinion, in praise of unswerving devotion to justice, "I doe sometymes remember what is said of Levy. In poynt of right and truth, he tooke noe notice of father or mother. And that is the way to establish love and peace in this our Israel."

Master John Cotton, in his farewell sermon to the Lincolnshire group of departing Puritans leaving Southampton in 1630, took as his text 2 Samuel 7: 10: "Moreover I will appoint a place for my people Israel, and will plant them, that they may dwell in a place of their own, and move no more; neither shall the children of wickedness afflict them any more, as beforetime." Samuel Eliot Morison, *Builders of the Bay Colony,* 5th ed. (Boston, 1962) 71.

The immortal Puritan poet, John Milton, who arose at four or five in the morning to listen while one of his daughters would read a chapter of the Old Testament, thought of Cromwellian England as a latter day Zion. In his *Areopagitica,* he wrote, "Why else was this nation chosen before any other, that out of her as out of *Sion* should be proclaimed and sounded forth the first tidings and trumpet of Reformation to all *Europe* . . . for now the time seems come, wherein *Moses* the great prophet may sit in heaven rejoicing to see that memorable and glorious wish of his fulfilled, when not only our seventy elders, but all the Lord's people are become prophets."

Even a century and a half later Thomas Jefferson, that arch foe of theocracy, equated his country with biblical Israel when he wrote of George Washington, "I felt on his death, with my countrymen, that 'verily a great man hath fallen in Israel.'" See Second Samuel 3:38. Jefferson to Dr. Walter Jones, January 2, 1814. Quoted in *The Life and Selected Writings of Thomas Jefferson,* edited by Adrienne Koch and William Peden (New York, 1944), 176.

16. The Priestly Code includes the version of the Ten Commandments which appears in Exodus 20:2-14. They also appear in Deuteronomy 5:6-18. Robert H. Pfeiffer, *Introduction to the Old Testament* (New York, 1941), 228 ff.

17. A double share for the eldest son was of purely Biblical derivation. The common law prescribed primogeniture, by which the eldest son took the entire estate; and gavelkind, which was the custom of Kent, required equal sharing by all sons. Radin, *op. cit*, 407 *et seq.* See George Haskins, "The Beginnings of Partible Inheritance in the American Colonies," 51 *Yale Law Journal* 1280 (1942) at 1309-1311.

18. Julius Goebel, Jr., "King's Law and Local Custom in Seventeenth Century New England," 31 *Columbia Law Review* 416, 431: "We have seen how the so-called Mosaic law had been seized upon and exploited by the radical religious elements in England as the true guide of men's ethical behavior. There can be no doubt that the great things which had been accomplished at Geneva, supposedly on the basis of Old Testament jurisprudence, had stimulated this enthusiasm. For it was a cardinal point of Calvin's propaganda that God's Kingdom could be realized on earth only by the adaptation of Israelite models. There was but one law in the Kingdom and that was the law of God as revealed in the Old Testament."

19. *Ibid.*, 418-419 note 7. Professor Goebel refers the practice of seeking the opinion of a neighboring jurisdiction to "the practice in medieval Germany of reference to the mother city by the daughter cities of difficult legal questions for decision, Schroeder, Deutsche Rechtsgeschichten, 741,743." A precedent of longer standing and more congenial to Puritan predilections may be found in the responsa of the rabbis who from the third century, when Rabbi Johanan, head of the academy of Tiberias, Palestine (d. 279) carried on a juridical correspondence with Rab and Samuel of Babylonia, have turned to more eminent scholars for opinions on doubtful issues. Simon Hurwitz, *The Responsa of Solomon Luria*, 2d ed. (1938) xi; Irving Agus, *Urban Civilization in Pre-Crusade Europe* (New York, 1965) I, 31; Haim Cohn, *Jewish Law in Ancient and Modern Israel* (New York, 1971) XII-XIII.

According to Dr. Ronald Berman, Chairman of the National Endowment for the Humanities, a federal agency, in making a grant to the YIVO Institute for Jewish Research, "Responsa 'record in detail the oldest applied legal tradition in the western world and have great importance for the study of linguistics, literature, history, commerce, philosophy and anthropology.'" quoted in *The Jewish News*—New Jersey, June 27, 1974, 12, col. 4. Dr. Berman, referring to a grant for computer storage for use in research of a great mass of material contained in the Hebrew Responsa, stated there were some 500,000 Responsa written by an estimated 5,000 authorities in Asia, Africa and Europe, primarily in Hebrew, Arabic and Aramaic, over the last seventeen hundred years.

In Israel, the Weizmann Institute of Science is worikng on storing responsa in a computer memory bank so they may be programmed for computer recall.

20. Quoted in Howe, *op. cit.*, 181.

21. 1 *Winthrop Journal* 202. *Winthrop's Journal* for the years 1630-49 appears in James Savage, *The History of New England* (Boston, 1853).

22. Howe, *op. cit.*, 182.

23. Taken from the reprint in *Mass. Hist. Soc. Coll.*, 1st Series, V, 173.

24. Quoted in Howe, *op. cit.*, 188. The Talmud also moderated the forty lash penalty of the Old Testament (Deut. 25:3). Tosefta Maccoth V §12; Sifre II §286; Maccoth 22. S. Mendelsohn, *The Criminal Jurisprudence of the Ancient Hebrews*, 2nd ed. (1968) 172: "As the spirit of moderation and clemency pervades all Talmudic penal laws, this punishment likewise is not allowed to be

carried to extremes. Moses prescribed forty stripes as the highest number but the Rabbis took off one. When the convict's life is thought to be endangered by this number, a less number is apportioned, which must not be increased, even when it subsequently appears that he could stand the full count (Tosefta l.c. §13; Maccoth l.c.). And as the lash is applied over the shoulder blades and chest [three parts of the body], the number of stripes must be divisible by three; if inadvertently a number not a multiple of three is apportioned, it must be reduced to render it divisible. Thus if the court sentences one to receive twenty stripes, he receives eighteen only (Tosefta l.c. §12; Maccoth l.c.; Maimon. l.c.2)."

Many of the provisions in the Body of Liberties, derived from the Mosaic law, were more humane than those of contemporary English common law. "The Liberties of Servants, derived from the Pentateuch, are humanitarian in character . . . . Theft is not punishable by death, although in England robbery, burglary, and larceny above the value of one shilling, were then capital felonies . . . Although animals then had no protection in common law, 'The Bruite Creature' has a section of his own in the Body of Liberties. 'No man shall exercise any Tiranny or Cruelties towards any bruite Creatures which are usuallie kept for man's use,' and cattle drovers may rest or refresh their cattle in any field not enclosed, without trespass." Morison, *op. cit.*, 232.

25. 4 *Winthrop Papers* 349. *The Mass. Hist. Soc. Coll.*

26. Howe and Eaton, "The Supreme Judicial Power in the Colony of Massachusetts Bay," 20 *New England Quarterly* 1 (1947).

27. *Ibid.*, 4. Governor Winthrop's telling argument against a unicameral legislature was that it would be a democratic innovation: "If we should change from a mixt aristocratie to a mere Democratie, first we should have no warrant in scripture for it: there was no such government in Israel." Morison, *op. cit.*, 92. Prior to *Sherman v. Keayne* (1642), the Deputies and Magistrates sat together. An involved procedure calling for the selection of a committee which in turn was to choose an umpire might be resorted to "in doubtfull cases" where a majority of the General Court voted one way, but one of its constituent bodies was opposed. After *Sherman v. Keayne*, by an Act adopted in 1644, separate chambers for Deputies and Magistrates were provided and both bodies were required to concur for action taken to become law.

28. 4 *Winthrop Papers* 349, 351-352.

29. 2 *Winthrop Journal* 231.

30. 4 *Winthrop Papers* 468.

31. *Ibid.*, 472 *et seq.*

32. A number of Old Testament injunctions speak of judgment "before God" and the Talmudists dispute as to "whether the adjudicating agent mentioned is really God Himself or whether the name of God stands only for a human judge." Sanhedrin, 66a. "And it was later laid down that 'God', in this context, must be read to mean any judge." Rambam, *Hilkhot Sanhedrin*, 26,1. Cohn, *op cit.*, 19. Examples of appearances "before God" include Exodus 21: 6 wherein the slave who declares he wishes not to be freed after six years servitude is to be taken "before God" for his ear to be pierced; Exodus 22: 7 wherein the owner of stolen, unrecovered property is to depose "before God" that he is innocent; Exodus 22: 8 which requires in cases of misappropriation that both parties come "before God" for an adjudication of guilt to be made.

33. See Howe, *op. cit.*, 102.

34. *Ibid.*, 103.
35. 1 Osgood, *The American Colonies in the 17th Century* (1904) 141 *et seq.*
36. Hale, *op. cit.*, 260.
37. Howe, *op. cit.*, 232.
38. *Ibid.*, 219 *et seq.*
39. *Ibid.*, 221.
40. The codification of 1648 includes, *inter alia*, provisions relating to arrests, attachments, bills of exchange, fraudulent conveyances and other sophisticated divisions of law. The provision on "conveyances fraudulent," for example, is the forerunner of statutory recording systems for land conveyances presently in force in practically every state of the union. Professor Haskins in 97 *University of Pennsylvania Law Review* 842 (1949) describes the common law influence upon the colonial law of dower expressed in The Laws and Liberties of 1648.
41. Cardozo, at the conclusion of his lectures, published as *The Growth of Law* (Yale University Press, 1924) 143, quotes Roscoe Pound, "Law must be stable, and yet it cannot stand still." Cardozo proceeds, "The mystery of change and motion still vexes the minds of men as it baffled the Eleatics of old in the beginnings of recorded thought. . . The victory is not for the partisans of an inflexible logic nor yet for the levelers of all rule and all precedent, but the victory is for those who shall know how to fuse these two tendencies together in adaptation to an end as yet imperfectly discerned. I shall not take it amiss if you complain that I have done little more than state the existence of a problem." Strict constructionists and liberals are found in the development of Roman Law as well. "There too we find two schools, each named after a great scholar, the strict constructionists being the School of Sabinus and the liberals being the School of Proculius." Louis Ginzberg, *On Jewish Law and Lore* (New York and Phila., 1955) 103.
42. William Aspinwall's Preface to the 1655 edition of John Cotton's *Abstract of the Laws of New England*, Mass. Hist. Soc. Coll. Series I, V, 47.
43. Hermann L. Strack, *Introduction to the Talmud and Midrash*, 2d ed. (1965) 13. The Puritan magistrates in the early years of the Colony of Massachusetts Bay "were intensely reluctant to have any written laws made because by these their discretion would be restrained." Paul S. Reinsch, *English Common Law in the Early American Colonies*, (New York, 1970 reprint of doctoral thesis originally printed in 1899) 12.
44. *Ibid.*, 18. Strack emphasizes, however, that the view which prevailed favored the recording of Oral Law.
45. *Ibid.*
46. *Ibid.*, 17. A paradoxical modern manifestation of extreme orthodoxy in defense of divinity appears in modern Israel. Israel Supreme Court Justice Haim Cohn reports that when he was a legislator, shortly after the founding of the modern State of Israel, "I published a draft bill of succession and wills, which was based on—but, where necessary, also departed from—Jewish law, and which was formulated in the legal Hebrew of today; whereupon one of the outstanding orthodox spokesmen protested that Jewish law does not lend itself to any reformulation in a different version, as that might lead to the divine language of the ancient law being forgotten, and, furthermore, that there was no secular authority competent to restate, and, a fortiori, to change, Jewish law." Cohn, *The Jewish State and Its Problems* (Hebrew),

ed. by Yavne, (Jerusalem, 1949) 80. Cohn notes, in a comment reminiscent of the early Puritan radicals, "the purists want to keep divine law intact, untouched by the impure secular legislation".

47. See Cardozo, *op cit.*, 84-85. "The good of one generation is not always the good of its successor. For the lawyer as for the moralist, the generalizations that result from the study of social phenomena are not 'fixed rules for deciding doubtful cases, but instrumentalities for their investigation, methods by which the value of past experience is rendered available for present scrutiny of new perplexities.' " (Dewey, *Human Nature and Conduct*, 240).

48. "The Chancellor was nearly always a clergyman and usually a prelate, often one of the Archbishops. His deputy, the 'Clerk' or 'Master of the Rolls,' who became a permanent official with judicial authority during the fifteenth century, was also a priest. . . The fact that the judge in this court was a Churchman was not an accident. An appeal addressed to mercy and charity— as the Chancery bills were—would seem most appropriately communicated to a priest and most successfully dealt with by a priest." Radin, *op cit.*, 429; cf. 5 Holdsworth, *A History of English Law* 215-18, 2d ed. (1937); Plucknett, *op cit.*, 647.

49. Plucknett, *op. cit.*, 262.

50. Note 10 *supra*, 89 *et seq.*, quoting Chapter IX.

51. "In the Pentateuch and the Talmud there is no distinct term for ethics because. . . the goal of ethics and law coalesce. . . The prophets looked upon law, in the larger sense, as ethical jurisprudence. In its narrower sense it was part of the larger field of morals. In any event, they repudiated any antinomy between law and ethics. . ." Boaz Cohen, *Jewish and Roman Law*, (New York, 1966) I, 66, 75.

Jewish law envisages a society which embodies, in Cushing Strout's phrase, "civic religion," that point located "where liberty, law, religion and morality converge." Lerner, *New York Post*, July 12, 1974, 37, col. 1.

The Jewish law concept closest to "equity" is that of "yosher" which refers in a certain very limited set of circumstances to a standard of conduct beyond that which the law exacts.

In only two cases is "yosher" obligatory: (1) as in English and American equity, in granting the owner a right of redemption from foreclosure, and (2) in the preferential right to purchase granted a neighboring landowner. In all other cases "yosher" is voluntary, calling for a "standard of saintliness" in a number of instances well beyond the capacity of ordinary mortals. See Moshe Silberg, *Talmudic Law and The Modern State* (New York, 1973), ch. VII. Judge Cardozo has defined the common law relationship of works of supererogation to the legal norm: "The law will not hold the crowd to the morality of saints and seers." Quoted in S.v.J., 367 N.Y.S. 2d 405 (1975), 408.

52. During the fourteenth century, with the growth of the English bar, the making of new writs practically came to a halt, and new situations had to be met by the adaptation of an existing writ, or not at all. Radin sees the two developments as cause and effect, "a guild of professional lawyers—almost inevitably a force against innovation, if for no other reason than that the adaptation of existing writs challenged their ingenuity." Radin, *op. cit.*, 187.

53. Commentary to Sanhedrin IV, 6. The hardening of precedent occurred gradually at common law. By the time of Blackstone in the eighteenth century, he could write that it was "an established rule to abide by former precedents." See Radin, *op cit.*, 343 *et seq.* In mid-thirteenth century, Bracton had written,

"It is quite proper to be in doubt in regard to particular new matters."
Bracton, 16 (Woodbine's ed. II, 21).

54. Boaz Cohen, *op. cit.*, 68. Roscoe Pound in *Law and Morals* (1926) 27-29 cites Leviticus ch. 19 as a classical example of primitive undifferentiation.

55. Silberg, "Law and Morals in Jewish Jurisprudence," 75 *Harvard Law Review* 306, 311 (1961).

56. *Ibid.*, 308.

57. Cohn, *op cit.*, XXV.

58. Deut. 15: 1-2.

59. Horowitz, *op. cit.*, 496.

60. Makkot 3a; Mishnah Shevi'it x,2.

61. Cohn, *op. cit.*, XXVIII.

62. Deut 16:20; See Israel H. Levinthal, *Judaism* (New York, 1935) 123 *et seq.*; Louis Ginzberg, *Students, Scholars and Saints* (Phila., 1938) 28.

63. Silberg, "Law and Morals in Jewish Jurisprudence," *op. cit.*, 321.

64. *Ibid.*

65. Justice Holmes in Southern Pacific Co. v. Jensen, 244 U.S. 205 at p. 221 wrote, "I recognize without hesitation that judges must and do legislate, but they do so only interstitially; they are confined from molar to molecular motions." Cf. Herzog, The Main Institutions of Jewish Law, 2nd ed. (London, 1965) I, 13 *et seq.*

66. 2 *Winthrop Journal* 319-320.

67. *Ibid*, 288 *et seq.*

68. Leo Landman, *Jewish Law in the Diaspora* (Phila., 1968) 86 *et seq.*

69. "Now these are the ordinances which thou shalt set before them."

70. Howe, *op. cit.*, 102.

71. *Ibid.*, 186.

72. Landman, *op cit.*, 39: "The consensus of opinion among rabbis throughout the ages has been that 'the law of the Kingdom is the law' does not imply that such laws enter the Jewish legal system. The laws of any nation must be obeyed, but they do not assume the status of Jewish law."

73. One of the earliest records of suspicion of Jewish law as a pretext for persecution appears in the Book of Esther, written in the fourth pre-Christian century. See Esther 3:8-9. Haman, the King's chief minister, in asking the King's permission to destroy the Jews, urges as valid cause their allegiance to different laws: "There is a certain people scattered abroad and dispersed among the peoples in all the provinces of thy Kingdom; neither keep they the King's laws; therefore it profiteth not the King to suffer them."

Expulsion from England took place in 1290; from France in 1306, followed by intermittent readmissions and expulsions; from Vienna in 1421; Spain in 1492; Lithuania in 1496; Portugal in 1497; Venice in 1535; Naples and Sicily in 1540; The Papal States, being all of central Italy, except for Rome and Ancona, in the mid-sixteenth century; Frankfort in 1616. See Solomon Grayzel, *A History of the Jews* 2nd ed. (Phila., 1968) 356-7, 400, 497, 387-8, 355-7, 386-90, 485-6, 395-6, 416-17. In feudal terms "the Jewish 'serfs' were indeed free men living under royal protection but enjoying a considerable measure of self-determination and individual mobility." But on the one extreme lay the ever-present threat of expulsion and on the other, if legal pretext were invoked, lurked captivity. "Time and again the Kings of England, Castile, or Aragon threatened Jews with the loss of freedom in case of disobedience. Even at the height of legal discrimination against Iberian Jewry during the quarter century of 1391-1415, the anti-Jewish decree of January 2, 1412 tried to stem Jewish emigration by warning the would be culprits they would lose all their property and become 'My captives forever.'" Salo Baron, *A Social and Religious History of the Jews* (Columbia University Press, 1967) XI, 9.

74. *Ibid.*, 20.

75. *Ibid.*, 21.

76. William Bradford, *History of Plymouth Plantation, 1620-1647* (Mass. Hist. Soc., 1922) II, 326.

77. 2 *Winthrop Journal* 288-9.

78. Howe, *op. cit.*, 253.

79. Quoted in Johnson's *Wonder Working Providence* (1867 ed.) 102. Cf. C.J. Parker, in Pearce v. Atwood, 13 Mass. 324, 345-46 (1816).

80. *Supra*, note 37.

81. Jefferson, "Inquiry Whether Christianity is a Part of the Common Law," 1 *Jefferson's Reports* 137 (1829) quoting Finch.

82. *Ibid.*, 140.

83. *Ibid.*, 141 *et seq.* Jefferson had acquired a rather jaundiced view of Jewish ethics and law from a superficial work by Enfield which he quotes in a letter to John Adams, who was an admirer of Jewish influence. Where the New Englander had written to Jefferson ". . . in spite of Bolingbroke and Voltaire I will insist that the Hebrews have done more to civilize men than any other nation," (Quoted in Arnold Rogow, *The Jew in a Gentile World*, New York, 1961 at 242) Jefferson, in a letter to Adams, wrote "To compare the morals of the Old, with those of the New Testament, would require an attentive study of the former, a search through all its books for its precepts, and through all its history for its practices, and the principles they prove. As commentaries, too, on these, the philosophy of the Hebrews must be inquired into, their Mishna, their Gemara, Cabbala, Jezirah, Sohar, Cosri, and their Talmud, must be examined and understood, in order to do them full justice. Brucker, it would seem has gone deeply into these repositories of their ethics, and Enfield, his epitomizer, concludes in these words: 'Ethics were so little understood among the Jews, that in their whole compilation called the Talmud, there is only one treatise on moral subjects. Their books of morals chiefly consisted in a minute enumeration of duties. From the law of Moses were deduced 613 precepts, which were divided into two classes, affirmative and negative, 248 in the former, and 365 in the latter. It may serve to give the reader some idea of the low state of moral philosophy among the Jews in the middle age, to add that of the 248 affirmative precepts, only three were considered as obligatory upon women, and that in order to obtain salvation, it was judged sufficient to fulfill any one single law in the hour of death; the observance of the rest being deemed necessary, only to increase the felicity of the future life. What a wretched depravity of sentiment and manners must have prevailed, before such corrupt maxims could have obtained credit! It is impossible to collect from these writings a consistent series of moral doctrine'. Enfield, B.4, chapter 3." *The Life and Selected Writings of Thomas Jefferson, op. cit.*, 631.

84. Hale, *op. cit.*, 249.

85. James Kent was one of America's legal luminaries in the first century of United States independence. In 1804 he became chief justice of the New York Supreme Court and a decade later, chancellor. His judgments as chancellor, recorded in Johnson's *Chancery Reports* covering seven volumes of decisions, 1816-1824, form the basis of American equity jurisprudence.

86. People v. Ruggles, 8 Johns. 290 (1811). "The early state reports are full of cases in which decisions were affected and sometimes controlled by the thesis that Christianity is a part of the common law which we have inherited from England." Mark DeWolfe Howe, *The Garden and the Wilderness* (Chicago, 1965) 28, citing State v. Chandler, 2 Harr. (Del.) 553 (1837); 1 Story, *Life and Letters of Joseph Story* 431 (1851). See Chapter 4, *infra*, note 50.

87. *People v. Ruggles, supra,* 293.

88. *People v. Ruggles, supra,* 296.

89. *People v. Ruggles, supra,* 293-4. Ten years after his decision, Kent stoutly defended his action. "Surely we are a Christian people. 'Do not the ninety-nine hundredths of our fellow citizens hold the general truths of the Bible to be dear and sacred?' " he asked the delegates to the 1821 New York Constitutional Convention. "Any attack upon these truths is an attack upon the order of society, to the correction of which the Common Law is sworn." Perry Miller, *The Life of the Mind in America* (New York, 1965) 194. In 1838, Chief Justice Shaw of Massachusetts, another of the United States' early judicial giants, passed sentence for "blasphemous and profane libel" on Abner Kneeland, an exponent of eighteenth century rationalism, who delivered public lectures questioning the existence of God. "In one of the hearings the public prosecutor sneered at Jefferson as a 'Virginia Voltaire' and contended, successfully, that Christianity was part and parcel of the constitution of Massachusetts," as well as of the common law. Miller, *supra* 195.

In England it has been the rule since 1727 that an offense against religion was part of the common law. See Leo M. Alpert, "Judicial Censorship of Obscene Literature," 52 *Harv. L. Rev.* 40, 43-44, citing Dominus Rex. v. Curl, 2 Strange 789 (K.B. 1727) which overruled Queen v. Read, 11 Mod. 142 (Q.B. 1708).

2·

FROM BRIS
TO BURIAL

Train up a child in the way he should go
And even when he is old, he will not depart from it.

Proverbs 22 :6

THE STRENGTH OF Jewish family ties has been remarked upon
in social studies [1] and by casual observers. [2] The religious content of
Jewish domesticity has been its binding epoxy. From the dispersion
forward, following the Second Temple's destruction, "fences had to
be built in certain ages to protect the beautiful flowers of Judaism,"
and the religious hedge "became part of our legal code of life. Once
it becomes law, it cannot so easily be changed." [3] Thus, Jewish law
governing domestic relations has survived with a religious im-
mediacy absent from other of life's concerns; its adherents resisting
with near fanatic pertinacity secular legal inroads.

It is no surprise, then, to find that the preponderance of American cases in which Jewish law references appear relate to family
issues. [4] An emotional context for the most urbane disagreement,
the family dispute, involving at least one religiously committed
participant, makes for legal confrontation of Gordian knottiness.
Historically, the common law system has only recently enfolded
marriage and the family. The age of ecclesiastical jurisdiction is

39

not distant.[5] A further unsettling factor in United States jurisprudence, ever alert as it is to First Amendment infringements, is
the paradoxical solicitude in family cases for religious influence in
the home. The "sanctity of marriage" is a threadbare cliché, in
Christian theology a sacrament; but, nonetheless, while church and
state tread a slippery constitutional balance in schools and public
places,[6] state policy invites religion to stay at home with the
family.

The degree of importance which Jewish tradition attaches
to family formation is evident from the most cursory survey. The
very first duty which the most influential Jewish law code enjoins
in the first section of its first chapter is marriage.[7] In Orthodox
communities, "if a girl was poor or an orphan, and did not have
the wherewithal for a dowry, it was the duty of the community
to supply this and thus assure her marriage."[8] In a rabbinic commentary to Genesis a Roman matron asks Rabbi Jose bar Halafta:
"How long did it take the Holy One, blessed be He, to create the
world?"

"He said to her: 'six days.'"

"And from then until now what has He been doing?"

"The Holy One, blessed be He, is occupied in making marriages
. . . as difficult a task as dividing the Red Sea."[9]

The primacy of family and its community influence is revealed
in a Talmudic aphorism: "He who establishes peace in his own
family is as if he were establishing it for all Israel."[10]

Traditional Judaism is nourished through family ritual and
ceremony in an unending chain. The father must arrange for the
circumcision of his sons; have them taught their prayers and the
Pentateuch in Hebrew, by borrowing if necessary; prepare them
for *Bar Mitzvah;* and, in short, be an educator of Torah in its
broadest sense. The mother was also expected to educate by molding
character, imposing discipline and supervising religious observances. Children were required to observe the Commandment,
"Honor thy father and thy mother." Grandparents were obliged
to inculcate ethical and religious precepts in the young. The institution of the ethical will, a peculiarly Jewish product, makes
no disposition of money or other worldly goods but is an instruction manual in moral conduct which the testator leaves for
the guidance of his loved ones.[11] From birth to death, family was

the focus of religion and law. Its inter-relationships, rituals and practices were the subject of detailed regulation.

Circumcision

The American cases in which circumcision is a factor miss its significance in Jewish law. It is the oldest Jewish rite, beginning when Abraham circumcised members of his household in accordance with God's command, "And ye shall be circumcised in the flesh of your foreskin; and it shall be a token of the covenant betwixt me and you." [12] This oldest of Jewish rites was forbidden by the Seleucid King, Antiochus IV, provoking in part the Maccabean revolt of the second pre-Christian century; it was renounced by St. Paul who replaced it with baptism; it was denounced by Hadrian in the second century of Christianity, following Bar Kochba's rebellion; it was ridiculed by Juvenal, Horace and later Roman poets. Scorned and reviled through medieval and later times as a superstitious branding, circumcision has endured as an almost universal ritual among Jews, including the "highly assimilated and even free-thinking Jews of today." [13]

Although an uncircumcised male is still a Jew by birth under Jewish law, circumcision on the eighth day of life is a perpetual obligation.[14] "Circumcision is so important that it is even to be performed on the Sabbath or Yom Kippur. According to R. Joseph Karo, in the *Shulhan Arukh*, it is the most important positive commandment." [15] It is a ritual bound up with patriarchal antiquity and the tortuous path of Jewish history. Its performance is supercharged with religious and emotional associations.

In 1958 in Syracuse, New York the Orthodox parents of a newborn boy informed the hospital, according to their complaint, that he "was to be circumcised by a Rabbi in a ritualistic ceremony in accordance with the Jewish religion and Jewish custom and practice." [16] In fact, "the operation was performed by a person not qualified to perform it under Jewish religious law; the prescribed religious ritual was not observed; and the operation was performed prematurely on the 4th day, whereas the religious law requires it to be performed on the 8th day." [17] The complaint, though loosely drawn, was susceptible of being interpreted as alleging "the intentional or negligent infliction of emotional distress," [18] an expanding area of New York tort law. The lower court judge, however, whose decision was affirmed on appeal with but one dissent, chose to apply a technical reading of the distraught parents' claims.

They were held to be improper plaintiffs: "the conduct of the defendants, if a wrong in relation to the son, was not a wrong in its relation to the plaintiffs, remote from the event . . . the defendants . . . did not assume any risk of liability that their acts might violate the personal sensibilities of others, be they the son's parents, his co-religionists or the community at large." [19] The decision went on to reject any claim of statutory or constitutional violation; it restricted recovery for "mental pain and suffering" to the one assaulted, and, finally construed a recent decision of New York's highest court allowing recovery for "injuries, physical or mental, incurred by fright negligently induced" [20] as not intended "to provide a cause of action for interested bystanders." [21]

Judge Halpern, in dissent, upon the parents' appeal, stated the case for relief: "The ceremony of circumcision is an elaborate one. It is to be performed by a specially qualified person who is to recite a prescribed prayer. The father and others present also recite prescribed benedictions or blessings. (Maimonides Code, Book II [Hyamson translation] pp. 164-a to 164-b; Gottlieb, a Jewish Child is Born, pp. 45-46, and Finkelstein, The Jewish Religion: Its Beliefs and Practices, in The Jews : Their History, Culture and Religion, vol. 4, p. 1376)." [22] After reviewing circumcision's religious importance, "we would have to conclude that the complaint is sufficient to charge serious and severe distress, when read in the light of the authoritative religious writings of which we can take judicial notice." [23] Judge Halpern cites cases supporting "the right to recover for the intentional infliction of mental anguish" as a recognized tort under New York law.[24] If not intentional, defendants "acted recklessly in disregarding the plaintiffs' express directions and proceeding with the operation in violation of the plaintiffs' religious belief" and "recklessness, under these circumstances, is the equivalent of intention." [25]

In response to the lower court's and majority view of the Orthodox parents as "interested bystanders," the dissenter points to defendants' "contractual relationship with plaintiffs" and, beyond simple contract, he charges the hospital with a "special duty to protect the emotional tranquillity of the [mother]." [26] In his analysis of the judicial enlargement of the tort of inflicting mental distress, Judge Halpern cites cases upholding recovery for emotional suffering by close relatives of a decedent whose body has been mishandled in violation of the plaintiff's "religious feeling." [27] This line of cases, once considered exceptional, is now in the mainstream of a liberalized judicial approach to recovery for mental distress in New York.[28]

Had the trial court and Appellate Division been more receptive to admitting Jewish law respecting circumcision, plaintiff's damages may well have been subject to substantial mitigation, for the performance of a circumcision by a medical doctor, in exceptional circumstances, may not violate Jewish law. "Two considerations would bar a non-Jewish physician: (1) if his intention were to harm the Jewish child; (2) If his intention were to perform a non-Jewish religious rite." [29] Neither consideration was present. In addition, under certain rabbinic construction, "the ritual of 'taking a drop of blood' (*hatafat dam brit*)" when performed on the eighth day by a man trained in ritual circumcision (*mohel*) would comply with Jewish law and cure the hospital's faulty actions.[30]

Since the *Kalina* case, the trend of New York cases has been to extend liability for infliction of mental distress. It has been held that parents may have a right of action against a school which has caused them mental distress by the unauthorized disclosure of confidential information concerning their child. The decision [31] cites cases supporting the general liberal trend permitting recovery and makes no attempt to distinguish *Kalina*, merely remarking, "On the other side of the coin, there is precedent for dismissing a complaint in mental distress for failure to state a cause of action." [32]

A second New York case [33] in which circumcision was pivotal, and its significance misconstrued, dealt with court approval of the placement of a four year old child who had been adjudicated "neglected." By statute, foster placement "must, when practicable, be with or in the custody of a person or persons of the same religious faith or persuasion as that of the child." [34] The boy, born to a Jewish mother and Greek Catholic father, had been circumcised in accordance with Jewish law. Four years later his father had him baptized, without maternal knowledge or consent, as a Roman Catholic. Why the father chose Roman Catholicism was never satisfactorily explained in the father's testimony, although he remained insistent that his son was a Roman Catholic. The opinion of the Children's Court Division of the Domestic Relations Court stated the issue and conclusion:

> The question to be decided here is whether the boy concerned in the proceedings is Jewish or Roman Catholic. It is asserted and testimony submitted that this child has been circumcised according to Jewish rites in the year of 1948 and therefore he is of Jewish faith. Circumcision, of itself, does not mean that a child is of Jewish faith. Much medical authority believes that it is also a health measure. However, when a child is circumcised within the tenets and rules prescribed by the Jewish religion, the circumcision establishes and completes the Jewishness of the child as to his religion.[35]

The judge's mistaken view that the order of ritual, circumcision preceding baptism, determined the child's faith is, of course, contrary to Jewish law. The decisive factor, from the Jewish standpoint, was the mother's Jewishness.[36] This the court never alluded to, placing an erroneous emphasis on circumcision and purporting to rely on Jewish law in so doing.

Child Rearing and Support

Traditionally, the merit of a father was judged by the children he had raised and the goals toward which they were directing their lives. Judah ibn Tibbon, a rabbinic sage, asked his son, rhetorically: "What is the honor I so clearly wish for? It is to be remembered for good, both in life and in death, because of you, so that others, observing you may say: 'Blessed be the father who begot this son: blessed be he who raised him!' "[37]

The older English common law similarly granted to the father the right to guide a child in religious training.[38] But, in the United States the courts have tried to remain aloof from intervening in child rearing. The judicial inclination is stated in a New York opinion:[39]

> Dispute between parents when it does not involve anything immoral or harmful to the welfare of the child is beyond

the reach of the law. The vast majority of matters concerning the upbringing of children must be left to the conscience, patience and self-restraint of father and mother. No end of difficulties would arise should judges try to tell parents how to bring up their children.

However, there are occasions when the courts are either unavoidably obliged or irresistably tempted to direct the nature of a child's rearing, if only by way of construing contractual or statutory child support provisions. A 1961 Illinois appellate court decision [40] enforced the terms of an antenuptial agreement calling for the rearing of children of a broken marriage as Jews in the face of the divorced mother's disregard of the contract. Mary Jane Gottlieb insisted on raising her son, Steven, as a Catholic. For two years litigation between Mary Jane and her ex-husband, Jerry, dragged on before the Illinois lower courts. Finally, Mary Jane won modification of the custody provisions of the divorce decree permitting the enrollment of Steven in a Catholic parochial school. Upon the father's appeal, the appellate court uncovered "a discernible design on plaintiff's part to repudiate and breach the agreement and decree," and ruled that "the provision for [the children's] religious rearing was a determination that their well-being would be best served by raising them in the Jewish faith." The court reversed the lower court's modification of the divorce decree holding that "in the absence of clearly established circumstances indicating that the best interests of the child would be served by modification we do not feel that solemn agreements incorporated in a decree and sanctioned by the court should be so lightly cast aside." Ironically, the decision favoring the Jewish father and directing a Jewish upbringing for his children, is at odds with Jewish law which declares the religion of the mother controlling. The case is illustrative of the inability of reluctant courts to avoid engagement in religious aspects of domestic quarrels, and of their harried efforts to make secular peace on religious battlegrounds.

Paradoxically, a 1955 Massachusetts case [41] which followed the Jewish law view that the religion of the mother governs the religion of her children, led to a harshly criticized [42] holding denying a Jewish couple adoption of twins born to a woman "raised as a Catholic." Despite proof that the mother, contrary to Catholic doctrine, had obtained a civil divorce, openly cohabited with another man without benefit of Church dissolution of her marital ties, and had not baptized her twins, the court found "the mother did not cease to be a Catholic, even if she failed to live up to the ideals of her religion."[43] The mother's consent to adoption by Jewish foster parents notwithstanding, the court strictly construed a Massachusetts statute reading:

> In making orders for adoption, the judge when practicable must give custody only to persons of the same religious faith as that of the child. In the event that there is a dispute as to the religion of said child, its religion shall be deemed to be that of its mother.[44]

It found the mother's Catholicism an "inborn status," dictating adoption by Catholics only.

Inescapably drawn into the vortex of religious controversy in custody and support cases, not all jurisdictions follow the rigid approach of Massachusetts. New York and Wisconsin, in particular, have looked to factors which temper the religious identification of the adoptive parents. New York would not have followed the Massachusetts ruling since the natural mother had made a legal declaration of her unconcern that the adoptive parents were Jewish.[45] Wisconsin puts "the religious requirement . . . within the broader standard of the general welfare of the child."[46] Such views, of course, tend to minimize the need for secular court investigation of religious law definition.

One New York case, in particular, proved irresistible on its facts to an extended judicial rebuttal. In *Kaplan v. Kaplan*,[47] papers in a divorce action were accepted as an application by the wife for temporary support and counsel fees and the application was granted under New York law. The judge went further and responded to the defendant husband's contentions that under Jewish law "it would be tantamount to blasphemy to compel him to exceed his annual trust and annuity income in providing for the support of his wife and three daughters." The husband had pursued "a life devoted exclusively to Hebrew studies" and cited Jewish law sources as authority for his claimed exemption from any obligation of family support under those circumstances. The court's withering response was to hoist the defendant by his own petard:

> Defendant's references to the "Kethubah," the Jewish contract of marriage, to the "Yoreh Dayoh Hilcoth Talmud Torah" Chapter 246, paragraphs 21, 25, "Hagah" are distortions of the law to suit himself, and defendant is best described by a famous quote of Nachmanides, "a scoundrel within the limits of the Torah."
> At the outset, the example (now established Hebraic law) set by one of the greatest scholars in Rabbinic history, Rabbi Akiba, who would not devote his life to study without his wife's express consent, forbids defendant from pursuing his newly chosen "life's work" in Monsey, New York . . . Defendant's reference to "Yoreh Deah" perverts and traduces its moral teaching that it is meritorious for a man to work for his sustenance and devote the remainder of his free time to study. He is not to devote his time to study that he must seek "charity" or rely on the largesse of others . . .
> The nadir of defendant's conduct is his reference to the "Kethubah," the Jewish contract of marriage. Its clarity and preciseness require no Hebrew scholar to comprehend the husband's basic obligation: "I will cherish, honor, support and maintain thee in accordance with the custom of Jewish husbands who cherish, honor and support their wives in truth . . . and I will also give thee food, clothing and necessaries . . ." This is a sacred promise to care for his wife, not in the manner to which she was accustomed, but in accordance with his station in life.
> The court commends to defendant a reading of Exodus, Chapter XXI, verse 10; Maimonides, "Nashim," section "Ishuth," Chapter XII, paragraphs 1, 2 and 5; and the Shulhan Aruch (Code of Jewish Law), Even Ha'Eser, Chapters LXIX and LXX, which make it mandatory for a husband to support his wife in accordance with his economic status.

The court then went on to direct the husband to pay an amount for support and maintenance which left him with but $2,000 for himself in annual trust income. "Should defendant find such sum inadequate," the opinion concludes, "he has a simple remedy of invading the corpus of his trust fund or using his educational background and talents to pursue mundane employment in the honored profession of a religious teacher."

That a father's family support obligations take precedence over the costs of self-support, albeit for the worthy purpose of "a life devoted exclusively to Hebrew studies" is a judicial finding supported by American and Jewish law. A more difficult legal issue concerning child custody under Jewish law was presented to the New York Appellate Division in a 1969 case.[48] The technical question was "whether the custody of the child shall be arbitrated in accordance with the provisions of the separation agreement" between the parties, the salient terms of which the court summarized: [49]

> . . . in conformance with Jewish religious law, the petitioner [wife] shall have custody of their son until his sixth birthday, at which time the respondent [husband] shall have custody. Finally, it provides that any controversies arising between the parties shall be arbitrated under Jewish religious law by three persons, one to be chosen by the petitioner, one to be chosen by the respondent, and the two so designated to choose an orthodox rabbi as the third, all of whom are to be versed in Jewish religious law, and that, if the three arbitrators cannot agree, the decision of two shall be final.

It was the mother's contention that it was in the best interest of the child that she retain his custody past the age of six and "that in her belief, Jewish religious law does not provide that the respondent must have custody after the child reaches his sixth year." The father, on the other hand, "asserted that in his opinion both parties would violate their religious code if he did not obtain custody of their son at age six . . . To his answer was attached a decision of a rabbinical court, signed by three rabbis, stating that according to Jewish religious law the custody of a male child over six years of age belongs to his father." [50] Refusing to be drawn into an examination of Jewish law on the merits of the substantive question, the court saw a broader issue posed: How far to carry judicial recognition of foreign, in this case Jewish, law, privately contracted for, in the resolution of domestic litigation. It determined that considerations beyond the agreement prevail. "The basic principles governing the custody of infants are beyond debate. The State, succeeding to the prerogative of the crown, acts as *parens partriae.*"[51] The court went on to ignore the agreement between the parties, and declared the limiting of "the area of decision to one relevant factor alone—the effect of Jewish religious law" too restrictive, and likewise nullified the agreement's narrowing "the choice of arbitrators to those versed in Jewish religious law."[52] For whatever impelling motive, or combination of motives, whether the prospect of arbitrators usurping the role of domestic relations adjudicator, the invocation of Jewish law, their conjunction, or some unexpressed cause, the vehemence of the opinion certainly strays from the New York inclination to leave a "dispute between parents when it does not involve anything immoral or harmful to the welfare of the child . . . beyond the reach of the law."[53]

But not every New York court has given short shrift to Jewish law or failed to recognize the controlling role of the mother in determining the Jewishness of her offspring. In *Gonzalez v. Gonzalez,*[54] an action for divorce, the court gave effect to an agreement between the parties allowing the offspring of the terminated marriage to adopt the mother's maiden name. The agreement read in part:

> That MIGUEL GONZALEZ consents that the issue of the marriage, DAVID LAWRENCE GONZALEZ' name may be changed to DAVID LAWRENCE ROSENTHAL and that in the event there is a divorce and MAXINE ROSENTHAL GONZALEZ remarries, MIGUEL GONZALEZ hereby consents to the legal adoption of the issue of his marriage by her new husband.

The court found "a showing of compelling reasons warranting" a name change in "the best interests of the infant" on the mother's urging, correctly, that "In Jewish law . . . the newly born child assumes the religion of its mother,"[55] and since she intended that David "be raised in a Jewish home environment as a Jewish child and will be sent to Jewish religious schools and will be

known as a Jew and as the son of Maxine Rosenthal" it would be
in his best interest to be known as David Lawrence Rosenthal.

The much debated decision in *Wener v. Wener* [56] revolved about
the effect to be accorded the terms of a Jewish marriage contract,
Ketubah, insofar as it may obligate a husband to care for a child
in the home. The lower court had emphasized the right of husband
and wife to rely upon their contractual matrimonial document and
the trial judge took the unusual step of defending that decision
in a legal journal,[57] his defense appearing at about the same time
as a critical Appellate Division review. The Appellate Division affirmed, but admonished,[58]

> New York cannot apply one law to its Jewish residents and
> another law to all others. If our law does not require a hus-
> band to support a child whom he has never agreed to adopt,
> the court cannot refuse to apply such law because the tenets
> of the parties' religion dictate otherwise.

In his defense, Judge Multer stressed the parties' contractual
choice of law.

> The mere novelty of the problem was not the reason for
> calling Jewish law from the wings to play a dramatic role in
> this dispute. Even though alternate theories for reaching the
> same result may have been available, it was proper to look
> to the Jewish law for evidence of the intent of the parties.
> The Ketuba, the marriage agreement of the parties, established
> that intent as forcefully as their acts and conduct did. The
> agreement of the parties was that they be bound by Jewish
> law.
> If they had agreed that their rights be governed by the
> laws of Israel, or England, or Louisiana, or of any other
> jurisdiction, the court would have been required to enforce
> the agreement accordingly.[59]

Taking judicial notice of Jewish law, or accepting its proof
on the testimony of expert witnesses, presented no problem to Judge
Multer: [60]

The cases are legion where civil courts have not hesitated to enforce the rights of religious groups and members of such groups, *inter se,* as well as against others. In such cases, the courts have taken the proof of what the religious orders required, and what the members of the church or synagogue had agreed. The cases were decided accordingly.

In the view of the trial judge, "the *Wener* decision merely directs: 'Do what is required of you in accordance with your agreement, regardless of whether it is in Hebrew, English or Chinese.'" The particular agreement it was his lot to interpret happened to come in Hebrew and direct the application of Jewish law.

A New Jersey judge,[61] in a sympathetic exposition, equated the Ketubah with what English law designates as "marriage articles" and entertained a divorced wife's suit to enforce a traditional purpose of the Ketubah, the return of her dowry upon termination of the marriage:

If we lay aside the terms, unusual to our ears, in which the documents are couched, we have what is familiar to English law under the name of marriage articles, and we have a case of the legal situation, which so often arises out of marriage articles, of an executory trust . . .

The court was untroubled by any constitutional "establishment clause" doubts and gave effect to the Ketubah's intent, returning to the wife the $5,000 dowry she had brought to her groom in brighter days.

Education

At the time Hitler's *Judenrein* policies were moving swiftly toward the total extinction of European Jewry and his machinations were sweeping the civilized world toward its fatal rendezvous with organized barbarism, the State Education Department of The University of the State of New York commenced proceedings to extinguish the lamp of learning in New York's Jewish religious schools, the yeshivos. On March 17, 1939 and March 20, 1942 the

Board of Regents passed resolutions looking toward charter revocation of "private or parochial schools that operate with a session carried on in a foreign language during the forenoon, with only an afternoon session in English." The yeshiva, authentic successor and link to age-old institutional education in the doomed ghetto, stood imperiled in its American city of refuge.

All twenty-six affected yeshivos in New York City retained in their defense the learned and deeply committed counsel, Louis J. Gribetz, to persuade the Board of Regents to withdraw its proceeding. He succeeded. In an impassioned brief,[62] drawing on the ethos of his people, Gribetz described for the State Education Department the life force of Judaism—religious education. He described its history, folk-lore, objectives, its crucial importance to Jewish survival and its means of institutional transmission, the yeshivos. He explained the religious basis for morning classes in Hebrew and afternoon instruction in English and preserved the yeshivos' existing educational program. The proceeding was terminated and Jewish religious education continued to be conducted as it had been before.

In the words of the brief,[63] "This proceeding is of no ordinary character and interest. It is momentous and invested with unusual consequences." An adverse Regents determination would have closed the yeshivos, leaving the ugly implication that their programs had been officially found un-American. To counter such innuendo, intensified by the charged patriotism of wartime, a section of the brief was addressed to "The Yeshivos and Americanism": [64]

> The yeshivos stress the identity of the ideals of Americanism and Judaism, the spiritual affinity between them. They show that Americanism derives its great ideals from the Bible and other Jewish sources and that there is no incongruity or incompatibility between Jewish tradition and the American way of life.

The principles of the Declaration of Independence and of the Constitution were likened to "the Jewish conception that all men are free and equal before the law and in the sight of God." [65] A reference is made to the Colonial period and the Reverend John Cotton whose "laws for New England gave marginal references to the Bible for each law." Shortly after Lexington and Concord, Samuel Langdon, President of Harvard College, delivered a sermon attacking monarchical government upon the authority of Israel's experience, which is quoted in part: [66]

> The Jewish government, according to the original constitution, which was divinely established, . . . was a perfect republic. And let those who cry up the divine right of Kings consider that the form of government which had a proper claim to a divine establishment was so far from including the idea of a King, that it was a high crime for Israel to ask to be in this respect like other nations, and when they were thus gratified it was rather as a just punishment for their folly . . . The civil polity of Israel is doubtless an excellent general model, allowing for some peculiarities; at least some principal laws and orders of it may be copied in more modern establishments.

The State Education Department is directed to Biblical influence on lesser known works of the Founding Fathers: [67] "Franklin, Adams and Jefferson, who had been appointed to prepare the seal, selected a design which represented the Egyptians engulfed in the waters of the Red Sea and Moses guiding the Jews and commanding the waters to close over Pharaoh." The choice of the motto on the seal of the United States, "Rebellion to tyranny is obedience to God" derives from "Elijah's condemnation of Ahab's tyranny." [68]

To utterly confute any implication of foreign, un-American or disloyal impulses stemming from education at yeshivos, the brief stressed in magniloquent phrases the secular disciplines and civic training they inculcate: [69]

> The yeshiva has not been and is not merely a school of religion or theology. It has ever been an institution for general education. Every product of mind and spirit, every facet of the complex and multiform relations of humanity, every problem of man's shoreless and bottomless ocean of existence and endeavor, has occupied the minds of the sages at the yeshiva and has been included in its curriculum. Lit-

erally, whatever was worth teaching or knowing was developed, discussed and learned in this institution.

Through the yeshivos came conceptions and ideals of life which constituted the very fundamentals of civilization. Aided by the yeshivos the people who gave to the world the Bible and the Talmud became the people not only of the Holy Book but of the book.

The Jews' devotion to books, however, was not merely as an intellectual occupation. Their acquisition of knowledge was for the purpose of disseminating it for the betterment of mankind, to fill the world with a sense of right, law and order. Another main purpose was to prepare themselves for a life of action and service for the community. The Talmud and other religious literature is replete with passages showing how the Rabbis insisted rigorously on activity and service. They scorned any one who lived in a world of intellect alone. Following are some of the declarations in the Talmud and other Hebrew literature on the subject.

Maimonides, in Yod, Talmud Torah, 3,10 said: "The student of the Talmud who devotes himself to its investigation in order to escape the duty of toil and self-support, desecrates the honor of God; he disgraces the Talmud, extinguishes the light of faith, brings evil fate down upon himself, and forfeits his portion of the world to come." Elsewhere it is said: "The study of the Talmud combined with good works possesses atoning powers." Education which does not produce character and service is a failure. They merely pay lip-allegiance to the Talmud who preach but do not practice its teachings. The sages said: "Great is that learning which calls forth a practical life," and "Wisdom does not enter the heart which is not pure."

The Rabbis of the Talmud strongly urged upon the Jews the pursuit of secular studies. In Shabbat, 75a, it is said: "The man who understands astronomy and does not pursue the study of it, of that man it is written in the Scriptures: 'They regard not the work of the Lord, neither have they considered the operation of His hands.' " In Berakot, 58b, Samuel said: "The streets of the heavens are as familiar to me as the streets of Nehardea" (his birthplace).

The Jews specialized in medicine, in the anatomy of the human body, in knowledge of animal and plant life. Whole tractates in the Mishnah are devoted to studies which indicate a thorough knowledge of natural history. Church Father Jerome criticized the Jewish scholars of his age for spending so much time in the laboratory of the physician.

The Rabbis were masters of language and spoke many tongues. The Rabbis of the Talmud say: "There are four languages that one ought to use: Greek for the art of poetry, Latin for the terms of military command, Aramaic for elegies, and Hebrew for daily speech." Rabbi Elijah of Vilna, the greatest exponent and the quintessence of the excellence of rabbinic Judaism, said that to understand the Torah one must be well-versed in secular knowledge. He encouraged the translation of Euclid and Josephus into Hebrew. He studied mathematics, astronomy, anatomy. His works include treatises on astronomy, trigonometry, algebra and grammar. Members of the Sanhedrin, or tribunal of judges, were required to possess universal wisdom. R. Johanan b. Zakkai, and R. Akiba were considered great in universal wisdom. Greek wisdom was fostered in the house of the great Rabbi Gamaliel.

The Rabbis gave labor a new dignity, and their conception of labor caused great advance in civilization. The advice given by Rav to one of his pupils was: "Flay a carcass in the market place, receive thy wages, and do not say: 'I am a great man, and it is below my dignity to do such a thing.'" (Baba Bathra, 110a.) Berakot 8a contains this precept: "He who enjoys the toils of his hand is greater than he who fears God." In Mekilta 46b the sages taught: "The world is pleased with him who pursues business in an honest way, and such a man is regarded as if he fulfilled the entire Law."

The Rabbis exalted independence and self-support. They themselves practised the humble trades of tailor, shoemaker, baker, blacksmith, etc. It is recorded that upwards of one hundred sages and teachers of the Talmud engaged in manual labor and many others in professional callings. The labor of the hands is raised to a high religious virtue. All study of the Law without work must in the end be futile and become the cause of sin (Pirke Abot 2.2). In fact, labor is a commandment of the Torah, or religious law. The people were charged to do work on the six days just as they were ordered to rest on the seventh day. The Rabbis said that just as God works for the perpetuation of the world so man must work in order to preserve the world.

It is a sobering reflection of the times, the temper of which Gribetz had judged accurately, that an appeal to patriotism and civic virtue was the route to success in the proceeding. Thirty years later the United States Supreme Court[70] would affirm the constitutional right of the Amish, whose reliance on faith it likened to that of the Jews,[71] to deviate from state compulsory education laws on religious grounds, and withdraw their children from all public educational standards after the eighth grade of elementary school.

But it is precisely in the area of religious faith, with religious education as its bedrock, that the fervent eloquence of the brief makes its most moving, as well as legally compelling, plea. Jewish religious education is described as co-extensive with and essential to Judaism from an historic perspective:[72]

> From time immemorial the yeshiva occupied and was accorded a foremost position in Jewry and Judaism. This institution was coeval with the Jewish people and coexistent with and productive of their great literature. In point of origin and significance, the Talmudic expression, "The tradition of Moses from Sinai," is applicable to it. The Temple, the Patriarchate, the yeshiva, have been at all times an essential unity.
>
> This institution accompanied the Jew everywhere. Never did it forsake or desert him. It defied and outlasted persecution and worlds of hostility, interdictors and censors, momentous global changes. The Jew's sentiment for the yeshiva barbarism could not stifle, subjugation could not eradicate. Western education could only enhance it. No people has ever clung so passionately, so desperately, and so fondly to an educational institution as the Jews to the yeshiva. They called it by the most endearing names: "vineyard of the Lord," "spiritual eye of the soul," "mountain of holiness."
>
> One cannot understand Judaism and its literature and

life without knowledge of this institution. No other institution is so deeply rooted in Judaism, or so clearly reveals and interprets its character, or so harmonizes with the Jewish conception of life and God. It has become an inseparable and indispensable part of the Jew's intellectual and spiritual existence . . .

Over a period of 800 years, the renowned scholars at the yeshivos produced the monumental contribution of the Jew to the world—the Talmud . . .

The Encyclopedia Britannica (Vol. 26, p. 384) writes:

"***in the development of European science and philosophy it (the Talmud) played a necessary part, and one can now realize that again the benefit was for common humanity rather than for the Jews alone."

The role of the yeshivos in transmitting Jewish education is the subject of another section of the brief: [73]

The importance and the strength of the yeshivos were an outgrowth of the reverence and love of the Jew for education. Education held an indispensable and exalted role in Jewish life.

The late Charles W. Eliot observed:

"From earliest to the latest, the Hebrew race has been, to a remarkable extent, a literate people passing from father to son and from generation to generation, the art of reading and writing, the love of letters, and a strong belief in education."

Education was a religious duty. In the Bible, Talmud and other sacred literature of the Jews are repeated injunctions on them to devote themselves to learning. Their very place of worship, the synagogue, was in Biblical and pre-Talmudic times called "the place for instruction." The greatest personalities—including the prophets and the priests—acted as teachers. One of the functions of the priests was the dissemination of education. "For priest's lips should keep knowledge and they should seek the law at his mouth for he is a messenger of the Lord."

No language is as rich as Hebrew in the number of root

words referring to or implying the idea of teaching. At least thirty-four root words in Hebrew connote the concept of teaching. Throughout Hebraic literature perhaps no words were more frequently used than "teach" and "teacher."

A basic place in Jewish life was reserved for the instruction of the young. Indeed, it may be said that elementary school education had its roots in the Hebrew tradition and practice. The education of youth began even prior to school age. Isaiah suggested that it should begin when the child is weaned (Isaiah 28:9). Philo observed that "They are taught, so to speak, from their swaddling clothes." As soon as the child could lisp he was taught to recite prayers and proverbs and to chant psalms.

The Bible stringently commanded every Jewish father to teach his children diligently. "Teach thy son" has become a fundamental doctrine in Judaism. So strong is the concept of education in Jewish life that Jewish legends relate that Jewish saints, while still being nursed, were able to pronounce the Hebrew blessing over the milk they drew from their mothers' breasts. Even begging was sanctioned if the object were to provide education. "Though you have to secure the means by begging, be sure to provide for the instruction of your children."

It became a sacred custom for every Jewish father to provide in his last will and testament that his children should provide for instruction of their children. It was a rule in Jewish life that no Jew who pretended to the title of Talmid Chochim (man learned in the law) should live in a place where there were no teachers for children. The phrase in the Psalms, "Touch not my anointed," refers to school children, and the phrase, "Do not offend my prophets," refers to teachers.

It was essential for every Jew to have an accurate knowledge of the law. All Jewish sages and leaders condemned ignorance as synonymous with sinfulness since the ignorant man could not possibly be good or pious.

In obedience to the divine command to teach the child, the Jewish people were the first to institute a system of free universal education.

H. G. Wells observes in his "History of the World" that

"The Jewish religion***led to the first efforts to provide elementary instruction for all the children of the community."

In Eby and Arrowood, "The History and Philosophy of Education, Ancient and Medieval," the authors, in stressing the importance of instruction and the teacher in Jewish life, state:

"The Jews held all teaching in greatest reverence, particularly elementary instruction, which was universally despised by other peoples. Teaching was to them a sacred office; for as God, the first teacher, gave the law to Israel, so the teacher gives it to the children. The Talmud inquired, 'What does God do in the fourth hour?' 'He teaches little children,' is the reply. A famous rabbi declared, 'The world is only saved by the breath of school children.' A city in which there was no school was a forbidden place of abode for a Jewish family.

"Not only instruction but also the teacher was exalted. 'Respect your teacher as you would God,' was a common admonition to the young. A Talmud ruling decreed, 'The teacher precedes the father; the wise man, the king.' If the parent and teacher are both in need or in prison, as spiritual father, the teacher has prior claim over the natural father.[74] If one's father and teacher are bearing burdens, one must help the teacher first. The rabbis took the highest rank everywhere."

The Jewish system of education is characterized by them as follows:

"The fact that it has outlasted every other system whatsoever makes it the most successful educational experiment ever staged in the history of civilization."

Reference is made to them by the educational historian, Dittes, who declared:

"If ever a people has demonstrated the power of education, it is the Hebrew people."

Isaiah's command, "All thy children shall be taught" was given solemn, intensive and practical realization in the yeshivos established by the Jews.

Addressing himself to the narrow issue of morning Hebrew instruction and afternoon English lessons, Gribetz respectfully referred the Regents to the integration of Hebrew morning prayer with Hebrew lessons and the readier availability of English instructors in the afternoons.[75] But, on broader grounds, counsel had sought to establish attendance at yeshivos as a constitutionally protected religious practice, and had succeeded in depicting yeshivos as bearers of Judaism itself. His presentation had set the context within which citation of legal precedent came almost as an embellishment.

Eight years after the New York Board of Regents withdrew its charter revocation proceedings, a New York Domestic Relations Court convicted a Jewish parent of violating the State Education Law "in failing to cause his school age child to attend school instruction between September 12, 1949 and May 12, 1950." [76] The child had attended "a small religious school in New York City maintained by persons of the Jewish faith. The only instruction given by this school was in the Bible, Talmud and elementary Jewish law." [77] In his defense, the child's father relied on the First Amendment, proclaiming his religious belief that all secular education was sinful and a child's study should be confined to the study of Torah.

The factual setting differed in significant respects from the earlier Board of Regents proceeding.[78]

> The instructor did not possess minimum qualifications for secular instruction required of a teacher . . . English was not the language of instruction; the textbooks used were not written in English, and no formal or systematic instruction was given in ten basic subjects, all of which were required by section 3204 of the Education Law. No records of attendance at this school were kept . . .

The trial court rejected the First Amendment claim of the parents: [79]

> It seems clear therefore that the religious convictions of respondents herein must yield to the total public interest. Compulsory education laws constitute but one of many statutes of a government, dedicated to the democratic ideal, which are

universally enacted for the benefit of all of the children within the realm of government. Child labor laws and laws making it criminal to abandon or neglect children, are similar instances of governmental intervention for the protection of children. Religious convictions of parents cannot interfere with the responsibility of the state to protect the welfare of children.

The Court recited other illustrations of constitutionally valid interferences with religious liberty in support of its decision, including the United States Supreme Court anti-polygamy ruling,[80] a conscientious objector opinion,[81] a disturbance of the peace case,[82] and a decision upholding compulsory vaccination.[83]

A pathetic by-product of the criminal case was a custody dispute revolving about a child of one of the several convicted fathers. At the instance of his ex-wife, as one who had violated the Education Law he was adjudged unfit to retain custody of his son.[84] That a father who would risk punishment for his religious beliefs concerning his son's education should in consequence lose both the education he believed in as well as his child is a triumph of technical construction over paternal devotion.

A father of less ardent commitment to Jewish education received better treatment on religious grounds at the hands of a Buffalo, New York court in a 1926 case.[85] He had enrolled his son in an Ohio military academy and while the boy attended daily chapel, he would not attend compulsory Sunday church services. For this minimal adherence to his own faith he was expelled and the school brought suit to recover from the father the balance of tuition then owing. While the school claimed its catalog describing the school's curriculum clearly mandated Sunday church attendance and was therefor part of the contract made between school and father, the court was less certain of the clarity of this alleged proviso. In addition, the City Court of Buffalo found that even if there was a contract,

> It is plain to me that the strenuous effort of the plaintiff to compel the defendant's son, a boy of Jewish faith, to attend the church services of various Christian churches in the village of Germantown, against his will, and in opposition to

his religious faith and convictions, is clearly a violation of his constitutional rights. This, to my mind, is so unless the language of the Bill of Rights of the State Constitution of Ohio is composed of empty words, and the ideas and ideals of the American People as to freedom of conscience through all these years has been but a pleasant dream.[86]

Miami Military Institute was denied recovery of its tuition bill.

MARRIAGE

Prohibited Marriages

Under Jewish law a man may not marry:[87]

a) His mother, grandmother and ascendants; the mother of his grandfather; his stepmother, the wife of his paternal grandfather, and of his ascendants; and the wife of his maternal grandfather.

b) His daughter, granddaughter, great granddaughter and her descendants; his daughter-in-law; the wife of his son's son, and descendants; and the wife of his daughter's son.

c) His wife's mother or grandmother; the mother of his father-in-law, and ascendants.

d) His wife's daughter or her granddaughter and descendants.

e) His sister, half-sister, his full or half-brother's wife, divorced or widowed, except for levirate marriage with the widow of a childless brother (Deut. 25:5-10); and the full or half-sister of his divorced wife in her lifetime.

f) His aunt, and uncle's wife (divorced or widowed), whether the uncle be the full or half-brother of his father or mother.

g) A married woman, unless proper divorce has been given; and his divorced wife after her remarriage (her second husband having died or divorced her).

h) Anyone who is not a member of the Jewish faith; the issue of an incestuous or adulterous union; the married woman guilty of adultery with him; and the widow whose husband died childless, until the ritual directed in Deuteronomy Chapter 25 (*Chalitzah*) has been performed.

i) A Kohen (descendant of the ancient priests of Israel) may not marry a divorced woman, a *Chalitzah* widow, or a proselyte.

Thus a man may marry, among relatives:

a) His stepsister, his stepfather's wife (divorced or widowed), his niece; and his full or half-brother's or sister's daughter-in-law.

b) His cousin; his stepson's wife (divorced or widowed) ; and his deceased wife's sister.

A woman may not marry:

a) Her father, grandfather, and ascendants; her stepfather; and the husband of her grandmother, and of her ascendants.

b) Her son, grandson, great grandson; her son-in-law, and the husband of her granddaughter and descendants.

c) Her husband's father, or grandfather, and the father of her father-in-law and ascendants; and the father of her mother-in-law.

d) Her husband's son or grandson, and descendants.

e) Her brother; half-brother; her full or half-sister's divorced husband in her sister's lifetime; and her husband's brother and her nephew.

f) A married man, unless properly divorced; and her divorced husband after the death or divorce of her second husband.

g) Anyone who is not a member of the Jewish faith; the issue of an incestuous or adulterous union; and the man guilty of adultery with her as a married woman.

Thus, a woman may marry, among relatives:

a) Her stepbrother; and her stepmother's former husband.

b) Her cousin; and her deceased sister's husband, whether of a full or half-sister.

c) Her uncle.

At common law a man may marry the daughter of his wife's brother or his wife's sister; but not the daughter of his own brother or sister.

American case law has had occasion to deal with two of the prohibited classifications, marriage to a non-Jew and marriage between uncle and niece.

Intermarriage

Testators have made bequests to a beneficiary provided he or she marries within the Jewish faith. A number of such prospective legatees, faced with difficult choices between heart and *halachah* (Jewish law), have determined to have their wedding cake and eat it with papa's silver spoon. The Surrogates' Courts of New York have given them indigestion. Although restraints on marriage are generally forbidden, will provisions of the type described generally have been sustained:[88]

> Conditions in partial restraint of marriage which merely impose reasonable restraint upon marriage are not against public policy. Conditions not to marry a person of a particular faith or race are not invalid.

A Queens County, New York, Surrogate reached a like result[89] under a will providing: "If any person or persons to which any bequest or benefit is given herein . . . shall at the time of my death be married to any person born or begotten of parents other than of the Hebrew religion and faith, then . . ." such bequest was to be reduced.

Judge Irving Lehman of New York's highest court invalidated a will provision, however, the intent of which was to deny an inheritance to a family member who married a non-Jew, for the reason that the restriction was not so phrased.[90] Instead, the testator, "an orthodox Jew," made his bequest to a son, who had twice "married women of a different faith" in his father's lifetime, contingent upon the marriage of that son "with the consent and approval of the executors and trustees named in the will." Although the father's intent was clear, the formulation of the condition was too broad to be sustained and the court ordered it stricken. So Isaac Liberman's son, Harry, was free to marry Margaret Jones, his inheritance intact (less considerable legal fees).

Marriage to a non-Jew in *Gluckstern v. Gluckstern*[91] took an unusual turn. Married as Jews, Mrs. Gluckstern confided to her husband that she was converting to Christian Science. He argued the conversion violated his wife's marriage vows[92] and he was no longer obligated to support her. He alleged, "prior to and at the time of the marriage the parties agreed that they would maintain their home and conduct their lives in accordance with the tenets of the Jewish faith." To be married to a non-Jew was contrary to his religion. The court found no basis in fact or civil law for any conclusion that there was any prenuptial agreement concerning [Mrs. Gluckstern's] religion . . . If the defendant contends that such a contract is implied, then I hold that (with due deference to but) notwithstanding the Jewish or Hebraic or Mosaic law or tradition it is not the secular law in this or any other state in the Union.

Had Mrs. Gluckstern made her decision for Christian Science following a civil marriage ceremony, but before a religious one which she and her intended spouse had previously agreed to, the result would have been different in New York.[93] Where an Orthodox Jew sued to annul his civil marriage because his Episcopalian wife refused to go through with conversion to Judaism "and be married by a rabbi," the annulment was granted. The New York court declared "decisions in this state have uniformly held that a marriage may be annulled for any fraud or deception which would invalidate or authorize the cancellation of any contract." [94] Other states do not share New York's attitude toward granting annulments under similar circumstances on the grounds that "secular courts should not force a party to engage in a religious act, i.e. a religious ceremony of marriage." [95]

Uncle-Niece Marriage

Practically every state in the Union prohibits marriages between uncles and nieces as incestuous. Jewish law, however, permits such marriages. The Rhode Island statute governing prohibited degrees of consanguinity makes an exception for marriages valid under Jewish law.[96] Under these circumstances, it should come as no surprise to report litigation growing out of Jewish weddings between non-Rhode Island uncles and nieces celebrated in that state.

In one such New York case [97] the issue arising upon the uncle's death was whether his surviving "spouse" was entitled to have letters of administration issued to her. Upon appeal from the Surrogate's decision denying letters to the niece, the Appellate Division upheld the validity of a marriage valid in the state where the ceremony was performed. Marriage between uncle and niece, said the court "is still lawful in many jurisdictions in our country and abroad throughout Christendom. It was not interdicted by Levitical or Talmudical law and is presently sanctioned by Jewish faith and doctrine." [98] It is therefore "incestuous" by New York statutory

designation merely and is not repugnant to public policy as poly-
gamy, for example, would be. New York's highest court, the Court
of Appeals, affirmed.

A Maryland court, faced with similar facts, reached the same
result, but with less confidence.[99] It held the Rhode Island marriage
between uncle and niece voidable, but since any action to invalidate
it was required to have been brought in the lifetime of the parties,
the marriage was sustained against collateral attack by disgruntled
relatives after the uncle's death.

The uncle-niece relationship lay at the core of 1968 New
York litigation over the testamentary rights of the niece-
"spouse."[100] In the course of their lives, a Jewish marriage ceremony had taken place which was later annulled at the uncle's
instance on the legal ground that the parties were uncle and niece
of half blood. On the subsequent death of the uncle, his niece
claimed rights in his estate under the terms of their antenuptial
agreement which provided it was to become effective "only in the
event that the contemplated marriage between the parties shall
be solemnized." Denied recovery at the intermediate appeal level,
the case went to the Court of Appeals where the outcome hinged
on two issues, both resolved favorably to the niece. First, New
York's highest court treated the validity of an antenuptial agreement contemplating marriage between uncle and niece:[101]

> That the contract itself is valid is not open to doubt.
> It did not prescribe where the marriage was to be solemnized.
> It was not only valid by Jewish law, but it would be valid at
> least in some jurisdictions outside of New York, where it
> could have been performed, and hence the contract was not
> interdicted as an unlawful agreement . . .

Secondly, the court analyzed whether there was a sufficient performance of the terms of the antenuptial agreement "to require
decedent's estate to pay the amount contracted to be paid." Performance depended on whether a marriage between the parties had
been "solemnized," and the court found it had:[102]

> The parties undoubtedly believed the marriage which
> had been solemnized by a Rabbi between them according to

Jewish law was valid. Each stated in the application for the marriage certificate that no legal impediment existed. They lived together as husband and wife for a substantial part of a year when the decedent, apparently contemplating another marriage, brought the action to annul the marriage with petitioner.

The essential conditions of the antenuptial agreement had been satisfied.

Significantly, New York's highest court—majority and both dissenters—framed its inquiry in terms of finding the true intention of contracting parties who had conditioned their antenuptial contract on the "solemnization" of a contemplated marriage. The majority upheld that contract in the face of a subsequent "marriage" void under New York law as incestuous, but valid under Jewish law. The dissenters contended the parties had in mind a marriage valid under civil law. Neither majority nor dissenting opinions recognize any constitutional impediment to the parties invoking a Jewish law test of "solemnization."

Conversely, Jewish nuptials, complete with caterer and Ketubah, rather than confirming the parties' antenuptial agreement, were asserted by the surviving spouse to have abrogated that agreement in a 1974 New York case.[103] The widow argued the Ketubah superseded her prior waiver of widow's rights, and the 100 *zuzim* to which she contractually became entitled "have no monetary value of any kind, but represent the intestate share" which New York law allows.[104] Her late husband's estate responded, not by denying the efficacy of the Ketubah as a contract, but by alleging his more than full and generous compliance with its terms: "the surviving spouse having conceded the receipt by her, as joint tenant, of 200 shares of Occidental Petroleum Corporation, 100 shares of American Oil Corporation and 100 shares of Gulf & Western Corporation, has already received more than the present value of '100 zuzim.' "[105]

Submitted for the estate in defense of the antenuptial agreement was an affidavit of the rabbi who officiated at the wedding. Rabbi Derby's neat accommodation of State and Jewish law provided the Court with an appealing avenue for resolving the contest: "The Ketubah in this case having been executed in today's times, must necessarily be interpreted under today's laws and applying the Jewish legal axium 'The Law of the land is the law,' the Jewish Law says the widow is entitled to that which the law of the land (New York State) allows her." [106] The court emphasized the affidavit, cited *Wener v. Wener* [107] and quoted from *The Spirit of Jewish Law* by George Horowitz to fashion a decision which blended three basic positions, none favorable to the wife. First, the Ketubah was not inconsistent with the antenuptial agreement. Second, under New York law the Ketubah's effect on property rights is not binding and Jewish law references New York law. Finally, quoting Horowitz, "even for the observant and the orthodox, the Ketubah has become more a matter of form and a ceremonial document than a legal obligation, [recalling] ancient and hallowed memories of a time when the Jews constituted a people with a distinctive body of their own laws." [108] The antenuptial agreement was sustained and the widow lost her claim.

Jewish Marriage Ceremonials

Whether a particular form of Jewish marriage ceremony is to be recognized by secular law has been the subject of several civil litigations. A 1927 New York case [109] turned on the validity of a Jewish religious marriage ceremony known as a *shtille chuppe*. Not solemnized by a rabbi, the ritual is marked by the presentation of a ring in the presence of witnesses, the chanting of a prayer and a ceremonial dinner. The parties to these exotic nuptials, performed elsewhere, thereafter cohabited in Canada as man and wife. The woman, who left her first "husband" and remarried some seven years afterward in New York, denied the validity of the *shtille chuppe* in laying claim to widow's rights of inheritance to the estate of her second "husband" when he died. Number two was her one and only, she now saw clearly in her grief and brief. She was opposed by children of the deceased. The Surrogate's Court held the *shtille chuppe* marriage valid under Jewish law and therefore "had this ceremony taken place in the State of New York it would have been valid." [110] It also found that although the *shtille chuppe* marriage would not be recognized as valid under Canadian law, their cohabitation in Canada validated the marital status of the parties under the laws of that jurisdiction. Since the *shtille chuppe*

DIVORCE

The legal tribulations of matrimony often reach a climax in divorce proceedings. The orgin of divorce has long been identified.[119]

Hurrah! I have just found the solution.
Yes, I have delved to the very source
And now I can tell you that "marriage"
Is the principal cause of divorce.

As long as marriage continues in the form presently known to the Western world, divorce and its ramifications will contribute to bulging case reports.[120]

Compelling a Jewish Divorce

A complication of divorce, absent when a religious wedding ceremony takes place, is that civil divorce has no simultaneous Jewish law impact, and conversely, a *get,* or Jewish law divorce, is not statutorily recognized by civil authority. Therefore, cases arise respecting the obligations of the parties following a civil divorce where no *get* has been obtained, as well as where the course of marriage amiss has followed the reverse pattern of a *get* absent a civil decree.

To the Jewish woman, civilly divorced, but without a *get,* re-marriage is adultery. An observant Jewish man would not marry her, and should she remarry civilly and have children, such children in Jewish law would be subject to certain marriage disabilities as offspring of a prohibited union.[121]

In the United States, concern for the plight of the civilly divorced woman whose husband reneges on a promise to appear before a religious court, or *Bet Din,* is legally complicated by constitutional compunctions. Other common law jurisdictions have exerted pressure on the reluctant husband to comply with his Jewish law obligations without the need to heed a superintending First Amendment establishment clause.

A 1973 Canadian case[122] faced the issue squarely of whether a civil court legally could order a recalcitrant husband to appear before a Bet Din at the instance of his civilly divorced wife as part of a

Jewish law proceeding to compel the husband to deliver to her a *get,* or bill of divorce. Both parties to the action were Orthodox Jews. The wife had remarried another Orthodox Jew in a civil ceremony, which they were anxious to follow with a religious wedding. Furthermore, unless a *get* was obtained by the applicant-wife, children, which the applicant and her new husband intended to have, would bear the stigma of being "bastards (Mamzerim) in the eyes of the Jewish religion, as will the descendants of such children."

Preliminarily, the trial court observed [123] that while it

> will not essay to quiet disputes within a religious congregation, or between individual members of that congregation where those disputes arise upon and affect only matters of religious dogma or belief, yet the Court will hear the case where the consequence goes beyond that . . . In the instant case there is no conflict of dogma . . . Orthodox Jewish religion itself is not divided upon the subject.

The court then proceeded to incorporate in its opinion an agreed upon "statement of Jewish law": [124]

> According to traditional Jewish law, when a Jewish man and a Jewish woman wish to marry in accordance with traditional Jewish practices, they must enter in *a marriage contract ("Kethubah") prior to the marriage ceremony.* The Kethubah is explained to the parties and then it is executed.
>
> The Kethubah contains the declaration which is made by the man: "Be thou my wife according to the laws of Moses and Israel." This same declaration is made by the man to the woman at the marriage ceremony. After the marriage ceremony, the Kethubah is read aloud to those assembled. It is then given to the wife.
>
> The Kethubah contains the obligations and duties of both the husband and wife pertaining to marriage.
>
> *The laws of marriage and divorce are completely related to Jewish law. Even at the time of marriage, the possibility of divorce is contemplated.* The Kethubah guarantees the rights of the wife in case of a divorce by providing for maintenance for the wife in case of a divorce. At the end of the

marriage ceremony, the man breaks a glass. This is a symbolic act signifying that even in happy times, there may be sadness and that the union may be broken.

The declaration made by the man binds the two people in marriage. At the same time, according to Jewish law, the man declares that he accepts all rules and regulations pertaining to marriage and divorce because these rules and regulations are contained in the laws of Moses and Israel. The Talmud, a body of laws comprising part of the laws of Moses and Israel, states that the continuance of the marriage is dependent upon rabbinical jurisdiction. According to Jewish law, by presenting himself to the Rabbi and entering the Kethubah, the man is submitting himself to Jewish law pertaining to both marriage and divorce.

The Jewish law states that the man must initiate the divorce proceedings. As this law is believed to be divinely given, it is immutable.

The requirement that there be a divorce exists whenever the marriage ceases to exist factually. Consequently, if there has been a civil divorce, there must be a Jewish religious divorce. Because of the civil divorce, the man has relinquished his rights and duties as a husband and the woman has relinquished her rights and duties as a wife. Factually, the marriage has ceased to exist and the husband and wife must obtain a Jewish religious divorce.

Historically and biblically, rabbinical courts had the right to compel the parties to be divorced. The rabbinical courts had the power to impose physical sanctions in the form of imprisonment and beatings to compel the husband to initiate the necessary proceedings for the Jewish divorce. The rabbinical courts no longer have the power to impose physical sanctions and it became acceptable for the rabbinical courts to turn to the civil courts for enforcement of their orders and, in fact, there is authority in Jewish law which permits rabbinical courts to request the assistance of civil courts in enforcing their orders.

This authority is to be found in the *Mishna, Tractate of Gitten,* cap. 9, para. 8, and Maimonides: *Laws of Divorce,* cap. 2, para. 20.

The Mishna states:

"A Bill of Divorcement obtained through coercion by a Jewish court is valid, by a non-Jewish court, it is invalid. If non-Jewish courts inflict punishment on him and say to him 'Do what the Jewish court requires,' this is valid."

Maimonides states:

"He whom the law requires to divorce his wife and does not so wish, a rabbinical court, in any locality and at anytime should inflict stripes until he says 'I so desire,' and proceeds to write the Bill of Divorcement. Such a Bill of Divorcement is valid and thus, if non-Jewish courts beat him and say to him 'Do what the rabbinical court orders' and the rabbinical court pursues him through the non-Jewish jurisdiction until he issues the Bill of Divorcement, such a Bill of Divorcement is valid. If the non-Jewish court on their own initiative, not in conformity to Jewish law, force him until he issues a Bill of Divorcement, this is an invalid proceeding.

"Why is the first instance valid when there he is also forced by non-Jewish or Jewish jurisdiction? Because we do not classify as coerced anyone except he that is pressured and forced to do something which he is not required according to the divine law, as for example, he who is beaten until he will sell or buy something. But he whose evil drives have led him to disregard a commandment or to commit a transgression and is beaten until he does that which he is required to do or until he removes himself from doing that which is prohibited, this is not classified as coercement, but his initial behavior is considered as having been coerced through his original faulty thinking. Therefore, he who does not desire to divorce his wife, since he desires to be part of the Jewish people and desires to do that which is right and to put distance between himself and that which is wrong, and his base desires motivated him, and he was beaten until that base desire was weakened and he says 'I so desire,' this is considered a divorcement from free will.

"If the law did not require his divorcing his wife

and a rabbinical court erred or non-qualified persons forced him until he would give a Bill of Divorcement, this Bill of Divorcement is invalid as it is classified as prohibited coercion; and if non-Jewish courts pressured him to give a divorce not in conformity with Jewish law, this is not considered a valid Bill of Divorcement even though he stated before the non-Jewish court, after the pressure had been applied, 'I so desire' and he told the rabbinical court, 'Write and sign the Bill of Divorcement,' since the Jewish law does not require it and the non-Jewish court applied prohibited coercion, this is not considered a valid Bill of Divorcement."

Rabbinical courts interpret the above quoted passages as authority for them to turn to civil courts for enforcement of their orders and to request the assistance of civil courts in enforcing their orders.

In the case of the applicant and respondent, the rabbinical court (Beth Din) considered the factual situation and concluded that because the applicant and respondent are now civilly divorced and the applicant intends to be remarried according to traditional Jewish practices, there must be a religious divorce. The respondent was not present before the Beth Din when it considered the factual situation. The Beth Din attempted on several occasions to communicate their decision to the respondent but the respondent refused to discuss the same with the rabbis.

Until such time as the applicant is religiously divorced in accordance with traditional Jewish practices, she cannot be remarried according to traditional Jewish practices. The Jewish laws do not recognize the civil divorce as dissolving the religious marriage and therefore consider the applicant and respondent still to be married. The fact that the applicant has remarried civilly is of no consequence religiously and this civil marriage is not recognized in accordance with Jewish laws.

Children born of a union not recognized by Jewish law are regarded as bastards ("Mamzerim"). A "mamzer" is considered to be less than a whole or complete person in Judaism. The "mamzer" is not permitted to marry according to traditional Jewish law and as a result all descendants of the non-recognized union will be "mamzerim" for generations ever-more and will be ostracized from the main stream of Jewish life.

As the tenets of Jewish law require a divorce in this instance, the rabbis would not look upon an order from this Court compelling the respondent to initiate proceedings for a Jewish divorce as an interference with their religion. On the contrary, there is authority in Jewish law for the asking of assistance from civil courts.

There are no Jewish religious grounds upon which the respondent can refuse to initiate proceedings for a Bill of Divorcement.

The Jewish religious precepts of a person professing to be a Jew would not be offended by the making of the order sought. From a religious point of view there is no religious reason why the applicant and respondent should not be religiously divorced.

The rabbis, as spiritual leaders of the Jewish community would welcome a civil court making an order compelling a man to institute proceedings for a Bill of Divorcement where the Beth Din has determined that the same is necessary.

The Canadian lower court, unencumbered by any constitutional "establishment" doctrine, and relying upon the Canadian Bill of Rights, interpreted the Ketubah as "tantamount to a prenuptial contract," enforceable as such in accordance with "freedom of religion." The husband was ordered to "present himself before the Beth Din to institute inquiry whether a bill of divorcement is necessary as between the parties, and to institute proceedings for the same should the Beth Din so determine." [125] Greatly aiding the court in avoiding entanglement in dogma was the united rabbinic "statement of Jewish law." The court then felt at liberty to refer to their choice of law, by freely contracting parties, as controlling. An additional factor, absent from the United States' cases which decry reliance on Jewish law as risking church-state entanglement, was the unanimity of rabbinic authority on the point at issue. From the form of the Ketubah "apparently prepared by a stationery office in Chicago" to the traditional ceremony itself,

to the rabbis' quoted statement of law, there was a uniformity
of practice, an unbroken heritage, which impressed Judge Wilson,
and to which he unhesitatingly referred. Making a comparison
which must have struck him as instructive, he wrote: [126]

> Not infrequently, in recent years parties to the Christian
> marriage are seen to vary the ceremony as it was known
> to their parents, striking out some of the customary avowals
> or adding phrases which they feel of particular significance
> . . .[127] But in the traditional Jewish marriage, the Kethubah
> and its delivery prior to the actual ceremony are unvarying.

On appeal to Manitoba's highest court,[128] Judge Wilson's
faith in a monolithic Judaism failed to sway his reviewers. Over
the dissent of Manitoba's Chief Justice, his four colleagues reversed Judge Wilson with three separate opinions. One of the
majority was put off by dissension among Jewish authorities, contrary to Judge Wilson's impression and contradicting the "Statement of Jewish Law" he relied upon, as to the consequences of a
civil court's compelling Bet Din attendance. "An article by Dr.
M. M. Brayer, professor of biblical literature and religious education at Yeshiva University" is referred to, which

> includes the following comment:
>> "However, if a non-Jewish court or other methods
>> of compulsion are used, the divorce is invalid, even if it
>> contain rabbinic requirements, because it would be an
>> instrument made out by one who acts not as a free agent."
>> . . . the Court is faced with a contrary opinion as to the
>> propriety of intervention by a civil court. That must be
>> taken into account in considering whether this is a proper
>> case for exercise of the Court's discretion in favour of the
>> applicant . . . It should be noted that reform rabbis, those
>> less constrained by orthodox tenets, will officiate at a mar-
>> riage ceremony notwithstanding absence of a Get.[129]

Three of the majority balked at courts giving "judgments that
cannot be enforced." While "Mr. Morris could be fined or imprisoned
for contempt if he failed to appear before the rabbinical court,

[t]hat would not accomplish the performance of the so-called contract." [130]

Two of the majority, exercising a familiar protectiveness toward civil matrimonial jurisdiction, with nationalistic overtones, declared:

> in the context of marriage and divorce, we in Canada, over the past century, have developed our own laws . . . the law relating to marriage and divorce in Canada is a Canadian civil matter and cannot be allowed to become uncertain or schismatic by reference to various sects or religions . . . We are bound to administer the law of Canada as it is written, and the power of the civil courts of justice should not be extended to assist rabbinical courts or, indeed, any religious sects, to enforce their orders. [131]

The same two judges countered the enforceability of the Ketubah as a contract on two grounds. First, both judges found the mutual pledges of the Ketubah much the same as those in the Anglican marriage ceremony, the United Church of Canada vows and those of the Roman Catholic Church, [132] leading them to conclude "the so-called pre-nuptial statement or Kethubah is not all that definite or clear-cut *as a contract*." Secondly, Mrs. Morris

> is now living with another man, by her own choice, and yet comes before this Court of equity to make her first husband deliver a bill of divorcement or "Get" so that she will not suffer shame in the eyes of her religious community . . . [133]

and although "Canadian law will uphold and enforce a contract" [134] it will not do so at the instance of one who fails to come to a court of equity with clean hands, "and in the light of the facts we have in the present case, Mrs. Morris does not." [135]

One of the majority took the view that the court could only construe the Ketubah as a contract under Canadian law if "civil rights" were involved and "in the present case the right sought to be declared and enforced, in my opinion, affects no civil rights enjoyed by Mrs. Morris." [136] Another judge thought the assertion of such rights was "somewhat tenuous." [137]

In dissent, Chief Justice Freedman, would have sustained Judge Wilson.[138]

> The wife seeks nothing here which would have the effect of displacing or superseding the general law of the land or of annexing Jewish law to it. What she does ask is the assistance of the Court in enforcing her marriage contract. An order made by the Court granting such an application would leave the general divorce law of the land intact and unimpaired.

In summary, a majority of Manitoba's highest court was most troubled by a belief that the remedy sought by Mrs. Morris was inappropriate for a civil court, which could only deal with non-compliance by imprisonment for contempt as its most severe weapon.[139] This concern apart, a majority of the court, if it had been convinced of the clarity of Jewish law on the subject, might well have leaned toward affirmance.

An English court in 1969 was called upon to render judgment in similar circumstances.[140] The wife had obtained a civil divorce and her ex-husband refused her a *get*, thereby impairing her remarriage prospects. In consequence, the court ordered the former husband to make a lump sum support payment of 30,000 pounds to the wife within two weeks, and 2,000 pound weekly payments thereafter until her remarriage, if ever there should be one. However, if the husband would grant a *get* to his spouse, the lump sum payment would be reduced by $16\frac{2}{3}\%$ and weekly payments increased slightly until remarriage. By such court-exerted financial pressure the husband was induced to consider seriously a Bet Din appearance. Legal justification for the monetary difference in support payments rested on the ex-wife's reduced remarriage prospects without a *get*.

A New York court[141] confronting a version of the same problem ordered the balking husband to appear "before the Rabbinate to answer questions and give evidence needed by them to make a decision . . ."[142] However, the court order in his case was made easier by a specific proviso in a settlement agreement executed by the parties just prior to the wife's successful action for marriage dissolution, that "whenever called upon, and if whenever the same shall become necessary" both parties agree

to appear before a Rabbi or Rabbinate selected and designated
by whomsoever of the parties who shall first demand the same,
and execute any and all papers and documents required by
and necessary to effectuate a dissolution of their marriage
in accordance with the ecclesiastical laws of the Faith and
Church of said parties.[143]

Enforcing such an agreement in accordance with its terms
did not enmesh the court in First Amendment "establishment" or
"free exercise" difficulties, contrary to the husband's contention.
"Complying with his agreement," wrote the court [144]

would not compel the defendant to practice any religion,
not even the Jewish faith to which he still admits adherence
. . . His appearance before the Rabbinate to answer questions
and give evidence needed by them to make a decision is not
a profession of faith. Specific performance herein would merely
require the defendant to do what he voluntarily agreed to do.

But the State of New York is inconsistent if not befuddled
in its willingness to enforce agreements between husband and wife
which provide for submission by the spouses to Bet Din jurisdiction
for Jewish divorce purposes. The basic confusion and indecision
lie in the application of the Constitution's religion clauses to the
Jewish law procedure contracted for by the parties. If the reference
is regarded as one to a religious rite imported into a secular judicial
proceeding, then recoil with all due constitutional revulsion is the
dictated response. On the other hand, a judge who sees Jewish law
as a system entire and complete in itself, functioning as any other
legal system but which happens to coincide with a body of religious precepts,[145] has no problem in accepting contractual references to Jewish law by the disputants as binding upon them and
enforceable by secular courts.

A 1973 New York Appellate Division decision [146] illustrates
the constitutionally based negative reflex in a dissenting opinion
(as well as confused uncertainty by the majority), while a New
York Family Court opinion [147] in the same year by a judge obviously
at ease with Jewish law eruditely reconciles it with First Amendment standards.

Margulies v. Margulies posed the difficult problem of dealing with a recalcitrant husband who repeatedly refused to honor his stipulation to appear before a Bet Din to participate "in a Jewish ritual divorce." [148] In consequence of his disobedience, the husband was twice held in contempt of court orders and fined. His defiance at length brought a third order, this time of commitment for fifteen days in jail "with the opportunity to purge himself of the contempt if he appeared and participated in a Jewish ritual divorce." [149] The husband appealed. The majority appellate court decision stands squarely on both sides of the constitutional and Jewish law issues raised. The defendant husband was freed from incarceration but his fines were allowed to stand. The majority found itself "without power to direct defendant to participate in a religious divorce, as such is a matter of one's personal convictions and is not subject to the court's interference." [150] At the same time, the fines were upheld because the defendant

> at the time when he agreed to participate in the religious divorce . . . was well aware of the consequences and nature of the act and that it could only be obtained upon his assertion to the rabbinical court that it was being sought of his own free will. Defendant was also well aware that plaintiff could not enter into a valid remarriage under Jewish law until the "get" had been granted.[151]

Consequently, the majority concluded, the defendant acted contumaciously in never intending "to carry out the terms of the open court stipulation and that he utilized the court for his own ulterior motives." [152] As far as Jewish law was concerned, the majority felt it was acting in accordance therewith "since a Jewish divorce can only be granted upon the representation that it is sought by the husband of his own free will" and "if obtained under compulsion by the court, would in any event be a nullity." [153]

The dissenter saw an insurmountable constitutional impediment to enforcement of any of the contempt orders appealed from, be they in the nature of fines or imprisonment.

> Religion, as well as religious laws, ceremonies and procedures are matters of individual conscience. The constitutional and

traditional complete separation of church and state is most
salutary and desirable. No erosion of this basic concept should
be permitted. . . . I am certain my brethren would not enforce
an order directing a litigant to go to confession or to say six
Our Fathers and four Hail Marys.[154]

Later in 1973, *Rubin v. Rubin* [155] presented Judge Stanley Gartenstein of the Bronx County Family Court with an opportunity
to review Jewish law of divorce, put it in perspective as a complete juridical *corpus juris*, distinguish *Margulies v. Margulies* and
locate Jewish law vis-à-vis the First Amendment. The case arose
upon the petition of a civilly divorced woman to enforce an Alabama
divorce decree. A consent order based on that decree granted her
monthly payments and arrears on condition she cooperate in
securing a Jewish divorce,—a condition she refused to carry out.
Nonetheless, she sought the relief otherwise ordered. Judge Gartenstein distinguished the *Margulies case* as one dealing with the punishment of a recalcitrant party whereas *Rubin* concerned a court's
obligation to act at the instance of a defaulting party.

In a learned opinion he outlined the emphatically contractual
nature of Jewish marriage and compared it to the "quasi-contract-
ual relationship" which characterizes marriage under Anglo-Saxon
jurisprudence.[156]

Indeed, if the Ketubah (marriage contract) leaves the actual
or constructive possession of the wife at any time subsequent
to the effective commencement date of the marriage contract,
further cohabitation is forbidden (Ketubot 7; Even-Ha-Ezer,
66, 1).[157]

Following from this strongly contractual concept of marriage,
"the Get or divorce is a simple act of release nominally executed by
the husband for delivery to the wife 'freeing' her for marriage to
anyone else, having its Biblical origins in Genesis 21, verses 9-14
and Deuteronomy 22, verses 13-19." [158] The impression that a *get*
requires the appearance of both parties before a rabbinic court is
dismissed as fallacious. It is true that the *get* must be drafted
with the aid of "those learned in the law (Kiddushin 60)," [159] but it

is effective when executed by the husband and delivered to the wife by his agent.

The role of the Bet Din is explained. It

> was convened at the suit of the wife for injunctive relief direct-ing the husband to execute and cause delivery of the Get free-ing her. On the other hand, even where proceedings were at the instance of the husband, the staggering minutiae of tech-nical details requiring the assistance of experts (Kiddushin 60, supra), gave the rabbinical courts a res upon which to seize in acquiring judicial powers.[160]

As the repository of the necessary expertise to properly process a *get*, resort to a Bet Din became virtually unavoidable to insure a valid Jewish divorce. Divorce by consent had thus been recognized two thousand years before New York and other Ameri-can states concluded "that a dead marriage should be dissolved."[161] But where mutual consent was lacking, the Bet Din in the guise of "expertizing" devised protections against divorce of an unwilling wife unless certain grounds existed.

> This practice of rabbinical law, in existence for about a thousand years from earliest Talmudic times, was codified by Rabbenu Gershom in the approximate year 1000 of the common calendar."[162]

Judge Gartenstein in an aside even explains the origin of the word "get" as

> derived from the statutory formula connected with its execu-tion. Hebrew numbers, being expressed with the same letters which form words, every word has a numerical value. The word *Get* derives from a combination of letter *gimel* having numerical value of 3 plus *tet*, value 9; total 12 corresponding to the statutory formula of a twelve-line instrument. . . . To underscore how repugnant the tragedy of divorce is, nowhere in the original Hebrew text of the Bible does the letter *tet* follow the letter *gimel*.[163]

In the absence of a *get,* neither party is free to re-marry. Certain restrictions on remarriage ensue even following a *get.* Since marriage to one with whom adultery has been committed is prohibited, "this can result in a religious prohibition against marrying the very same second spouse with whom a party has in fact been living." [164]

Judge Gartenstein in a tactful footnote [165] assumes that all the judges in *Margulies* were referring to a "no-fault" or mutual consent divorce when they took Jewish law to prescribe "that the *Get* can only be obtained on consent" of the husband. He points out that divorce proceedings

> under Talmudic Law are maintainable at the suit of the wife on certain enumerated grounds (Kethuboth 77; Mishne Torah, Marriages XXV; Even Ha-Ezer 154: 118, 11 Rema; M. Kethuboth VII, 10; Even Ha-Ezer 134: I Rema; Even Ha-Ezer 154; 3 Rema) ; at the suit of the husband under circumstances where the financial emoluments of the Ketubah were forfeited (Kethuboth 72; Even Ha-Ezer 115, 4, 5) ; or by the court on its own suit against the wishes of the parties (M. Yevamot VIII, 3; Avodah Zarah 36 B; M. Yevamot II, 8)." [166]

Under the principles of Jewish law described by him, the Judge found the wife's refusal to manifest consent to a *get* made "the position of the husband under ecclesiastical law" untenable.[167] If she had merely refused to appear before a Ben Din, the husband's ability to obtain a *get* would have been unimpaired but her withholding of consent was critical.

Judge Gartenstein then grappled with the constitutional implications of denying relief to the wife for her failure to comply with a condition previously agreed upon, consent to a *get.* Like Manitoba's Chief Justice Freedman in *Morris v. Morris,*[168] Judge Gartenstein saw the basic dispute as a contractual one—"people are bound by the promises they undertake." [169] Furthermore, Judge Gartenstein then took up the First Amendment as a sword to ward off state action "which might interfere with religious disciplines and/or from any act which might interfere with religious tribunals." [170] In other words, the "free exercise" provision was invoked to keep the courts of the realm . . . from entering a dispute with religious implications where the matter has been the subject of litigation in the ecclesiastical courts.[171]

The court concluded it would not act at the instance of "the defaulting party to enforce other relief in her favor at a time when she refuses to perform a condition precedent thereto, which happens to be an act of religious significance."[172] The husband was ordered to "consult a Rabbi of his choice for the purpose of having a notice sent to petitioner either to appear or accept a *Get*."[173] If the *get* were completed within two weeks after notice, then the husband would have to make the payments required. If not, then the wife would be left to her own resources.

New York law is left in the ambiguous posture of withholding relief from a wife who will not cooperate in Jewish divorce proceedings after having agreed to do so,[174] while standing powerless to enforce relief through threat of incarceration against a recalcitrant husband who flouts his promise to grant a *get*,[175] a promise valid under Jewish law.

Recognition of Jewish Divorce

Unlike a Jewish marriage ceremony, expressly sanctioned by state laws, divorce in accordance with Jewish religious ritual alone has no standing in state law, but its validity must depend upon its recognition by some sovereignty. There are instances, however, when a Jewish divorce or *get* may have *collateral* legal ramifications.

A state court, preliminarily, in divorce cases looks to the threshhold question of whether jurisdiction has been properly obtained over the parties to the action. Ordinarily, it will recognize as valid a divorce regarded as valid in the state or country where it was obtained. It will decline recognition only when the proceeding suffers from a serious jurisdictional defect such as failure of the original divorce court to have both husband and wife or either of them as parties privy to its proceedings. A 1935 New York decision[176] denied legal effect to a Jewish divorce, valid under Russian law, obtained by the husband from a rabbi in New York while his wife was living alone in Russia. Similarly, in another

New York case,[177] a wife's annulment suit was sustained based
on the fact that her "husband" was already married when they
went through their "wedding" ceremony. The husband's defense
was that he had previously divorced his first wife in a New York
rabbinic divorce. The court declined to recognize such Jewish divorce on jurisdictional grounds because at the time it was granted,
the "divorced" spouse was domiciled and residing in Russia. The
converse situation leads to the same result. A *get* granted in Russia
at the instance of a husband, whose wife resided in another country
at the time, was equally jurisdictionally defective.[178] The fact that
such a divorce satisfied both Jewish and Russian law made no difference. Even in the Holy Land, as two reported New York cases
have held,[179] Jewish divorce did not necessarily receive recognition.
Palestine under the British mandate did not acknowledge rabbinic
divorce to alter the status of a party not a domiciliary of Palestine
at the time the *get* was granted.

On the other hand, where proper jurisdiction has been obtained,
state courts will give effect to a Jewish divorce or *get* recognized
by the sovereignty where it has been performed. Thus, an Ohio
court [180] examined into the effectiveness of a Jewish divorce granted
in Russia and upheld it as valid under Russian law, the couple
having both been within Russia at the time of the *get*. The court
quoted extensively from a work on Jewish law, Kadushin's *Jewish
Code of Jurisprudence*,[181] in support of its conclusion.

Sometimes a state court will be faced with a foreign law
interpretation requiring the guidance of expert witnesses. The
New York Surrogate,[182] in upholding the validity of a *get* which
terminated a first marriage of the decedent, took expert testimony
on the issue of whether Jewish divorce in Poland required the
imprimatur of secular review, or whether such divorce was given
effect in Poland without further secular Polish court proceedings.
The expert distinguished between contested Jewish divorce proceedings, which required Polish court review, and uncontested
Jewish divorce for which no such requirement existed.

On other occasions a state court, desiring an equitable result,
will make liberal inferences from contested or unclear testimony,
take judicial notice of foreign laws and indulge freely in legal con-
structions. When the "huddled masses yearning to breathe free, the
wretched refuse of . . . teeming shore" were inundating the Ameri-

can east coast at the turn of the century, a New York Surrogate[183] was asked to deny letters of administration to the presumptive widow of an immigrant from eastern Europe upon application of the decedent's father, who claimed his was the legitimate right. Though the father "signed by his mark," the Surrogate thought him "not lacking in shrewdness or a certain sort of patriachal dignity of demeanor."[184] However, if his claim were to succeed, "he will take the little estate away from [the woman Rachel], who has always in this country lived as the wife of his son."[185] To prevent the consummation of any such design, the chivalrous Surrogate indulged in presumption, inference and disparagement in fair Rachel's cause.

The Surrogate's distaste for the milieu of the parties colors his opinion:[186]

> The testimony taken illustrates one of the very curious phases of urban life in this cosmopolitan seaport, where of late years have come so many from the remoter parts of Europe . . . it was in Rumania that the family or marital relations of [the decedent] were constituted, quite in conformity, I think, with the curious license which in some European countries, and even under some insular American governments, is tolerated.

The "patriarchal" petitioner's testimony is belittled. "The testimony is in Yiddish, and the interpretation not very clear." In substance, Rachel is alleged to have been married originally to one Topelman, by whom she had a daughter, Goldie.

> Finally this Topelman went away as a soldier, and to a hospital as orderly, and then Henry [the decedent], the son of Moses [the petitioner], and Rachel eloped from his father's house. The father testifies in effect that he objected, as his son was betrothed to another girl, so he followed them to Bucharest, and consulted a "schochet, who kills calves," to get his aid to induce Rachel to leave Henry, and he says, "she would not." This is about all I can make of the father's testimony.[187]

The Surrogate finds Moses' testimony lacking in veracity. "He states he consulted an agent of his faith about his son's first re-

lations to Rachel. On examination I find," he declares triumphantly,
"a 'schochet' is not a religious officer, but one authorized by a
Jewish community to slaughter cattle for people of this ancient
faith."[188] The Surrogate misunderstood the religious nature of
the office of *schochet* in the Jewish communities of eastern
Europe.[189] Even more damaging to Moses' credibility, however, is
Moses' description of his "daughter-in-law," belied by her appearance when fair Rachel took the stand:[190]

> She testified that she was now 43 years old, which was con-
> firmed by her much younger appearance on the witness stand,
> although Moses would make her out a very old woman, 70 or
> more, a gross exaggeration, which shows bias, not enough
> to impeach him, but sufficient to affect the accuracy of the de-
> tails of his testimony.

Then the Surrogate essayed to prop his opinion on presumptions of law, common and Jewish.[191] Rachel had testified "that she
divorced Topelman 'by a rabbi and married by a rabbi,' " but she
produced no proof other than her own words.[192]

> None, I think was necessary, as one may always testify to
> his own status, if it is not objected to by the adversary party.
> A marriage or birth certificate is not necessary to establish
> those events. A "get" or Jewish "bill of divorce," is not, I
> think, essential to prove a Jewish divorce in the first instance.
> The necessity of producing records in our law refers to our
> records only, for in Jewish law itself the production of a
> "get" to prove a divorce was unnecessary.

Previously, the Surrogate had rejected the testimony of Moses'
sister that Rachel had "admitted to her that she was not married to
Henry" on the ground that "admissions claimed to be made to antag-
onistic witnesses are never a high order of evidence . . . A person's
admission of marriage is of no value on the question of status."[193]

Moses' petition rested on the common law presumption that
Rachel's marriage to Topelman continued. The Surrogate responded
that "presumptions of the common law" were "certainly formulated
for and by a very different civilization to that which the parties

to this proceeding originally belonged. Such common law presumptions have scant relevancy to the eastern institutions of Rumania
and Bulgaria." [194]

A presumption the Surrogate did recognize, however, rested
on the claimed status of husband and wife asserted by Rachel and
Henry upon their immigration to the United States. "I will take
notice of our own immigration laws," he stated, "requiring the
marital relations to be truly stated by immigrants before their
admission." [195]

He took judicial notice of the recognition of Jewish divorce
law by foreign lands.[196]

> In Russia, Rumania and parts of Austria the marriage and
> divorce laws are different from those of this common-law
> country. Although the parties offered no evidence of the
> foreign law, yet for the purposes of this application I should
> take notice of such difference, or a great wrong may be done
> to Rachel . . . A decision which abrogates a marital relation
> of long standing, at the instance of a third party vitally
> interested in the result, ought to be entered on by a court of
> justice, having no jurisdiction in marital matters, with great
> caution, especially when it may concern a foreign status,
> recognized and enforced in the country of the spouses' own
> origin. At this point I am concerned that our law shall not
> be brought into disrepute with people of this sort.

The Surrogate finds an additional presumption favoring
Rachel: [197]

> Topelman, the first consort of Rachel, or husband, if husband
> he was, disappeared from the matrimonial scene many years
> ago—more than 7—and it sufficiently appears, I think, that
> he has since given no sign of life. The presumption of the
> death of Topelman on an indictment of Rachel for bigamy
> would justify her acquittal after 7 years, if not before.

"But," concludes the Surrogate, "we need not, I think, rest
this matter on any mere refinement or disputable presumption of
law." Rachel had testified to her Jewish divorce from Topelman.[198]

Now divorces of those of the Jewish faith by their rabbis in Russia and Rumania, I will take notice for the purposes of this application, are valid, and the subsequent marriages of such divorced persons are consequently recognized as valid by the law of the *locus contractus,* to use our own technical phrase, or rather they are valid under the principle *"locus regit actum."* Status of marriage is ordinarily fixed by the law of the place of marriage. Rabbinical divorces, being recognized in Rumania, are valid in this jurisdiction. *Leshinsky v. Leshinsky,* 5 Misc. Rep. 495, 25 N.Y. Supp. 841; *Miller v. Miller,* 70 Misc. Rep. 368, 128 N.Y. Supp. 787; *Weinberg v. State,* 25 Wis. 370 (1870); *Sokel v. People,* 212 Ill. 238, 72 N.E. 382 (1904).

Although not so in this country, in Russia and Rumania the Jewish communities constitute a sort of *imperium in imperio,* as the state allows them to divorce themselves, according to their own laws, the Mosaic Code, embodied in the Pentateuch; and commented on or modified in the Talmud. The jurisprudence of so old and so great a people as the Jews is naturally not inferior to the jurisprudence of other cultivated races. One is apt to forget, what Renan pointed out in France, that modern law has three great originals—Greek, Jewish and Roman. Our own law owes most to the law of Israel. The lower classes of Jews, the peasants and the industrials of the towns in Rumania, avail themselves liberally of the permission indicated, although the Jewish nobility and the aristocratic people of the Jewish faith generally prefer for greater security to property the additional or ancillary sanction of the ordinary courts of a European country. But as this last is an obscure branch of Jewish law I need not enter on it, as it does not affect this proceeding.

It must not be forgotten that, as among people of all other faiths, the Hebrew community is not, in Europe, equalitarian. Some of them in the terms of the European sociology, have long belonged to the higher nobility, which in European countries still counts for much, although more are of the class known as *"petite noblesse,"* in Europe a negligible rank, but most are classed as bourgeois or peasants, as is the case with European peoples of other faiths. Now, religious obser-

vances and laws are—and it is unfortunate that it is so—
most strictly complied with in all races by the humbler classes
of any faith. Henry and Rachel Spondre were evidently Jews
of the lower order. She would doubtless feel obliged to resort
to the rabbi for a divorce, and both would resort to the rabbi
for their subsequent marriage, just as she testified was the
fact. I have already referred to the law regulating divorce
in Rumania, as well as to our own common law of marriage.
The Mosaic and Talmudical law of marriage and divorce can
be found stated generally in such works as Amrams' "Jewish
Law of Divorce" and Henriques' "Jewish Marriages and the
English Law," and Year Book, American Rabbis, Volume XXV,
and also in the "Treatise on the Jewish Law of Marriage and
Divorce" by Rev. M. Mielziner, of the great Hebrew College
at Cincinnati, all instructive and excellent books of the law.
Jewish law in Russia and Rumania constitutes what we know
in our own law as *"jus moribus constitutum,"* being recognized
as a particular law for a portion of the community only.

So Rachel had charmed the Surrogate. "When Rachel," he
wrote, "swore to a divorce and marriage by a rabbi, her testimony
at once challenged my attention. It introduced something of importance to her, and its validity ought fully to be considered or
justice may fail this poor woman." [199] The Surrogate saw to it
that justice would not leave Rachel's side. The late Henry's estate
would also cleave to her rather than to Henry's father.

Jewish Divorce—Collateral Aspects

Collateral ramifications of Jewish divorce appear where the
get itself would not receive secular recognition. Thus a New York
court [200] considered a separation agreement tainted and voidable
under New York's Domestic Relations Law, which forbids agreements to alter or dissolve a marriage, when the agreement included
a provision contemplating Jewish divorce.

The saga of Sarah Kantor [201] provides an excursion into *get*
ramifications through states of matrimony, "divorce," "widowhood,"
Czarist Russia, Connecticut and New York. It illustrates the inconsistent treatment Jewish divorce may receive at the hands of

secular courts, where it is a nullity per se, but its weight may be
felt in the court's balancing of equities.

"Sarah Kantor and one Solomon Rubin went through a form
of marriage ceremony in Russia in 1879 and lived together there as
Husband and Wife for about seven years, and had three children
born there." So begins the Supreme Court of Errors of the State
of Connecticut [202] in recounting with simplicity the first episode in
Sarah's legally full and intriguing career. "About 1886 Rubin came
to this country, and in 1889 or 1890 the plaintiff," for so Sarah
came to be known,

> and Rubin continued to live together as husband and wife
> until the spring of 1893, when, in consequence of domestic
> quarrels which finally culminated in Rubin calling the plain-
> tiff a vile name and telling her to get out, the plaintiff left
> Rubin and his home. About two months afterwards Rubin
> and the plaintiff, who are both of the orthodox Jewish faith,
> went before a rabbi in Brooklyn, who after an ineffectual
> attempt at reconciliation, performed the ceremony of rabbinical
> divorce.[203]

Both parties then remarried in Orthodox Jewish ceremonies.
Seventeen years later Rubin died and Sarah, who had become Mrs.
Kantor, claimed her statutory share of Rubin's estate. The Probate
Court denied Sarah's claim, invoking the Connecticut law forbidding an elective share to a spouse who has abandoned his or her
mate.[204] Sarah argued the legal effect of a *get* in Jewish law pre-
cluded a construction of abandonment. She claimed "that the rabbinical divorce of 1893 was in legal effect an agreement by the
parties for a permanent separation, with permission to marry again
according to the custom of their religion.[205] The Probate Court
rejected her claim and its decision was affirmed on appeal.

The first judicial tack taken by the appellate opinion was in
the direction of investing the *get* with a certain authority cognizable
by secular tribunals. "This plaintiff has twice solemnly and cere-
monially renounced all her marital rights and duties toward Rubin,
once by the rabbinical divorce of 1893, and again by the rabbinical
marriage to Kantor in the same year." [206] Then veering slightly,

the effect of the *get* is reduced by the court to a sort of quasi-legal separation:

> This plaintiff, by throwing aside the mantle of her religion and claiming now to be the lawful widow of Rubin, necessarily characterizes her rabbinical marriage with Kantor as adulterous; and if we regard the rabbinical divorce of 1893 as an agreement for a permanent separation it is not sufficient cause for the plaintiff's living in adultery with Kantor until Rubin's death.[207]

Finally, the *get* is construed as "abandonment" within the Connecticut statute:

> Of course, the plaintiff can have no standing in this or any other court founded on the claim that the rabbinical divorce was a mutual license to commit adultery . . . The rabbinical divorce between Rubin and the plaintiff was a separation, with intent never to resume their marital rights or duties.[208]

Regardless of whether the *get* was ever definitively construed, its existence was variously used by the Connecticut court to prevent a result which would allow Sarah to inherit from both the late Mr. Rubin and the unobtrusive Mr. Kantor.

Defeated in Connecticut, resourceful Sarah was undeterred. She next appeared in a 1917 New York trial,[209] asserting her dower rights against certain surprised purchasers of New York real estate from the deceased Mr. Rubin. They had been careful in their purchase to obtain a waiver of dower rights from a Mrs. Rubin, unaware that they were dealing with the second Mrs. Rubin. This time, Sarah asserted her Jewish divorce was a nullity under American law and, as the first and true Mrs. Rubin, she urged that she was entitled to dower in the real estate conveyed by her late husband. The secular court was once more put in the position of investing a *get* with legal implications. The appellate court, to which Sarah had appealed, affirmed the rejection of her claim, deciding that she was estopped from recovery on three grounds, the primary one being "(a) The rabbinical divorce, wherein she was the complainant." [210] The other two were "her knowledge of Rubin's remarriage with her acquiescence" and her own remarriage. The court stated:[211]

> The power to give a "get," or bill of divorce, though surrounded with forms to prevent hasty or capricious separations, was regarded as a matter of religious observance. Jewish writers required that the rabbi should be satisfied that there were sufficient grounds. He must, however, first seek to reconcile the parties. The rabbi's efforts for conciliation having been met by her refusal, he delivered to her the "get," which upon her marriage she gave to Kantor as a credential attesting her freedom to remarry. Such a "get" closes with the solemn words, in Hebrew:
>> "And this shall be unto thee, from me, a bill of divorce, a letter of freedom, and a document of dismissal, according to the law of Moses and Israel." Mielziner, "Jewish Law of Divorce," p. 129; Amram, "Jewish Law of Divorce," p. 158.
>> By Hebrew Law, the woman thus freed by divorce could not marry for 3 months thereafter. Amram, "Jewish Law of Divorce," p. 108. In 1791, Lord Kenyon received testimony of a Jewess (without producing any document) proving a divorce *more judaico* in Leghorn, and thus established the validity of her own divorce. Ganer v. Lady Lanesborough, Peake's Nisi Prius R. 17.

So dogged Sarah had come to litigations' journey's end. Married and divorced under Jewish law, she sought to deny its force. But Connecticut and New York, to which she appealed for secular succor, gave enough credence to her Jewish divorce to render all her claims nugatory.

The consequences of an invalid *get* under secular law are evident in naturalization proceedings which require the applicant for citizenship to be of good moral character.[212] A number of federal court proceedings have either denied naturalization applications or revoked citizenship of Jewish immigrants who had divorced spouses in rabbinic proceedings and then remarried. Such divorces, while invalid on secular jurisdictional grounds, are completely in accordance with Jewish law. The spouses, technically adulterers, if not bigamists, were often charged with moral turpitude, the consequence of which might be deportation.[213]

Judge Simon Rifkind, in a 1941 review of a petition for citizenship,[214] opposed by the government, ruled that an immigrant's ignorance of the secular invalidity of a *get* did not necessarily show deficient moral character. The petitioner had executed a marriage license application, following a rabbinic divorce, in which he responded affirmatively to the question of whether this was to be his first marriage. On appeal, the Court of Appeals remanded for trial the issue of the applicant's good faith belief that the *get* had undone his first marriage.[215] This case, at least, represents a more humane and realistic approach to the question of rating moral character than does indulging in common law presumptions of bad morals in consequence of participation in religious ritual unrecognized by civil authority.

Jewish divorce has achieved a degree of collateral recognition in civil court proceedings denied the *get* as an act of independent secular juridical significance. It is a solemn religious procedure of which the civil authority takes no immediate notice, but from which there subsequently may radiate imponderable legal ramifications under state and federal law.

DEATH AND BURIAL

The end of life is surrounded by Jewish ritual and hedged in Jewish law no less than is its beginning. Upon the death of a parent, sons are commanded to attend religious services in the morning, afternoon and evening for an eleven month period, and on the anniversary of the date of death thereafter as long as they may live. At such services *Kaddish*, the prayer for the departed, is recited. Next to the "Shema" ("Hear, O Israel"), it is revered as the most sacred of all Jewish prayers.[216] It is a usage current among American Jewry to retain an individual or religious society to perform memorial services on the anniversary days or *yahrzeits*.[217]

Yahrzeits and Kaddish

By his will, Sam Fleishfarb "gave the sum of $3,000 to his

executor 'to be deposited by him in trust for thirty (30) years for
the following purposes: That the annual interest thereon is to
be used annually for a Yahrzeit to commemorate the name of
my deceased wife.' " [218] This bequest was contested. "The executor
advances the contention that these provisions are wholly void,
which position is enthusiastically supported by all others connected
with the case, with the single exception of the court." [219] The Surrogate sustained the gift as one for "religious or pious uses" within
the scope of a public charity, the yahrzeit "prayer for the repose
of the soul of a dead person [being] similar in purpose to masses
in the Roman Catholic Church." [220] The analogy is well taken.
That part of the Kaddish which is the doxology became, in the
Latin Mass of the Roman Church, the Gloria and the Sanctus. The
Jewish custom, established in the Middle Ages, of burning a
memorial lamp for twenty-four hours on the yahrzeit, may well
have "derived from the [Catholic] practice of burning votive
lamps." [221]

The *Fleishfarb* case became established precedent. In 1939
it was followed by another Surrogate[222] against the desire of an
executor who "naively alleges . . . that 'conversations had with
the heirs indicate a desire to completely eliminate the [bequest].' "
The court disdainfully rejected the executor's request: ". . . the
desired annihilation of the legacy may not be secured by such
consent." The $500 given in trust for use of the interest to "keep
the Yahrzeit" was sustained as "a valid trust for religious uses." [223]

Not only sons may say Kaddish. The Talmud tells of Yochanan
ben Zakkai, who founded the little yeshiva of Yavneh after Titus
had destroyed the Second Temple in the year 70. On his death bed,
he cried out, "My sons died in their youth. Now there will be no
one to recite the Kaddish for me when I am gone!"

"Aren't we your sons?" reproached his disciples.[224]

Daughters also, where there was no son surviving, were authorized to say Kaddish by Joseph Caro and Moses Isserles of
Cracow, authors of sixteenth-century legal works. Caro's *Shulchan Aruch* remains the definitive legal code of orthodoxy.

Others conversant with Hebrew ritual and prayer were often
retained by mourners to say Kaddish. A payment of $100 for this
purpose was questioned as an improper funeral expense on a New
York estate accounting.[225] The court disallowed the expenditure,

insisting that Jewish law required the accounting administrator, the decedent's son, to say Kaddish:

> The objection made to an expenditure of $100 for the saying of Kaddish is sustained on the ground that this expenditure was voluntarily made by the accounting administrator, a son of the deceased, for a substitute who undertook for the son the performance of the filial duty resting upon the son as such under the Orthodox Hebrew practice. This expenditure was in no true sense an incident to nor part of the funeral service of the deceased.[226]

Interment

Applications for disinterment by close relatives of the deceased, often for the purpose of re-burial in a family plot, present courts with hard decisions. The petitions are addressed to the equity powers of the judiciary and one of the grounds for opposing exhumation of Jewish decedents is that Jewish law is thereby violated.

A learned New York justice was presented with a typical fact pattern in 1937.[227] The children of a deceased father sought a restraining order to prevent a synagogue from interfering with the disinterment of his body so that it might be re-buried in a plot where their recently deceased mother had been laid to rest. The synagogue opposed the application and the conscientious judge posed the issue of "whether, all other elements being favorable, an objection based on ecclesiastical law is sufficient to sway the mind of equity." [228] An earlier case had declared, "Ecclesiastical law is not a part of the law of this State, nor are equitable rights to be determined by it; on the contrary, when a court of equity exercises its powers, it does so only upon equitable principles, irrespective of ecclesiastical or any other law." [229] Nevertheless, the court reflected, "We may not and will not entirely discard the religious aspect of the question herein involved and decide it on purely secular grounds." [230] The court then proceeded to probe Jewish law: [231]

> Searching the testimony to inform ourselves of the religious belief, rites and ceremonials of the principals herein,

we learn that all concerned were and are Jews whose orthodoxy is of varying degrees. We discover that as a matter of pure religious law disinterment is a matter of grave consideration to Jewry and is abhorred as unthinkable desecration, except under certain circumstances. With this conception ready agreement is had, for to all civilized creeds the disturbance of the body of one who sleeps beyond mortal power to awaken is abhorrent and vigorously resented. Nevertheless, conditions arise making it necessary or desirable to exhume a body and reinter it elsewhere. This fact is recognized even by the strictest, most ancient, controlling and inexorable law of orthodox Jewry. That creed accepts as one reason excusing exhumation the desire to place the remains of a human being among his own. The interpretation of this provision of Jewish law apparently is not unanimous, even among the orthodox. The startling difference of opinion expressed by the rabbis leaves the court in a quandary as to what the Code of Karo, more commonly known as the *Schulchan Aruch*, the oldest compendium of Jewish law,[232] means by the doctrine of *"u'besoch shelo"* (among his own). Reference *in extenso* was had during the trial to an article written by an eminent Jewish scholar and rabbi anent the subject of disinterment. A study thereof does not dissipate the confusion regarding disinterment among orthodox Jews. Nor is any help to be had in accepting the advice of an ancient authority by asking a question of a rabbi when disinterment is sought. This was permitted at the trial and the result proved most discouraging, for one holy man said that to disinter the remains in question would be defilement, while the other confidently asserted that the proposed removal was entirely consistent with every requirement of orthodoxy.

The holding of the court was in favor of the synagogue, prohibiting exhumation. The facts did not justify a finding of "superior private rights or public reason" sufficient "to disturb the repose of the dead." The court concluded,[233] "while ecclesiastical law may not control equity, yet, mindful of the horror with which orthodox Jewry regards all exhumation, in the absence of a compelling reason for permitting what has always been considered a desecration abhorrent to the finer and humanitarian interests prevalent since the beginning of civilization, heed will be given to the religious inhibitions affecting the parties herein concerned."

Not all cases weigh Jewish law with the same gravity. A number of decisions on similar facts discount its importance considerably or completely.[234] A State of Washington case,[235] in declining to consider Jewish law, testimony of which was conflicting, offered as its rationale the absence of ecclesiastical courts in the state. A 1965 Ohio decision [236] relied upon a statute permitting disinterment upon application by next of kin. A clause in the burial contract forbidding disinterment was declared to be void as contrary to public policy. The synagogue's objection that the statute was violative of the First Amendment's free exercise provision as an interference with Jewish religious rights was also rejected.

In a number of cases, however, the courts simply assign overriding importance to the wishes of close family members desiring disinterment for reburial in a family plot.[237] In other cases an effort is made to reconcile Jewish law to that conclusion. *In re Katz* [238] seized upon the fortuitous death of Mrs. Katz while negotiations were pending for the purchase of a family plot, necessitating temporary interment elsewhere, as justification in Jewish law for exhumation. Reburial in these circumstances "will not contravene the tenets of the Jewish faith because: (1) the deceased had expressed a desire in her lifetime to be buried in the family plot; and (2) it is intended to bury the deceased in such a family plot." [239] The court quoted from the responsum of a rabbi, and amplified his Jewish law citations: [240]

> The *Schulchan Aruch* referred to in the above-quoted opinion is the basic code of Jewish Law. *Yoreh Deiah,* par. 363, literally translated, provides as follows:
>> "We are not permitted to move either a corpse or bones from an honorable grave to an honorable grave, nor from a contemptible grave to a contemptible grave, nor from an honorable grave to a contemptible grave, . . . but in the midst of his own it is permitted even from an honorable grave to a contemptible, for it is pleasant for a man to rest alongside of his fathers. Likewise it is permitted (to move him) for the purpose of reinterring him

in the Holy Land. If the body was placed there on the condition that it may be moved, it is permitted in any event; and, it is (also permitted) if it is not safe in that particular grave because of the fear that idolators may take out the body or that water may gather in the grave, or if the body is buried in a found (mistaken) grave, it may be removed."

It is stated in an abridged English translation of the "Code of Jewish Law (*Kitzur Schulchan Aruch*) A Compilation of Jewish Laws and Customs" by Rabbi Solomon Ganzfried, translated by Hyman E. Goldin, L. L. B., published by The Star Hebrew Book Company, U. S. A. 1928, c. CXCIX, p. 105, par. 11, concerning disinterment:

"The dead should not be removed (for burial) from a city where there is a cemetery to another city, unless it be from any country to Palestine, or if he had to be removed, to the burial ground of his fathers. *If he had commanded that his remains should be conveyed from one place to another, it is likewise permitted.*" (Italics mine.)

And in paragraph 12 thereof there is the statement:

"It is forbidden to open a grave after it has been closed, that is after the earth had been heaped upon the lid of the coffin, but, as long as the earth had not been piled thereon, it is permitted to open the coffin if there were occasion for it. If because of a very urgent reason it be required that the body of the dead be removed from a grave, an eminent Rabbi should be consulted."

In Vol. 4, p. 613, of the *Jewish Encyclopedia,* published by Funk & Wagnalls, there is a discussion on the question, which supports the contentions advanced by the petitioner, to the effect that where the burial took place with the intention of later removing the body, disinterment is permissible, and that, further, if the body is to be reinterred in a family plot, it is also permissible (even where it is not buried with the intention of removal). In the last instance it is stated that there is a difference of opinion among authorities even of the Orthodox Jewish faith, as to the interpretation of that portion of par. 363 of the *Yoreh Deiah,* which provides that "in the midst of his own it is permitted, even from an honorable grave to a contemptible, for it is pleasant for a man to rest alongside of his fathers." One group of Rabbis contends that the body may not be removed for reinterment in another cemetery in a plot which has been secured since the death of the deceased, and the other, that this can be done. In support of the latter view, the above-cited article in the *Jewish Encyclopedia* states: "Those who favor removal in such a case take the words: 'It is pleasant for a man to repose alongside of his fathers' in a larger sense, conveying the idea that to be buried in a family plot is presumably desirable to any man, and it matters not whether the family plot has been already brought into use or is to be consecrated for a future time. In corroboration of this view, they refer to the fact that the older Baraita in *Massek, Semahot,* l.c., as well as the *Kol Bo* makes no mention of 'alongside of his fathers', the former simply stating as the reason that, 'It is conferring an honor upon the dead.' (*she-zeh hu kebodo*)."

If eminent Rabbis differ upon the interpretation of this phrase, one group interpreting it strictly and the other liberally, it seems to me justified for this court of equity to be guided by the liberal point of view . . .

Other cases, taking *In re Katz* as a starting point, depart from its exploitation of the intended temporary nature of the original burial and proceed to find, "recognizing this difference of opinion among rabbis, . . . that our courts should 'be guided by the liberal point of view where, as here, all of the nearest of kin of the decedent desire the removal of the body to a family plot.' " [241]

Several holdings barring disinterment attempt to reach the decision the decedent would have made. A Virginia case [242] considered a widow's application. She had changed from Orthodox to Reform Judaism following her husband's death and wanted him to display the same flexibility and move to a Reform cemetery. After considering conflicting rabbinical testimony, the court ruled that although Reform beliefs would allow disinterment under the circumstances, such beliefs would not have moved the decedent in his lifetime and, *a fortiori,* thereafter. A New Jersey decision [243] was similarly based on divination of the decedent's intention. His tenaciously held Orthodox religious beliefs led the court to a denial of exhumation as his presumed controlling wish.

In New York State some cemetery corporations have been organized under the Membership Corporations Law and others under the Religious Corporations Law. A 1920 decision [244] drew a distinction between the two with respect to state court authority to direct exhumation of bodies buried in plots owned by them. Religious corporations were granted a special status with broader discretion in applying religious law to thwart family re-interment plans, while membership corporations remained amenable to judicial direction. It is a distinction which has not endured the test of time, in that religious corporations fare no better than membership corporations in the face of family pleas for reburial with other deceased family members in family plots.[245]

Religious scruples have been honored in the rejection of petitions to disinter Orthodox Jewish decedents for the purpose of cremation.[246] There being no conflict with a desire to re-inter in a family plot, courts are relieved of balancing religious law against a family's "devout and natural wish" for togetherness after life. Furthermore, while there is divided opinion among the Orthodox authorities as to whether the "doctrine of 'u'besoch shelo' (among his own)"[247] provides a reason excusing exhumation, there is no doubt that cremation "is not a form of disposal of the dead recognized or approved by the tenets of Hebrew faith."[248]

Despite protestations that religious law has no place in secular courts, that "ecclesiastical law is not a part of the law of this State, nor are equitable rights to be determined by it,"[249] upon close analysis civil court decisions often defer to religious law principles if they represent unanimous, heartfelt and unshakeable articles of faith.

NOTES TO CHAPTER 2

1. See *The American Jew: A Reappraisal* (Phila., 1964) edited by Oscar I. Janowsky, ch. II, C. Bezalel Sherman, "Demographic and Social Aspects," 37: "The marital bond, traditionally strong among Jews, appears to have retained much of its force in the United States, for the rate of divorce has been considerably lower than in the general population." A study by Nathan Goldberg based on the 1950 census is printed in support of the conclusion. But cf. *Rubin v. Rubin*, 75 Misc. 2d 776 (1973) in which a New York Family Court judge notes his recent experience: "With the sociological reality of a tremendously increased divorce rate upon us, a phenomenon which cuts across all levels of society, Orthodox Jews find themselves in matrimonial litigation more often. . ."

2. In the first century the Roman historian "Tacitus deemed it a contemptible prejudice of the Jews that 'it is a crime among them to kill any child.'" Joseph H. Hertz, *Pentateuch and Haftorahs* (London, 1965) 931; Josephus, in the same century argued with Rome, "We must not be treated merely as tolerated aliens simply because we honor our parents, respect old age . . . and strive to maintain family purity in our midst." A talmudic aphorism was: "Happiness in the home penetrates into the world outside." Nathan Ausubel, *The Book of Jewish Knowledge* (New York, 1964) 155.

Certain English Romantic novelists of the nineteenth century strove to awaken a degree of sympathy for Jewish characters by appealing to the acknowledged closeness of Jewish family ties. Sir Walter Scott, for example, in *Ivanhoe* puts a typical plea in the mouth of Isaac of York, "Think not so vilely of us, Jews though we be . . . the hunted fox, the tortured wildcat loves its young—the despised and persecuted race of Abraham love their children." Quoted in Montagu F. Modder, *The Jew in the Literature of England* (Phila. 1939) 142.

The ineluctable comparison is with Shylock in *The Merchant of Venice*, a quotation from which Scott employs at the head of the chapter in which Isaac is introduced. Shakespeare caricatured the Jewish usurer as one who wavered in primacy of affection between gold and daughter in "a passion so confused" crying now for the one, now for the other, "My daughter! O my ducats! O my daughter! Fled with a Christian! O my Christian ducats! Justice! the law! my ducats, and my daughter!" *The Merchant of Venice*, Act II, Scene VIII.

The contemporary Danish minister Poul Borchsenius has observed, "it is always dangerous to generalize, but there really is some truth in the belief that it is Jewish to be faithful in love." Commenting on Jewish life in the Golden Age of Spain, he has written, "The first duty of the communal authorities and above all, the Court, was to supervise the purity of family life and the chastity of the single." *The Three Rings* (London, 1963) 101, 189.

103

3. Israel H. Levinthal, *Judaism* (New York, 1935) 118-119.

4. In Jewish law itself, "Of a total of 2820 folio pages in the Babylonian Talmud, almost one-half (1302) belong to the two divisions primarily devoted to civil and marriage laws. More than a quarter (785) are assigned to benedictions and the observance of holidays in synagogue and home." George Horowitz, *The Spirit of Jewish Law* (New York, 1953) 38.

5. At common law "Canonical rules on what constituted a valid marriage were at first controlling. If the validity of a marriage was involved in the course of litigation in the Kings courts, the case for this purpose was transferred to the Church court for determination and the jurisdiction of the Kings court was resumed after the Church court had reached its conclusion." Max Radin, *Anglo-American Legal History* (St. Paul, Minn. 1936) 507. Later the common law and church rules diverged. But, nonetheless, even after Henry VIII's break with Rome the ecclesiastical courts continued to assert jurisdiction in marriage, family and probate matters: "The Church of England simply took over administration of the ecclesiastical courts." Harvey Zuckman and William F. Fox, "The Ferment in Divorce Legislation," *Journal of Family Law* 515, 518 (1973). Their jurisdiction did not end in England until the Matrimonial Causes Act of 1857. In the United States there is a split among the states concerning the extent to which the common law, at the time of its reception, included the substantive law developed by the ecclesiastical courts. New York, for example, rejected the law of divorce administered by the ecclesiastical courts. Missouri, on the other hand, accepted that body of law except as modified by statute. See Burtis v. Burtis, 1 Hopkins 557 (N.Y. 1825); Chapman v. Chapman, 269 Mo. 663, 666-70, 192 S.W. 448, 449-50 (1917); Stokes v. Stokes, 1 Mo. 320 (1823); Noah Weinstein, "Proposed Changes in the Law of Divorce," 27 Mo. L. Rev. 307, 317 (1962). However, ecclesiastical overtones have lingered in judicial consideration of family law even in New York. As late as 1929 the Court of Appeals, in upholding a marriage performed at sea by a ship's captain, referred to a "law of marriage. . . . common to all nations . . . marriage between the parties to this action was not subject to any bar imposed by the common voice of Christendom." Between parties capable of contracting, marriage is "of common right, and valid by a common law prevailing throughout Christendom." Opinion by Judge Kellogg in Fisher v. Fisher, 250 N.Y. 313, 317 and 320.

The issue of when reception of the common law from England took effect and when that effect ceased to have a continuing influence has been a problem common to the American states and The State of Israel. Judge Moshe Silberg in his opinion in Jakobovitz v. Attorney General, Cr. A. 125/50, 6 P.D. 514 (1952) wrote:

"I am very doubtful that Israeli courts are obligated to follow the innovations in law which were adopted in English courts after the establishment of the State [of Israel]. For if you so decide, you will have made Israeli jurisprudence subservient to the new winds blowing from day to day in the Courts of England. In my opinion, it is not this that the Israeli lawgiver intended when he wrote paragraph 11 in the Ordinance for the Administration of Government and Law—not a permanent dependence on the decisions of foreign tribunals. For the one is not the same as the other: the one-time admission of some foreign legal materials, fixed and limited, which became 'congealed' and was adopted at a certain, specified time, so as to develop it and refine it, through local courts within the boundaries of the State, is not like the acceptance of a body of alien law, unfixed and unspecified, that continues to be created and to be changed through the activity of foreign courts, outside the boundaries of the State. I am afraid that a broad acceptance of the latter situation would not be suitable to meet the particular needs of the inhabitants of the State, and is likely to become a dangerous restraint to the development of an independent original legal creativity." The United States in its infancy reached similar general conclusions. See Seeley v. Peters, 10 Ill. 130 (1848); Jesse Root, "The Origin of Government and Laws in Connecticut," Preface to Vol. I, *Root's Reports* (1798).

6. See Daniel J. Elazar and Stephen R. Goldstein, "The Legal Status of the American Jewish Community," *1972 American Jewish Yearbook* (Phila. 1972) Vol. 73, 71 *et seq.* recounting split United States Supreme Court decisions when state aid to religious institution issues arise. The degree of permissible state aid to parochial schools cannot yet be clearly formulated. In the Matter of Greve, 43 App. Div. 2d 851 (1974), a split New York court faced "the heart rending problem of having to determine whether a physically handicapped child" enrolled in a parochial school was to receive at public expense the services of an itinerant teacher, a service provided public school children. Against a strong dissent, the majority sustained the requested aid as constitutional. In a prescient 1949 article, Professor Arthur Sutherland reviewed the constitutionality of state aid to religious institutions in the wake of two crucial United States Supreme Court decisions, Everson v. Board of Educ., 330 U.S. 1 (1947) and McCollum v. Board of Educ., 333 U.S. 203 (1948). He concluded that various shibboleths such as "due process of law," "establishment of religion" and similar comforting phrases begin after a time "to look suspiciously vague," and new formulae are sought. "Each new phrase is more satisfying only because for a time it is less familiar. As each in its turn inevitably loses its potency, we find and substitute another." "Due Process and Disestablishment," 62 *Harvard Law Review* 1306, 1307. Justice Jackson in his concurrence in the McCollum case wrote: "It is idle to pretend that this task is one for which we can find in the Constitution one word to help us as Judges to decide where the secular ends and the sectarian begins in education. Nor can we find guidance in any other legal source. It is a matter on which we can find no law but our own prepossessions . . . we are likely to make the legal 'wall of separation between church and state' as winding as the famous serpentine wall designed by Mr. Jefferson for the University he founded." 333 U.S. 203 at 237-238. (Jefferson's design of the University of Virginia was the enthusiasm of his old age, embarked upon when he was past 80. See Wendell D. Garrett, *Thomas Jefferson Redivivus* (Barre, Mass., 1971) 179. His epitaph bearing the three achievements by which "I wish most to be remembered" reads "Here was buried Thomas Jefferson author of the Declaration of American Independence, of The Statute of Virginia for religious freedom & Father of the University of Virginia.")

7. *Shulchan Aruch*, "Eben ha-Ezer," ch. 1, sec. 1.; "The duty of building a home and of rearing a family figures in the Rabbinic codes as the first of the 613 Mitzvoth of the Torah." Hertz, *op. cit.*, 931.

8. Levinthal, *op. cit.*, 28.

9. Philip and Hanna Goodman, *The Jewish Marriage Anthology* (Phila., 1965) 37, quoting Genesis Rabbah 68.4. See also Sotah 2a.

10. Quoted in Ausubel, *op. cit.*, 155.

11. References to matrimony in ethical wills are reprinted in Goodman,

op. cit., 44 *et seq.* See also *Prentice-Hall Wills—Trusts* looseleaf service at ¶68.116 (1968). Instances of ethical testaments occur in the Bible (of Jacob, Moses and David, for example) and in the Talmud. In the Middle Ages they became quite common. A selection of ethical wills with English translations was published by Israel Abrahams in 1927. It is entitled *Hebrew Ethical Wills* (Phila., 1927) 2 vols.

12. Genesis 17:11.

13. Ausubel, *op. cit.,* 116.

14. See M. Nedarim 3.11.

15. David Novak, *Law and Theology in Judaism* (New York, 1974) 66; "Yoreh Deah," 260.1.

16. Kalina v. General Hospital of the City of Syracuse, 31 Misc. 2d 18, aff'd 18 App. Div. 2d 757 (1962) as quoted by the sole dissenting judge on appeal.

17. *Ibid.*

18. Blair v. Union Free School District #6, Hauppauge, 324 N.Y.S. 2d 222, at 223.

19. *Kalina v. General Hospital of the City of Syracuse, supra,* at 19.

20. Battalla v. State of New York, 10 N.Y. 2d 237 (1961).

21. *Kalina v. General Hospital of the City of Syracuse, supra,* at 20. Under Jewish law the parents are more than interested bystanders. "Preferably, a father ought to circumcise his own son as Abraham circumcised his sons, Isaac and Ishmael." See B. Kiddushin 29a, referred to in Novak, *op cit.,* 67. The father is to this day encouraged to "assist in the operation so that it could be said that he 'finished' it." *Ibid.* at 71. He is more an actual or symbolic participant in the ceremony than a bystander.

22. *Kalina v. General Hospital of the City of Syracuse, supra.* at 760.

23. *Ibid.* Whether the right to take judicial notice of "authoritative religious writings" is clear-cut is open to question. The same objections may be raised as those which presented themselves to a Harvard Law School professor of evidence with regard to admitting foreign law: (1) the difficulty of laying hands on a reliable version, and (2) "their presuppositions might be so strange that [the judge] could not by solitary perusal assure himself of the true legal meaning." John M. Maguire, *Evidence: Common Sense and Common Law* (Chicago, 1947) 169.

24. *Kalina v. General Hospital of the City of Syracuse, supra,* at 757.

25. *Ibid.* 758.

26. *Ibid.*

27. Mental distress has long been the basis for recovery by close relatives in suits for damages for mishandling of the dead. Jackson v. Savage, 109 App. Div. 556, 558; see also, Foley v. Phelps, 1 App. Div. 551; Hassard v. Lebane, 143 App. Div. 424; Grawunder v. Beth Israel Hosp. Assn. 242 App. Div. 56, aff'd 266 N.Y. 605; Beller v. City of New York, 269 App. Div. 642; Darcy v. Presbyterian Hosp. 202 N.Y. 259. See also, Gostkowski v. Roman Catholic Church, 262 N.Y. 320; Klumbach v. Silver Mount Cemetery Ass'n., 242 App. Div. 843, affd. 268 N.Y. 525; Note, 21 *Cornell L. Q.* 166; see also Finley v. Atlantic Transp. Co., 220 N.Y. 249; Lubin v. Sydenham Hosp. 181 Misc. 870. But disturbance or mishandling of dead bodies was also long regarded as a unique category of tort law. When public policy is set in motion to find the cause of death in suspicious circumstances, religious considerations generally give way. Statutes in most states embody this policy. See 17 A.L.R. 2d 770 *et seq.* A 1973 New York case, Wilensky v. Greco, 344 N.Y.S. 2d 77, however, held an autopsy unjustified where the object was to

determine which injuries caused the death of an Orthodox boy killed in a car crash, where there was no suspicion of criminality, despite §673 of the County Law requiring the coroner to investigate death caused by casualty. See also, Lott v. State of New York, 32 Misc. 2d 296 (1962), where Jewish and Roman Catholic decedents were mistakenly exchanged, and the body of Mrs. Tumminelli "placed on a 'Taharah' board, washed in accordance with religious rites and prayers said over it" in Hebrew, while the body of the Orthodox Jewish decedent was "embalmed, made up with cosmetics and . . . placed in a coffin with a crucifix and rosary beads in her hands in accordance with the rites of the Roman Catholic faith." The court, in permitting recovery by both families stated: "In decisions affecting this type of action, the courts are not primarily concerned with the extent of the physical mishandling or injury to the body per se, but rather how such improper handling or injury affects the feelings and emotions of the surviving kin."

28. Battalla v. State of New York, 10 N.Y. 2d 237 (1961), the New York Court of Appeals landmark decision, was construed to extend the right of recovery to all mental distress intentionally or negligently inflicted with "the principle limitation implicit in the Battalla decision . . . that the emotional distress must be of a serious character." *Kalina v. General Hospital of City of Syracuse, supra*, at 760. The Court of Appeals in 1975 expanded its holding that psychological or nervous injury precipitated by psychic trauma is compensable. Wolfe v. Sibley, Lindsay & Curr Co., 36 N. Y. 2d 505.

29. Novak, *op. cit.*, 67.

30. Isserles and Shakh to Yoreh Deah 264.1 contra Taz in the name of Rashba.

31. Blair v. Union Free School District #6, Hauppauge, 324 N.Y.S. 2d 222 (1971).

32. *Ibid.*, 225.

33. In re Glavas, 203 Misc. 590, 121 N.Y.S. 2d 12 (1953).

34. §88, subd. 2. N.Y.C. Domestic Relations Court Act.

35. In re Glavas, 203 Misc. 590 at 593.

36. "Sharing with Roman Law the realistic view that *mater semper certa est,* Jewish law views descent from a Jewish mother as decisive in this connection." Benjamin Akzin, "Who is a Jew? A Hard Case," 5 *Israel Law Review* 259, 261 (1970). On the issue of Jewish legal identification, see also Ginossar, "Who is a Jew: A Better Law?" 5 *Israel Law Review* 264; Tamarin v. State of Israel (I) 26 P.D. 197 (1972); 8 *Israel Law Review* 286 (1973); See also *The Jewish News* (N.J.) Feb. 17, 1972, 19, col. 1; *New York Times,* Jan. 24, 1970, 1, cols. 3,4. The comments in each publication were prompted by Shalit v. Minister of Interior et al (II) 23 P.D. 477-608 (1969), an Israel High Court decision with nine separate opinions. Following the *Shalit* case, the Knesset established, in effect, that only persons who qualified as Jews under rabbinic law might be enrolled in the State Population Registry as Jews by nationality. In a challenge to that law a Jew alleging atheism attempted to be recognized officially as "Israeli" The High Court in Jerusalem rejected that claim. *New York Times,* Jan. 21, 1972, 14, col. 3.

37. Ausubel, *op cit.*, 157.

38. Hawksworth v. Hawksworth, L.R. 6 Ch. 539-40 (1871).

39. People *ex rel.* Sisson v. Sisson, 271 N.Y. 285, 286, 2 N.E. 2d 660, 661 (1936).

40. Gottlieb v. Gottlieb, 31 Ill. App. 2d 120, 175 N.E. 2d 619 (1961).

41. Petition of Goldman, 331 Mass. 647, 121 N.E. 2d 843 (1954), cert. denied, 398 U.S. 942 (1955).

42. See "Interfaith Adoption: A Symposium," 3 *Osgoode Hall Law Journal* (Toronto), 14 (April, 1964); Monrad G. Paulsen, "Constitutional Problems of Utilizing a Religious Factor in Placement of Children" in *The Wall Between Church and State* (Chicago, 1963) 117-141.

43. The Massachusetts court's view parallels the Jewish experience. "In the non-Jewish world there is a tendency to view as Jews even those who have converted to other faiths," a point of view that "has some basis even in Jewish religious law. See Mr. Justice Silberg, in his opinion in Rufeisen v. Minister of Interior (1962) (IV) 16 P.D. 2428," an Israel Supreme Court decision. Akzin, *op. cit.*

44. Annotated Laws of Massachusetts 6B C210 §5B.

45. Matter of Krenkel, 278 App. Div. 573, 102 N.Y.S. 2d 456 (1951).

46. See State *ex rel.* Strachota v. Franz, 163 N.W. 191-92 (1917). The subject is discussed succinctly in a special article entitled "The Legal Status of the American Jewish Community," by Elazar and Goldstein, *op. cit.*, 7-12.

47. *N.Y. Law Journal,* March 13, 1972, 19 col. 2.

48. Agur v. Agur, 32 App. Div. 2d 16, 298 N.Y.S. 2d 772.

49. *Ibid.*, 17.

50. *Ibid.*, 18.

51. *Ibid.*, 19.

52. *Ibid.*, 21.

53. See note 39, *supra.*

54. 354 N.Y.S. 2d 854 (1974).

55. *Ibid.*, 856.

56. 59 Misc. 2d 957, 301 N.Y.S. 2d 237 (1969), affd. 35 App. Div. 2d 50, 312 N.Y.S. 2d 815 (1970).

57. Abraham Multer, "Further Comment on *Wener v. Wener,*" 5 *Israel Law Review* 463 (1970).

58. Wener v. Wener, 35 App. Div. 2d 50, 54, 312 N.Y.S. 2d 815, 819 (1970). Judge Multer's comment and the Appellate Division affirmance both appeared in July, 1970.

59. Multer, *op. cit.*, 464. Judge Multer's reference to the recognition of the foreign "laws of Israel or England or Louisiana" may have been chosen at random, or he may have had in mind the case of Har-Shefi v. Har-Shefi (No. 2), P. 220, 2 All E.R. (1953) in which an English court granted recognition to a *get* "valid according to the law of the domicile," Israel; the case of Joseph v. Joseph 1 W.L.R. 1182, 2 All E.R. 710 (1953) in which a Canadian court recognized the efficacy of a Bet Din's grant of a *get* in London; and Matter of Seixas, 73 Misc. 488 (1911), in which the Surrogate's Court of New York County recognized the validity of a holographic will under Louisiana law made by a Louisiana resident sojourning in New York. The Surrogate stated: "The tendency at present is to give a sort of personal status to foreigners within this jurisdiction . . . our law has the power to recognize if it choose his personal law. It is very curious that the modern legislation thus extending extraterritoriality is only a recrudescence of a very old status observable everywhere after the subsidence of the Roman Empire. It was Savigny, I think, who first made this point abundantly clear to the world, and it has never since been questioned." The testator, Henry O. Seixas, was a Sephardic Jew and one of the early members of the exclusive Boston Club, a venerable

New Orleans institution. See Eli N. Evans, *The Provincials* (New York, 1973) 236.

60. Multer, *op. cit.*, 466.

61. Goldstein v. Goldstein, 101 A. 249 (1917).

62. The author is deeply indebted to Lester Lyons, Esq., a practicing New York attorney who was of counsel to the late Louis J. Gribetz in his argument before the New York State Education Department in his successful plea, for furnishing the brief submitted on that occasion.

63. Brief on Behalf of Yeshivos and Other Interested Parties in Opposition to the Contemplated Action of the Regents, 2.

64. *Ibid.*, 15.

65. *Ibid.*, 16.

66. *Ibid.*

67. *Ibid.*, 17.

68. *Ibid.*

69. *Ibid.*, 10-12. Dr. Solomon Grayzel, the noted historian, has challenged the broad secular interest claimed for yeshivos as an "historically doubtful generalization."

70. Wisconsin v. Yoder, 92 S. Ct. 1526 (1972).

71. Chief Justice Burger's majority opinion states, "the Old Order Amish religion pervades and determines virtually their entire way of life, regulating it with the detail of the Talmudic diet through the strictly enforced rules of the church community." 406 U.S. 205, 216. Adult baptism among the Amish "occurs in late adolescence, . . . the time at which Amish young people voluntarily undertake heavy obligations, not unlike the Bar Mitzvah of the Jews." 406 U.S. 205, 210.

72. Brief, *supra*, 4-7.

73. *Ibid.*, 8-10.

74. The complete midrashic statement is: "If a man is in captivity with his father and his master, he comes before his master, his master comes before his father. His mother comes before them all." Nahum N. Glatzer, *Hammer on the Rock* (New York, 1962) 65.

75. Brief, *supra*, 24-27.

76. People on Complaint of Shapiro v. Dorin, 199 Misc. 643, 99 N.Y.S. 2d 830, affd. 278 App. Div. 705, 103 N.Y.S. 2d 757, affd. 302 N.Y. 857, 858, 100 N.E. 2d 48, 49, appeal dismissed Donner v. People of State of New York on Complaint of Silverman, 72 S. Ct. 178, 342 U.S. 884, 96 L. Ed. 663, holding that N.Y. State Education Law §3212 was constitutionally applied

77. People of the State of New York v. Donner *et al.*, 302 N.Y. 857 at 858 (1951).

78. *Ibid.*

79. People on Complaint of Shapiro v. Dorin, 199 Misc. 643, 99 N.Y.S. 2d 830 at 838. Similarly, Pennsylvania has held that a Moslem parent could be prosecuted for keeping his child home from public school on Fridays. Commonwealth v. Bey, 166 Pa. Super. 136, 70 A 2d 693 (1950).

80. *Ibid.* at 836, citing Reynolds v. U. S., 98 U.S. 145, 25 L.Ed. 244; Davis v. Beason, 133 U.S. 333, 10 S.Ct. 299, 33 L.Ed. 637.

81. *Ibid.*, citing Hamilton v. Regents of the University of California, 293 U.S. 245, 262-263, 55 S. Ct. 197, 204, 79 L. Ed. 343.

82. *Ibid.*, citing Chaplinsky v. State of New Hampshire, 315 U. S. 568, 62 S. Ct. 766, 86 L. Ed. 1031.

83. *Ibid*, citing Jacobson v. Commonwealth of Massachusetts, 197 U. S. 11, 25 S. Ct. 358, 49 L. Ed. 643, 3 Ann. Cas. 765.

84. Auster v. Weberman, 278 App. Div. 656, 102 N.Y.S. 2d 418, affd. 302 N.Y. 855, 100 N. E. 2d 47, 342 U.S. 884, 72 S. Ct. 178, 96 L. Ed. 663.

85. Miami Military Institute v. Leff, 129 Misc. 481, 220 N.Y.S. 799.

86. *Ibid.* at 810.

87. Adapted from Hertz, *op. cit.*, 559.

88. In re Silverstein, 155 N.Y.S. 2d 598, 599 (1956).

89. In re Harris' Will, 143 N.Y.S. 2d 746 (1955), citing 2 *Jarman on Wills*, 6th ed., 47.

90. Matter of Liberman, 279 N.Y. 458 (1939).

91. 148 N.Y.S. 2d 391 (1955).

92. Although not incorporated in the Ketubah, the following recital is frequently read under the *huppah*, the marriage canopy, because it represents the spirit of a Jewish marriage: "And the said bride has plighted her troth unto him in affection and sincerity and has thus taken upon herself the fulfillment of all the duties incumbent upon a Jewish wife." Logic dictates one of such duties is to remain Jewish.

93. Watkins v. Watkins, 197 App. Div. 489 (1921); Rozsa v. Rozsa, 117 Misc. 728, 191 N.Y.S. 868 (1972).

94. Rutstein v. Rutstein, 222 N.Y.S. 688 (1921). In Tenner v. Tenner, Sp. Term, Kings Co. #21499/73 (1974), the New York Supreme Court annulled a marriage where the wife had misrepresented to the husband before the wedding that she was a widow when in fact she had been divorced. When her Orthodox Jewish husband discovered the truth (which constituted a violation of Jewish law since, as a *Kohen*, marriage to a divorcee is forbidden), he gave his wife a *get* and thereafter successfully instituted civil annullment proceedings.

95. Elazar and Goldstein, *op. cit.*, 13.

96. General Laws of Rhode Island 15-1.4 (1956). Rhode Island's founder set the tone for Jewish accommodation. In Roger Williams' view it was the obligation of Christians to initiate reconciliation between Jews and Gentiles. It was, he said, "The *Duty* of the *Civil Magistrate* to break down that superstitious *wall* between us Gentiles and the Jews, and freely (without their asking) to make way for their free and peaceable Habitation amongst us." Clarence Saunders Brigham, *The Fourth Paper Presented by Maj. Butler*, 18. See Abram V. Goodman, *American Overture* (Phila. 1947) 34. Williams' fondness for "wall" metaphors is most memorably immured in the wall which separates church and state. See ch. 5, note 1.

97. In re May's Estate, 110 N.Y.S. 2d 430, revd. 280 App. Div. 647, 117 N.Y.S. 2d 345, affd. 305 N.Y. 486, 114 N.E. 2d 4 (1953).

98. *Ibid*, 117 N.Y.S. 2d at 348. "Marriage to a niece is strongly deprecated in Rabbinic law—though it is valid. It is rare among Jews." *A Rabbinic Anthology*, ed. by C. G. Montefiore and H. Loewe (New York, reprinted in 1974) 508.

99. Fensterwald v. Burk, 129 Md. 131, 98 A. 358 (1916).

100. In re Estate of Simms, 31 App. Div. 2d 644, 296 N.Y.S. 2d 222, revd. 26 N.Y. 2d 163, 309 N.Y.S. 2d 170. See also In re Saffer's Estate, 39 Misc. 2d 691, 241 N.Y.S. 2d 681 (1963); Weisberg v. Weisberg, 112 App. Div. 231, 98 N.Y.S. 260.

101. In re Estate of Simms, 309 N.Y.S. 2d at 172.

102. *Ibid.*
103. Matter of White, 78 Misc. 2d 157.
104. *Ibid.*, 158, citing New York Estates Powers and Trust Law §5-1.1.
105. *Ibid.* The Court took the value of a *zuz* "at about 15 cents, a sum which in ancient times was a considerable amount," referring to George Horowitz's *The Spirit of Jewish Law* (New York, 1953) as its authority. It referred to the "ancient statutory minimum" of 200 *zuzim* obligatory for a virgin as having an estimated value of thirty dollars, citing the same source. It is not a simple matter to establish the value of a *zuz*. In S. Krauss, *Talmudische Archaelogie* (Leipsig, 1911) II, 406-07 a *zuz* is described as equivalent to a silver *dinar* of Roman coin, which means half of a gold *dinar*. A gold *dinar* may well have been a pound of gold in weight and a very high value indeed, since gold was rare in Roman times. In *A Rabbinic Anthology* edited by C. G. Montefiore and H. Loewe (reprinted New York, 1974) a pound weight of gold is equated with 400 *zuzim* in Talmudic times. See pp. 505, 664. During the Middle Ages the Jews evidently did not consider a *zuz* worth much since it became customary among them, even while using the traditional wording of the Ketubah, to write an "additional Ketubah" in which a different and higher sum was added to the 200 *zuz* for a virgin and the 100 for a widow or divorcee. A rabbinical ordinance of the fourteenth century, on the basis of an ordinance dating from several centuries earlier, added 300 florins for a widow and 600 for a virgin. Dr. Solomon Grayzel has concluded that the traditional *zuzim* of the Ketubah ceased to have any significant financial importance as early as the tenth century when the "additional Ketubah" became a frequent practice. The Jews of the Middle Ages adjusted themselves to the moneys of the lands and periods in which they lived. The "additional Ketubah" went out of style as the Jews of Europe, especially Eastern Europe, became impoverished. Whether *zuzim* or florins, whether 100 or 200, 300 or 600, all were equally out of reach. The subject of the additional Ketubah is discussed in Irving A. Agus, *The Heroic Age of Franco-German Jewry* (New York, 1969) 292-293. See also Louis Finkelstein, *Jewish Self-Government in the Middle Ages* (New York, reprinted in 1964) 74-75, 254.
106. Matter of White, 78 Misc. 2d. at 158-159.
107. See note 58, *supra.*
108. *The Spirit of Jewish Law*, §176.
109. In re White, 129 Misc. 835, 223 N.Y.S. 311.
110. *Ibid.*, 223 at 313.
111. In re Cossin's Estate, 126 N.Y.S. 2d 363.
112. Sturm v. Sturm, 111 N.J. Equity 579, 163 A. 5 (1932).
113. New York Domestic Relations Law §11, e.g.
114. It takes a flagrant flaunting of absent credentials to disqualify a "clergyman." Ravenal v. Ravenal, 338 N.Y.S. 2d 324 (1972) supplied the necessary elements. "The parties and the person performing the ceremony were members of an Encounter group." The "clergyman's" principal "occupation was as guitarist and folk singer." He also claimed to be a minister of Universal Life Church, Inc., a body without traditional doctrine. "We recognize everyone's belief. . . We will ordain anyone without question of their faith, for life for a free-will offering." Charters were furnished to "anyone" for "a free-will offering of $1.00 per month."
115. In re Diana Steinberg, deceased, *N.Y. Law Journal*, Feb. 7, 1974, 19 col. 7F.

116. In re Silverstein's Estate, 190 Misc. 745, 75 N.Y.S. 2d. 144.

117. *Ibid.*, 75 N.Y.S. 2d at 145-146.

118. I.N. Tuchman, *Jewish Law and Custom and The Courts of New York State*, Masters Project submitted to the Faculty of the Bernard Revel Graduate School (1971) 60.

119. Quoted from an anonymous source in Tilton, *Lawyers Strategy in Matrimonial Law.* See Harvey L. Zuckman and William F. Fox, "The Ferment in Divorce Legislation," 12 *Journal of Family Law* 517 (1973).

120. As divorce laws become more liberalized throughout the world, the volume of divorce proceedings will accelerate. E.g., New Jersey's liberalized divorce law adopted September 13, 1971 found divorces doubling within several months. *New York Times,* Feb. 6, 1972, 75. The 1969 California law which abandoned "accusatory proceedings" led to an increased rate of divorce. The national rate was four for every 1,000 persons in 1972, while the California rate was 5.4, an increase over the pre-1969 California rate. *New York Times,* July 8, 1973, 31, col. 3. The year 1971 set a record, to that date, for total United States divorces according to a *Wall Street Journal* page one article of Jan. 17, 1973. Whether liberalized divorce laws are causing the trend, or whether social demand for divorce is bringing about legislative change, or whether the two forces feed on each other, is a subject of debate. See *New York Times,* Jan. 5, 1974, 15. The trend is not limited to the United States. Britain, on January 1, 1971 commenced allowing divorce for "irretrievable breakdown" of marriage. Italy on May 12, 1974 voted, by popular referendum drawing some thirty-eight million voters, to retain its 1970 divorce laws. See *The Wall Street Journal,* April 23, 1974, 48. It had previously appeared that there was no country in the world in which anti-divorce sentiment was as strong. When the 1970 divorce law was pending a suit was brought by a Rome housewife against the Italian Premier, the Minister of Justice and the Mayor of Rome to guarantee her marriage would not end in divorce. *N.Y. Post,* Nov. 23, 1970, 52, col. 1. She did not prevail. The Archbishop of Belem in Brazil, the world's largest Roman Catholic country, has conceded that divorce is inevitable in that country. According to the Brazilian Public Opinion Institute a 1974 poll in Rio De Janeiro and Sao Paulo, Brazil's biggest cities, showed 74 per cent in favor of legalizing divorce. *New York Times,* Feb. 20, 1975, 9, col. 1. Australia has recently adopted one of the world's most liberal divorce laws, a no-fault arrangement requiring only a year's separation. *New York Times,* Nov. 28, 1974, 6, col. 1. On the other hand, the rate of marriage in the United States appears to be declining. For the first quarter of 1974 the marriage rate was 4 per cent below that of the year earlier period, and this seemed to represent the continuation of a trend. Research Institute of America, Inc., *Recommendations,* Vol. 25, No. 23.

121. See (h), Prohibited Marriages, p. 62. In the light of Maimonides' advocacy of corporal punishment to induce a husband's consent to a *get* (see Maimonides, *Laws of Divorce,* quoted at p. 74), the ultimate treatment center for a Hasid assaulted "by five other Hasidic Jews" on a Brooklyn street for his refusal to accede to a religious divorce is ironic. The victim, suffering from "two broken ribs and facial cuts and bruises," was admitted to Maimonides Hospital. In *The New York Times* of May 16, 1973, 43, col. 2, the account of the indictment of the five for kidnapping recounts "they allegedly pummeled their captive because he had obtained a civil divorce from his wife" and denied her a religious one. "This under a law of the Hasidic sect, pro-

hibited her from remarrying." The article gives no indication of whether the accused acted under some colorable claim of legitimacy as agents of a Bet Din or impulsively from spontaneous, if collective, personal religious outrage.

122. *Morris v. Morris*, decision by Justice Wilson of the Manitoba Court of Queens Bench rendered March 16, 1973, reported in 3 W.W.R. 526 (1973).

123. *Ibid.*, 8.

124. *Ibid.*, 9-16.

125. *Ibid.*, 25.

126. *Ibid.*, 17.

127. " 'Modern couples think weddings should be personal statements between the two people married instead of institutional bashes' explains the Rev. William Taylor, a Presbyterian minister in Chicago who encourages couples to innovate in the way they marry." *The Wall Street Journal*, Sept. 25, 1970, 1, col. 4. Even more radical changes are afoot. *The Wall Street Journal*, May 1, 1972, 1, col. 3, reported the offer of a one-year trial marriage "by a Tampa, Fla., Unitarian minister to couples who vow to love, honor and practice contraception." The Rev. Adrian Melott "said the traditional marriage rite is archaic. . ." A random sampling of the newspapers' social columns will disclose to the casual eye home-made, avante-garde ceremonials. *The New York Times* of Oct. 8, 1972, 92, reported the marriage of the nephew of the Roman Catholic Bishop of Portland (Me.) to the daughter of the Episcopal Bishop of New York. "Mr. Gerety and his bride wrote and performed their own ceremony, which she described as 'not religious in the traditional sense' . . . They called on their 200 guests as witnesses . . . The festivities began with the ringing of a bell as the bridal couple came into view from around the point on Lake Silver and paddled their canoe to a dock on the Moore property, where members of the wedding party awaited them, the men clad in white cotton tunics and brown corduroys with belts of sleigh bells and the women in long green velvet skirts and white cotton blouses. . ." Rather than a best man and honor attendants, all members of both families were included as "best people." They were then led "to a nearby field where the service took place."

Legal agitation for reform of matrimonial laws to permit personal contractual arrangements has endeavored to keep pace with social practice. In 1971 two women legislators introduced a bill in the Maryland State Legislature which would have allowed a Maryland couple to choose between traditional marriage and a three-year renewable marriage contract which could be canceled by either party on expiration. A 1972 study entitled "The Future of Marriage and the Family" by Harvey Cary Dzodin, submitted in behalf of the Harvard Law School's third year writing requirement, analyzes the prospects for such arrangements in detail. It is summarized in Dzodin, "A Marriage Proposal," *Harvard Law School Bulletin*, February, 1974, 19-21. The July-Sept., 1974 *California Law Review* carries a 120 page article entitled "Legal Regulation of Marriage: Tradition and Change," subtitled, "A Proposal for individual Contracts and Contracts in Lieu of Marriage." It is replete with an appendix of personal marriage contract clauses. Talmudic authority in support of marriage contracts for a limited term may be found in B. Yevamoth, 37b, Eben ha Ezer 2:10. There is nothing in Jewish law to prevent a temporary marriage, either for a term of days or months, or with a view to dissolving it at an unspecified future date. Justice Haim Cohn (Israel Supreme Court), *Jewish Law in Israeli Jurisprudence* (Cincinnati, Ohio, 1968) 16. See Bernard

J. Meislin, "The Jewish Law of Marriage in American Courts," 11 *Journal of Family Law* 271, 275 (1971).

128. Morris v. Morris, 2 W.W.R. 193 (1974).

129. *Ibid.*, at 218-219.

130. *Ibid.* at 212. Also see 220.

131. *Ibid.* at 210, 212.

132. *Ibid.* at 209.

133. *Ibid.* at 211.

134. *Ibid.* at 212.

135. *Ibid.*

136. *Ibid.* at 216.

137. *Ibid.* at 219.

138. *Ibid.* at 208.

139. In Israel the same concern is present. "On application by the Attorney General to the District Court, in proceedings similar to those of contempt of court, a husband may be imprisoned until due compliance with the order of the Rabbinical court" in pursuance of Jurisdiction of Rabbinical Courts Law, 1953, sec. 6. "However, even this measure is not foolproof. One husband we know of has now been imprisoned for five years without the desired result." Isaac Shiloh, "Marriage and Divorce in Israel," 5 *Israel L. R.* 479, 496 (1970).

140. Brett v. Brett, 1 W.L.R. 487.

141. Koeppel v. Koeppel, 138 N.Y.S. 2d 366 (1954).

142. *Ibid.*, 373.

143. *Ibid.*, 369-370.

144. *Ibid.*, 373.

145. The anti-establishment clause of the First Amendment "does not ban federal or state regulation of conduct whose reason or effect merely happens to coincide or harmonize with the tenets of some or all religions." McGowan v. Maryland, 366 U.S. 420, 442 (1961). But cf. United States Supreme Court Justice Powell's opinion in Committee for Public Education v. Nyquist, 37 L.Ed 948, 969 at note 39.

146. Margulies v. Margulies, 42 App. Div. 2d 517, 344 N.Y.S. 2d 482 (1973).

147. Rubin v. Rubin, 75 Misc. 2d 776, 348 N.Y.S. 2d 61 (1973).

148. *Margulies v. Margulies, supra,* 517.

149. *Ibid.*

150. *Ibid.*

151. *Ibid.*

152. *Ibid.*, 518.

153. *Ibid.*, 517.

154. *Ibid.*, 518, Judge Emilio Nunez dissenting.

155. 75 Misc. 2d 776, 348 N.Y.S. 2d 61.

156. *Ibid.*, 779. See Bernard J. Meislin, "Jewish Law of Marriage in American Courts," 11 *Journal of Family Law* 271 (1971).

157. *Rubin v. Rubin, supra,* 779.

158. *Ibid.*

159. *Ibid.*, 780.

160. *Ibid.*

161. *Ibid.*

162. *Ibid.*

163. *Ibid.*, 779.

164. *Ibid.*, 781.
165. *Ibid.*, 781, note 3.
166. *Ibid.*, 781.
167. *Ibid.*
168. See p. 79.
169. *Rubin v. Rubin, supra,* 781.
170. *Ibid.*, 782, citing a United States Supreme Court decision, Watson v. Jones, 13 Wall [80 U.S.] 679 (1871).
171. *Rubin v. Rubin, supra,* 782.
172. *Ibid.*
173. *Ibid.* 783.
174. See also Pal v. Pal, N.Y.L.J., July 25, 1973, 13, col. 5., rev'd 45 App. Div. 2d 738 (1974).
175. The confusion sown by the majority opinion in Margulies v. Margulies, 42 App. Div. 2d 517, 344 N.Y.S. 2d 482 (1973), is evident in Pal v. Pal, 45 App. Div. 2d 738 (1974) which cites *Margulies* for the proposition that a civil court may not convene a Bet Din. A strong dissent cites *Margulies* as standing for a civil court's right to punish a recalcitrant husband through fines but not by incarceration. It also disagrees with the majority's conclusion on the ground that the parties should be held to their contractual commitments. It is unclear as to whether fines will stand up. Israel is confronted with the same dilemma. See note 139, *supra.*
176. In re Goldman's Estate, 156 Misc. 817, 282 N.Y.S. 787.
177. Chertok v. Chertok, 208 App. Div. 161, 203 N.Y.S. 163 (1924).
178. Saperstone v. Saperstone, 73 Misc. 631, 131 N.Y.S. 241 (1911).
179. Albeg v. Albeg, 259 App. Div. 744, 18 N.Y.S. 2d 719 (1940); Greenman v. Greenman, 262 App. Div. 876, 966, 28 N.Y.S. 2d 535 (1941).
180. Machransky v. Machransky, 166 N.E. 423 (Court of Appeals of Ohio, Cuyahoga Co., 1927).
181. New York, 1915.
182. In re Rubenstein's Estate, 143 Misc. 917, 257 N.Y.S. 637 (1932).
183. In re Spondre, 98 Misc. 524, 162 N.Y.S. 943 (1917). (Surrogate Fowler.)
184. *Ibid.*, 945.
185. *Ibid.*
186. *Ibid.*
187. *Ibid.*
188. *Ibid.*
189. The *shochet* in Eastern European communities was "a semi-ecclesiastical functionary of a specialized kind" with a thorough knowledge of "prescribed religious laws and regulations." Ausubel, *op. cit.*, 404. He is "learned in matters of Jewish law and, as a rule, is a man of piety." Cecil Roth and Geoffrey Wigoder, eds., *The New Standard Jewish Encyclopedia,* 4th ed. (New York, 1970) 1746. For a slaughtered animal to be kosher it has to be slaughtered by a man who has been certified by a recognized rabbi as pious and knowledgeable in the laws of *shehitah* as prescribed in the *Shulchan Aruch.* Cf. *The Jewish Encyclopedia,* XI, 306 and 311.
190. In re Spondre, *supra,* 945-946.
191. The Surrogate also throws in a Roman law allusion for good measure, in the nature of an estoppel, to support the validity of Rachel's claimed marriage: "There is a curious and extremely instructive decision on the effect of

such a representation and one entirely familiar to Roman lawyers. The classical case was in brief this: Certain slave dealers, landing a cargo at Brindisium, a port of entry, some two thousand years ago, had among their cargo a young slave of great value by reason of his intellectual culture; but, fearing that the custom house officers would lay hands on him, the slave dealers represented the youth, contrary to the fact, to be free. It was held at Rome that he was a free man by reason of the misrepresentation. This judgment strikes me as most just. So here, if Henry Spondre and Rachel took themselves to be husband and wife in order to come under this government, they should, I think, be concluded in the courts of this government by their representation. . ." In re Spondre, *supra*, at 949.

192. *Ibid.*, 946. The Surrogate cites a 1790 English decision of Lord Kenyon in support. Ganer v. Lady Lanesborough, Peake's N.P. Cas. 17.

193. *Ibid.*, 945.

194. *Ibid.*, 946.

195. *Ibid.*

196. *Ibid.*

197. *Ibid.*, 948.

198. *Ibid.*, 950.

199. *Ibid.*, 951.

200. Gordon v. Gordon, 140 N.Y.S. 2d 878 (1957), interpreting Domestic Relations Law §51.

201. As reported in Kantor v. Bloom, 90 Conn. 210, 96 A. 974 (1916) and in Kantor v. Cohn, 98 Misc. 355, 164 N.Y.S. 383 (1917); 181 App. Div. 400, 168 N.Y.S. 846 (1918).

202. Kantor v. Bloom, 90 Conn. 210 at 211.

203. *Ibid.*

204. §391 Conn. Gen. St. 1902.

205. Kantor v. Bloom, *supra*, at 213.

206. *Ibid.*

207. *Ibid.*, 216.

208. *Ibid.*

209. Kantor v. Cohn, 98 Misc. 355, 164 N.Y.S. 383.

210. Kantor v. Cohn, 181 App. Div. 400, 168 N.Y.S. 846 at 848 (1918).

211. *Ibid.*, 847-848.

212. 8. U.S. Code 1427 (1924).

213. See In re Spiegel, 24 F. 2d 605 (S.D. N.Y., 1928); Petition of Horowitz, 48 F. 2d. 652 (E.D.N.Y., 1931); U. S. v. Zaltsman, 19 F. Supp. 305 (W.D.N.Y. 1937).

214. Petition of Schlau, 41 F. 2d 161 (S.D.N.Y.).

215. 136 F. 2d 480 (2d Cir., 1943).

216. Ausubel, *op cit.*, 237.

217. Tuchman, *op. cit.*, 25-26. The practice of hiring a Kaddish-sayer who is not of the family has been criticized as "contrary to the very spirit of Judaism." Dr. Solomon Grayzel has written, "Mourner's Kaddish originated with the desirability of a son rising in the congregation and reciting a rabbinic formula to testify to his proper Jewish upbringing. The formula has nothing to say about death or parents or anything of the kind. It was an old formula to signify the conclusion of a service in the synagogue and was later adopted for pietistic use. . . Its use by someone outside the family is a bit of superstition which I consider an excrescence."

218. In re Fleishfarb's Will, 151 Misc. 399, 271 N.Y.S. 736 (1934), opinion by Surrogate Wingate.

219. *Ibid.*, at 400.

220. *Ibid.*

221. Ausubel, *op. cit.*, 497.

222. In re Steiner's Estate, 172 Misc. 950, 16 N.Y.S. 2d 613.

223. *Ibid.*, at 952.

224. Ausubel, *op. cit.*, 238.

225. In re Feifer's Estate, 151 Misc. 54, 270 N.Y.S. 905 (1934).

226. *Ibid.*, at 55.

227. Justice Peter Schmuck in Seifer v. Schwimmer, 166 Misc. 329, 1 N.Y.S. 2d 730 (1937). In the same year Justice Schmuck on somewhat different facts reached the same result. Klahr v. Nadel, 166 Misc. 288, 1 N.Y.S. 2d 733. He stated, ". . . no doubt exists that under the circumstances here indicated [disinterment] would transgress a cardinal principle of orthodox Jewry as conceived by many a scholar and rabbi of the Jewish faith. Although ecclesiastical law cannot control equity, yet it is impossible to set at naught with heedlessness and indifference the traditions and rules of any religion, particularly so long established a creed as that of Jewry."

228. Seifer v. Schwimmer, 166 Misc. 329, at 330.

229. Cohen v. Cong. Shearith Israel, 114 App. Div. 117, 119, 99 N.Y.S. 732, affd. 189 N.Y. 528, 82 N.E. 1125 (1906).

230. Seifer v. Schwimmer, 166 Misc. 329, at 331.

231. *Ibid.*

232. The *Shulchan Aruch* is hardly the oldest compendium of Jewish law. Excluding the Talmud, it is preceded by, among other works of Jewish law, Isaac Alfasi's *Halakot*, compiled in the eleventh century, Nahmanides' glosses and novellae on the Talmud and his *Milhamot Adonai* of the thirteenth century, a commentary on Alfasi's work. There is, of course, Maimonides' *Mishneh Torah*, often called in English *The Code of Maimonides*, written in the twelfth century and compared to Blackstone's *Commentaries on the Law of England*. See Horowitz, *op. cit.*, 52.

233. Seifer v. Schwimmer, 166 Misc. 329, at 332.

234. Cohen v. Cong. Shearith Israel, 114 App. Div. 117, 99 N.Y.S. 732, affd. 189 N.Y. 528, 82 N.E. 1125 (1906); Matter of Schechter, 261 App. Div. 926, 25 N.Y.S. 2d 434 (1941).

235. Herzl Cong v. Robinson, 142 Wash. 469, 253 P. 654. (1927).

236. Tamarkin v. The Children of Israel, 2 Ohio App. 2d. 60, 206 N.E. 2d. 412.

237. Yome v. Gorman, 242 N.Y. 395, 403, 152 N.E. 126, 129, 47 ALR 1165 (1926); Application of Rosenwasser, 120 N.Y.S. 2d. 287 (1953); Petition of Isidore Davis, 192 N.Y.S. 2d 174 (1959); Matter of Bobrowsky, 266 App. Div. 849, 42 N.Y.S. 2d 36; Matter of Schechter, 261 App. Div. 926, 25 N.Y.S. 2d 434; Application of Sherman, 107 N.Y.S. 2d 905, affd. 279 App. Div. 872, 110 N.Y.S. 2d 224, reargument and appeal denied 279 App. Div. 919, 110 N.Y.S. 2d 919, affd. 304 N.Y. 745, 108 N.E. 2d 613.

238. 167 Misc. 301, 3 N.Y.S. 2d 754 (1938).

239. *Ibid.*, at 756.

240. *Ibid.*, at 757-758.

241. Raisler v. Krakauer Simon Schreiber Congregation, 47 N.Y.S. 2d

938, 939 (1944), citing Yome v. Gorman, 242 N.Y. 395, 403, 152 N.E. 126 (1926).

242. Goldman et al. v. Mollen et al., 168 Va. 345, 191 S.E. 627 (1937).

243. Friedman v. Gomel Chesed Hebrew Cemetery Association, 92 A. 2d 117 (1952).

244. Application of Bleistift, 193 App. Div. 477.

245. See In the Matter of Sherman, 304 N.Y. 745; also see §89 of the Membership Corporations Law.

246. In re Harlam, 57 N.Y.S. 2d 103 (1945); In re Herskovits, 48 N.Y.S. 2d 906 (1944).

247. Seifer v. Schwimmer, 166 Misc. 329 at 331.

248. In re Harlam, 57 N.Y.S. 2d 103 at 106.

249. Cohen v. Congregation Shearith Israel, 114 App. Div. 117 at 119.

3.

JEWISH INSTITUTIONS

Reduce things to the first institution, and observe wherein and how they have degenerate; but yet ask counsel of both times; of the ancient time, what is best; and of later time, what is fittest.

Francis Bacon

In the culture of the nation and especially in its highest expression, religion, two factors only count: Institutions and great individuals.

Louis Ginzberg,
"Students Scholars and
Saints."

Bet Dins

The crushing case load which a complex society has thrust upon the United States' court system has driven the Chief Justice of the United States Supreme Court to seek outlets for the relief of America's judicial distress. In an address delivered in 1971,

119

and mindful of the assistance Arbitration Associations, Workmens Compensation Boards and other administrative agencies have rendered the courts by adjudicating within areas of their respective expertise, Chief Justice Burger stressed the work remaining to be done in reducing calendar congestion:[1]

> We need a comprehensive re-examination of the whole basis of jurisdiction in order to eliminate whenever possible all matters which may be better administered by others so as to restore the courts to their basic function of dealing with cases and controversies.

There is a judicial body to which resort may be had "as old as the Bible itself,"[2] with special competence to decide matters of Jewish law submitted to it by consent of the parties. For a variety of reasons, not always articulated nor necessarily persuasive, the reaction of judicial reviewers to Bet Din decisions represents something less than the warm embrace with which one would expect the beleaguered oppressed to greet an emancipator.

In Chapter 5, on *Kashruth,* secular treatment of Bet Din decisions will be seen to have reflected a changing course as uniformity of definition of the term "Kosher" warped under strain. As a parade of expert rabbinical witnesses marched to and from the witness stand with conflicting testimony of what constituted compliance with "orthodox Hebrew requirements,"[3] secular judicial deference yielded to understandable perplexity. Acknowledgment of Bet Din supremacy crested in the *S.S.&B. Live Poultry*[4] decision and retrenchment from rabbinical recognition soon followed in subsequent civil "Kashruth" cases.[5] Uneven judicial treatment of Bet Din decisions characterizes other areas of application as well.

Origin and Development of Jewish Courts

Moses may have been the original overburdened judiciary, sitting in judgment on the people "from the morning into the evening."[6] Jethro, his Midianite father-in-law was shocked. " 'What is this thing thou doest to the people? Why sittest thou thyself alone. . . .' "[7] So, on Jethro's counsel, his son-in-law chose able men out of all Israel, and made them heads over the people, rulers of thousands, rulers of hundreds, rulers of fifties, and rulers of tens. And they judged the people at all seasons: the hard causes they brought unto Moses, but every small matter they judged themselves.[8]

In the Book of Deuteronomy God commands:[9]

Judges and officers shalt thou make thee in all thy gates, which the Lord thy God giveth thee, tribe by tribe; and they shall judge the people with righteous judgment. Thou shalt not wrest judgment; thou shalt not respect persons; neither shalt thou take a gift; for a gift doth blind the eyes of the wise, and pervert the words of the righteous. Justice, justice shalt thou follow, that thou mayest live, and inherit the land which the Lord thy God giveth thee.

From their Biblical beginnings, Jewish courts grew in complexity and sophistication over the centuries. At the time of the Second Commonwealth, in the several centuries preceding the Christian era, an independent institution was created to deal with matters of religious law. It was called Bet Din, or court, and better known by the Greek name *synedrion—sanhedrin.* The Bet Din, or Sanhedrin, was made up of different branches. The Great Sanhedrin, or *Bet Din ha Gadol,* was a legislative body which interpreted existing law and enacted new laws. It had seventy-one members and exercised religious authority "not only over the Judaeans in Judea, but no matter where they lived in the then-known world."[10] Other Bet Dins of twenty-three members were established in every city of importance, including three in Jerusalem. A special Sanhedrin, or Bet Din, tried political offenses. Another Bet Din had limited legislative jurisdiction over priestly matters, and yet another emergency Bet Din was set up by Judah Maccabee and his brother Jonathan for the trial of Greek sympathizers, during the second pre-Christian century at the time of the Maccabean revolts against Antiochus and his successors. In addition, there were other courts composed of three members with civil jurisdiction, which at the time extended to cases of theft, injury and mayhem, all regarded as private wrongs.

With the destruction of the Second Temple, Jewish life and institutions passed to Babylonia and along the Mediterranean, later infiltrating first Western and then Eastern Europe. During this long period, the authority of judges shifted its source from the Great Sanhedrin to three-rabbi courts, even, on occasion, to individual rabbis who ordained disciples as rabbinical judges. The Babylonian period, from the seventh to eleventh centuries, saw the universal recognition of Babylonian rabbinic authorities as supreme arbiters of controversy by sheer dint of scholarship, and difficult legal questions came as a matter of course to be referred to them for legal guidance. The scope of the power of courts in exilic communities broadened considerably to adjust to the increased demands for their authority in Jewish life. Rabbinic counsel was sought to preserve Jewish national character, for it was through *halachah*, Jewish law, that a people without a land was to endure until the restoration of Zion.[11] Outstanding rabbinic scholars kept Jewish law and Judaism afloat and responsive during the darkest of the Dark Ages in an unequalled feat of socio-political hydroponics. The sustaining nutrients were undifferentiated law and religion[12] as a people flourished without roots in any land.

During the Middle Ages, particularly after the Crusades began, resort to secular courts incurred Jewish community penalties. Medieval German and Spanish Jewish authorities, as early as the eleventh century, subjected an offender to excommunication. "It was forbidden to frequent Gentile courts even when their law coincided with Jewish law."[13] The reasons for shunning secular courts were numerous. There was the antipathy brought on by the heightened fervor of crusading persecutions. Medieval secular courts were notoriously corrupt. Bribery was common. Oath taking and other judicial features were Christian oriented. The law, itself, applied in secular courts would not be Jewish law.[14]

Jewish courts or Bet Dins, which developed in Europe were of three types. There were permanent three-rabbi courts; there were three-rabbi courts empanelled for the occasion, by each party choosing a judge and the two so chosen picking a third; and there was the single rabbi acting as sole judge. They were guided by the Talmud, legal codes, and those *responsa* of other authorities known to them. If the matter in issue was of a purely civil nature, the principle of *Dina D'Malkhuta Dina* (the law of the land is the law) applied. When the law of the land and Jewish law parted, the Bet Din "would make a strong effort to harmonize" the two, but would adhere to Jewish law if secular law was discriminatory or extortionate as it applied to Jews.[15] Criminal matters were beyond the competence of Jewish courts, except as the crimes charged related to "informing," a particularly imperiling danger to the community, and certain other domestic and business violations punishable by rabbinic authority with tacit secular consent. Wife-beating, coin-clipping and similar transgressions were punishable by flagellation and different types of excommunication. Homicide and theft were virtually unknown to the Jewish community.[16]

American Bet Dins

Based on European models, Bet Dins in America today are of the three-man variety, either standing or ad hoc. However, by reason of American division on denominational lines, Orthodox, Conservative and Reform, Bet Dins have not traditionally served a distinct geographic area as they did in the Old World.[17] There is, however, a standing Bet Din for matrimonial and business cases serving the Orthodox German Jewish community of New York City's Washington Heights. The largest permanent Bet Din is that of the Rabbinical Council of America which has a national constituency. The Conservative movement has a National Bet Din located in the Jewish Theological Seminary. The Orthodox Rabbinical Council of America has local Bet Dins under its auspices in Boston, Chicago and Philadelphia. Conservative rabbis in Chicago, Los Angeles and Philadelphia have sponsored Bet Dins in their respective cities. Ad hoc Bet Dins created by choice of the parties, with a third member chosen by the two previously selected, are also frequently constituted.[18]

The local Bet Dins of the Rabbinical Council of America will refer difficult decisions ultimately to a national *Bet Din Zedek* composed of the most highly qualified rabbis. The Reform movement has no organized Bet Din system. However, the national rabbinical organization of Reform Jewry, and the Union of American Hebrew Congregations both have machinery for resolving disputes between congregations and their rabbis through arbitration.[19]

Bet Dins function generally in areas of Jewish ritual such

as Kashruth; domestic relations, particularly with regard to Jewish divorce; conversion; on occasion, business disputes; employer-employee issues, especially in the area of Jewish education; and disputes between rabbis and congregants or congregations.[20]

Secular Recognition of Bet Din Decisions

Secular acceptance of Bet Din Kashruth decisions is hereafter reviewed at some length.[21] It is typical of the reception given the decisions of rabbinical courts in other areas of law as well. The skepticism courts bring to bear on Bet Din adjudications is reflected in a federal court "Kashruth" opinion. A meat packer, sued for negligence in delivering alleged non-kosher meat to a kosher dealer, claimed a Bet Din had passed favorably on its actions. The court, in denying the defense as so stated, called upon the defendant to "plead the nature of the rabbinical authority, by virtue of what mandate it operates, the nature of the proceeding before it, the parties thereto, and the judgment upon the matter in controversy." [22]

There are gradations of jaundiced skepticism, however, and the rejection rate with respect to Bet Din adjudications in legal fields seized by the civil courts from original ecclesiastical jurisdiction is almost total, whereas that rate is somewhat lower in commercial matters. The two traditional fields over which the church once held sway are matrimonial and probate law.[23] It is precisely in these fields that the decisions of Bet Dins are practically anathema to the civil judiciary.[24]

Stated Orthodox Jewish policy cites the Talmud for authority in seeking resolution of disputes by arbitration before rabbinical judges, if at all possible. The virtues of arbitration are affirmed by Maimonides: [25]

It is commendable at the outset of a trial to inquire of the litigants whether they desire adjudication according to law or settlement by arbitration. If they prefer arbitration, their wish is granted. A court that always resorts to arbitration is praiseworthy. Concerning such a court, it is said: "Execute the justice of peace in your gates" [Zechariah 8, 16]. What kind of justice carries peace with it? Undoubtedly, it is arbitration. So too, with reference to David it is said: "And David executed justice and charity unto all his people" [II Samuel 8, 15]. What kind of justice carries charity with it? Undoubtedly, it is arbitration, i.e. compromise.

A 1953 work on Jewish law reports the current state of Orthodoxy's attitude toward secular courts: [26]

> Even today, among the orthodox everywhere from New York to Bombay, it is considered a disgrace for a Jew to summon a fellow-Jew before the courts of the land. A decent respect for Jewish observances still requires that the aggrieved party should first apply to a rabbinical court to have the matter adjudged there. Only after the defendant ignores the Rabbinical summons, is it proper to sue in the courts of the land.

In furtherance of this policy, a will probate contest was sought to be compromised before a three-man rabbinical court. Their decision came before a New York Surrogate in the course of an accounting proceeding.[27] The Surrogate summarily dismissed the objectant's attempted ouster of his jurisdiction, stating: [28]

> Whatever position the Jewish law may take today regarding the probating of wills and settling of estates, the civil law of the State of New York must be applied and is the only law this court can consider. . . . The probate of an instrument purporting to be the last will and testament of a deceased and the distribution of an estate cannot be the subject of arbitration under the Constitution and the law as set forth by the Legislature of the State of New York [29] and any attempt to arbitrate such issue is against public policy.

Equally adamant opposition to Bet Din arbitration marks the judicial response to rabbinical arbitration of matrimonial and custody matters. A 1969 New York case [30] raised the question of "whether the custody of the child shall be arbitrated in accordance with the provisions of the separation agreement." That agreement provided for the arbitration of disputes by three persons "all of whom are to be versed in Jewish religious law, and that, if the three arbitrators cannot agree, the decision of two shall be final." [31] This procedure was followed by the parties and the decision of three rabbis in favor of the father's right to child custody was appended to his answer in the case. The court somewhat testily dismissed the purported arbitration, emphasizing that "The basic principles governing the custody of infants are beyond debate. The state, succeeding to the prerogative of the crown, acts as *parens patriae.*" [32]

Where the issue in a matrimonial dispute is more narrowly confined to financial wrangling, the decision of a Bet Din has a better chance of acceptance. The Berks had agreed to a Bet Din submission with respect to the financial aspects of their marriage difficulties. But before the Bet Din could complete its work, Mrs. Berk started an action in the City Court of New York [33] to recover monies she alleged were due to her. In justification she claimed that Mr. Berk had violated the terms of the arbitration agreement and, furthermore, the resignation of one member of the three-man rabbinical body prevented its continuance under Jewish law. On the petition of Mr. Berk, the New York Supreme Court stayed Mrs. Berk's City Court suit pending a Bet Din adjudication:

> The issue of whether or not the parties have breached their agreement to arbitrate by violating the terms thereof or by neglecting to continue or complete the arbitration and whether the powers of the "Din Torah" have been terminated should not be decided on conflicting affidavits. Surely the rabbinical board is competent to pass on these questions, to hear witnesses, including petitioner and respondent, and to appraise the value to be given to the testimony of any witness and to render a just and speedy determination respecting the rights of the parties. The board can apply the legal, moral and religious law to the dispute between the parties which is what the parties contemplated and intended when they agreed to arbitrate their dispute before such board. The suit in the City Court, involving a financial dispute between the parties, and being among those matters upon which the parties agreed to arbitrate, will be stayed pending the determination by the board of arbitrators as to the rights of the respective parties. [34]

Bet Din decisions on matters of ritual, unrelated to matrimonial or probate issues and free of internecine religious disputation, receive a more respectful hearing from secular tribunals. We may instructively compare the defamation litigation arising from rabbinic denunciation of Kashruth violators, branded as such by Bet Dins,[35] with a New York appellate court's dismissal of a libel action brought against publicizers of plaintiffs' disqualification by a Bet Din from conducting tests for *"Shatnes."* [36] Jewish law forbids the Orthodox to "wear a mingled stuff [Shatnes], wool and linen together." [37] This is one of the more abstruse Biblical commandments, "the etymology and meaning of which are both uncertain." [38] However, to the Orthodox, as a divine command, it must be obeyed.

A Bet Din's determination of qualification to test for Shatnes appears to have been accepted in *Berman, et al. v. Shatnes Laboratory, et al.*[39] Unlike "Kashruth" defamation cases, the rabbinic arbiters of Shatnes were not challenged as to their own understanding of "orthodox Hebrew requirements." [40] No rabbinical expert witnesses took the stand to subvert the Bet Din's competence or rebut its opinion. The plaintiff did, however, take exception to the publicizers of that Bet Din decision, suing them for libel. The New York Appellate Division sustained the rabbinical court and dismissed the action: [41]

> The parties to this appeal, by submitting the issue of plaintiff Berman's qualifications to test for Shatnes to a Din Torah, made their own procedure and established the basis upon which their differences would be resolved. . . . The determination of the Din Torah was in the nature of a common law award in arbitration . . . and acts as a bar to relitigating essentially the same issue that was decided thereby in the guise of the instant libel action. . . .
>
> Moreover, as the parties chose to resolve their differences in an ecclesiastical tribunal, temporal courts should not interfere with the binding results therein. . . .

Civil courts are likewise more inclined to be sympathetic to Bet Din adjudications of commercial disputes, although often finding non-compliance with statutory arbitration definitions. The result is that the party seeking enforcement of a Bet Din decision

may lose his civil case on technical grounds while receiving counsel
as to available alternative procedures.

The opinion in *Kozlowski v. Seville Syndicate, Inc.*[42] is a case
in point. It records a dispute between stockholders of a real estate
corporation and the efforts of one to assert a legal right to inspect
the corporate books. The parties had entered into an agreement
in "Talmudic Hebrew" signed by all three stockholders, which
according to the translation in evidence, reads as follows:[43]

> We each submit ourselves to the decision of Rabbi Israel
> Yitzchok Piekarski: It is Rabbi Piekarski's privilege to take
> to himself two other rabbis and whatever will be the decision,
> whether by Din Torah or by compromise similar to Din Torah,
> we undertake to obey such in all respects. Furthermore, with
> respect to the matter of the corporation (problem) we rely on
> Rabbi Piekarski to consult an attorney with respect to what
> he may suggest as best in both matters.

Rabbi Piekarski held at least several of the hearings contemplated by the quoted agreement and rendered his decision.
Against claims by the petitioner that the purported arbitration was
invalid because "Rabbi Piekarski was not sworn (CPLR 7506[a]),
nor were the witnesses (CPLR 7505); notice of the hearings was
not properly served (CPLR 7506[6]); the award was not in the
proper form, nor was a copy of the award served in the prescribed
manner (CPLR 7505)," the New York Supreme Court held all
these contentions failed.[44] "I therefore conclude," wrote Judge
Levy, "that the rabbinical decision is, from the standpoint of
procedure, a lawful award in a lawful statutory arbitration proceeding."[45] Citing Kadushin, *Jewish Code of Jurisprudence* (4th
ed., 1923), the court held "the written agreement of May 20, set
forth above, shows a clear intent on the part of the parties to have
Rabbi Piekarski arbitrate their controversy . . ., and that the
proceeding in question may constitute a statutory arbitration to
which the implementary provisions of Article 75 [of the New York
Civil Practice Law and Rules] are applicable."[46] The law countenanced in the arbitration is clearly Jewish law since the proceeding was either to be "by Din Torah or by compromise similar to
Din Torah," and as the court points out, "Jewish jurisprudence,

as it has developed over the millenia, has a number of devices for resolving disputes among persons of that faith. One method is by Din Torah, the traditional Jewish court of law, which proceeds according to Jewish law. . . ." [47] Ultimately, however, the court held the arbitration invalid because the award given by the rabbi was only "a partial one" and it was not possible to tell whether the hearings held by the rabbi covered all the claims submitted to him for decision.

In another arbitration case,[48] the parties had, on termination of their wholesale egg business, submitted certain disagreements to an Orthodox rabbi for determination. Rejecting the validity of the arbitration, the court principally based its decision upon the lack of "a written arbitration agreement or submission agreement in compliance with CPLR 7501." However, the court went beyond this chief defect in summarizing its grounds for upsetting the rabbi's decision, obliquely adverting with dissatisfaction to the application of Jewish law. "Clearly," wrote the court,[49]

> the proceeding before the rabbi was not intended to have and did not have the attributes of an arbitration coming within the provisions of Article 75, CPLR. There was absent the threshold requirement of a proper written agreement (see CPLR 7501) ; the rabbi did not take the required oath (see CPLR 7506[a]), and, in general, his proceedings were conducted in accordance with religious practices and customs rather than in compliance with statutory requirements.

But the court, by way of dictum, then went on to suggest that while statutory arbitration was unavailable, "common law arbitration" was a possible construction of the rabbinical proceedings which had taken place. However, since neither party to the proceedings had requested a hearing or remand to decide that issue, and because a remand was held unjustified since it would "endow this proceeding with the dignity of a plenary action" without a plenary action's procedural panoply of "proper pleadings and the usual pre-trial procedures," [50] the Appellate Division reversed the lower court's confirmation of the rabbinical judgment. The net result was frustration of the Bet Din determination.

An instance of Bet Din corruption resulting in a decree which the civil judiciary struck down, as it would have reacted to the fruits of any civil court corruption, appears in the New York case reports.[51] "The action is predicated on fraud and a conspiracy," Justice Cropsey begins. "It is somewhat unusual in its facts," [52] understates the judge. The unusual facts begin with the claims of a man named Nelson against his brother-in-law, the plaintiff. Nelson wanted "them disposed of by what is called a Din Torah." The three-man rabbinical court met and "made a verbal decision in favor of the plaintiff and against all the claims made by Nelson." Nevertheless, a subsequent written record of that decision contradicted it completely. The written record "stated that Nelson was entitled to have discharged a $6,000 mortgage which the plaintiff held on his property. . . ." [53] The confounded plaintiff began a civil action, alleging "that the signing of the written report by two of the Rabbis was procured through the fraud and misrepresentation of the third Rabbi (defendant Levy) and another party who was also a Rabbi as well as a lawyer (defendant Weisblatt), acting in conjunction with Nelson." [54] Plaintiff claimed damages in the amount of expenses he had incurred in successfully defending a prior action brought by his brother-in-law, Nelson, on the basis of the spurious Bet Din written "decision," to cancel the mortgage. The court made a preliminary finding of significance. Since the Din Torah (the rabbinical court session) did not comply with statutory arbitration requisites, the plaintiff was not bound by statutory limitations governing time within which to move to set aside an arbitration award. On the merits, Justice Cropsey found for the plaintiff against the conspiring rabbis. The law reports are silent as to the fate of the scoundrel brother-in-law, and as with many another rogue we must leave his ultimate judgment to the Ultimate Bet Din.

The Bet Din which has achieved the most publicity in the United States in applying Jewish law to a civil dispute is probably the Boston Bet Din which successfully adjudicated grievances between Negro tenants and Jewish landlords of some forty buildings in that city in 1968.[55] The Bet Din, consisting of five rabbis, was hesitant at first about departing from the usual subjects to which the approximately twenty-five American rabbinical courts have limited themselves, i.e., "refereeing internal religious squabbles and issuing routine rulings on religious questions raised by divorces of Jewish couples." [56] However, in the words of the *Wall Street Journal,* "since ancient Jewish law sets down some rules covering owner-tenant relations and since the owners of the apartments in this instance happened to be Jewish, the court decided to hear the case when the protesting tenants, Negroes and Puerto Ricans, approached it at the suggestion of a rabbi." [57] By terms of the decision, reached after almost four months of hearings, the landlords agreed to refrain from summary dispossess proceedings, to give two weeks' notice to tenants of intended action, and to provide certain janitorial and management services. The tenants agreed to refrain from wilful destruction of property and to control guests in this regard. Enforcement is built into the agreement reached between the disputants by a provision granting an Arbitration Board the right to hold rents in escrow. In addition, tenants' cooperation is encouraged under terms of the agreement which gives the tenants' organization, the South End Tenants Council, a right of first refusal to buy the buildings upon matching any bona fide third party offer. A consequence of such ingenious solutions has been that none of the Boston Bet Din's proceedings have been the subject of judicial review.

There is a natural, as well as Constitutional, reluctance on the part of civil courts to intervene in Bet Din proceedings. A Missouri decision [58] records a "show me" judicial response to a petition in a civil action to compel a Bet Din to speedily conclude its deliberations which had been dragging for two years and to "render a decision on an ecclesiastic dispute and grievance. . . ." The civil court declined to act. [59]

> It takes little discernment on our part to see that plaintiff's "Amended Petition for Mandatory Injunction" does not involve the use and control of church property, nor does it plead any facts that show a civil right of plaintiff is being transgressed. To the contrary, plaintiff's amended petition for mandatory injunction distinctly alleges that "an ecclesiastical dispute and grievance against another party, namely, Dovid ben Schloima (and Kaila)" is the matter involved. No facts are pleaded that would indicate the nature of the dispute and grievance that plaintiff has against the named parties and which he claims they have submitted to the defendants for

arbitration. In several places in his amended petition plaintiff
describes the grievance as a "moral" dispute and that this
dispute is to be tried by the defendants sitting as a Jewish
Court of Justice and their decision is to be based on Jewish
Biblical and Talmudic Law.

There is nothing in plaintiff's petition that shows that
any civil right of plaintiff is involved. It clearly shows, as the
trial court found, an ecclesiastical matter solely within the
jurisdiction of the defendants acting as a Jewish Court of
Justice. As we have pointed out in the authorities cited, the
civil courts have no jurisdiction in ecclesiastical matters and
are without jurisdiction to intervene in such matter.

The Synagogue and the Law

A recurrent quandary posed in religious disputes aired in secular
courts concerns the extent to which civil law principles of contract
should admit or exclude Jewish law as a determining factor. This
issue is raised in a case which concerns the institutions of Bet Din
and Synagogue, and the office of Rabbi. It deals with interpretation
of contract and with church-state relations. The case also serves
to introduce secular judicial treatment of disputes revolving about
a uniquely Jewish institution, without which Judaism as we know
it could hardly have survived, the Synagogue. The 1963 litigation[60]
details a rabbi's fight in a New York State court against ouster by
his synagogue after many years of service. The unspecified cause
of his troubles is referred to cryptically in the court's opinion as
"conflicts" which "developed between plaintiff and some officers
and members of the Congregation." [61]

The plaintiff rabbi first took his grievances, following receipt
of notice of his discharge, to a Bet Din which rendered "a written
decision, favorable to the plaintiff . . . and upon which this suit
for injunctive relief is predicated." The reaction of his Congregation did not betoken that joyful submission to the Bet Din's findings
which the Talmud expects of the litigant.[62] Instead, "the Congregation changed the locks on the doors of its Synagogue . . ." and thereafter held religious services elsewhere "without the presence of the
plaintiff Rabbi," [63] who, having exhausted religious channels, sought
civil intervention.

The New York Supreme Court first found nothing in the Congregation's Constitution and By-Laws governing discharge of a rabbi. It then looked to the New York Religious Corporations Law [64] which directs that dismissal must follow "a meeting of a church corporation" held upon due notice "according to the practice, discipline, rules and usages of the religious denomination or ecclesiastical governing body" of that religion. [65] Here the court was stymied. There was no "such practice, discipline, rule or usage" to be found in Judaism. There was no hierarchy to look to for authorization or approval of discharge. In fact, the rabbi, on investigation, appeared to be a supernumerary: "it is pertinent to observe that according to basic Jewish practices, only a quorum of ten men (minyon) is needed to conduct services and the presence of the clergy is neither required nor prohibited." [66] The court turned from the Religious Corporations Law to the Bet Din decision. It respectfully acknowledged "cognizance of the Beth Din over the religious life of the individual adherents of the Orthodox Jewish faith," but denied its civil jurisdiction over a corporate defendant.[67] The court also limited the Bet Din to its ecclesiastical function. "A Beth Din is an ecclesiastical court convoked to hear disputes between persons of the Jewish faith without resort to civil forums." [68] Thus, its injunction was not civilly enforceable.

The rabbi was left with a suit for breach of a civil contract, for which he was awarded $3,000. His discharge was illegal, having been voted at a meeting called without proper notice.

A 1955 Pennsylvania lawsuit [69] by a cantor against his Congregation-employer for breach of contract saw the reception in evidence of "the law of the Torah and other binding authority of the Jewish law." The cantor's claim was based on a change from separate to mixed seating of men and women between the time of execution of his contract of employment and the date he was to commence his duties. The change made it impossible for him "to officiate as cantor because 'this would be a violation of his beliefs.' " [70] The contract of employment was silent "as to the character of the defendant as an orthodox Hebrew congregation and the practices observed by it," [71] but the court accepted the unanimous uncontradicted testimony of three rabbis "learned in Hebrew law . . . to the effect 'that Orthodox Judaism required a definite and physical separation of the sexes in the synagogue' and . . . that an orthodox rabbi-cantor 'could not conscientiously officiate in a "trefah" synagogue, that is, one that violates Jewish law.' " [72] When the plaintiff signed his contract, the Congregation observed segregated seating. This became an implied condition of the contract and judgment was rendered in plaintiff's favor for damages for breach of contract. That judgment was affirmed on appeal. The usages of Jewish ritual were implied conditions of contract and the civil court necessarily entertained their proof.

A dispute between Synagogue and member over contract interpretation in which Jewish law was accepted as controlling appears in the Michigan Supreme Court reports. [73] The member had signed a building fund pledge which omitted the amount subscribed. Following certain disputes with other members, the pledgor "attempted to withdraw the pledge." [74] The Congregation brought suit. At a pretrial conference, the pledgor, and other members of his family for whom he had signed pledge cards and who were also joined in the action, proposed to amend their answers to the effect that:

> Jewish religious law and the custom and usage of plaintiff synagogue prohibits the institution of a lawsuit in a non-religious court before resort is had to Beth Din, or religious courts. There has been no effort on the part of plaintiff to seek relief in a Beth Din. Whether or not the cards on which plaintiff relies would otherwise form a legally binding contract, it was the intent of the parties that the Jewish law should govern the transaction. Since the Jewish law prohibits the institution of this suit, the parties did not intend to enter into a contract which is legally enforceable under Michigan law. [75]

Subsequently, a second affirmative defense was offered: "Jewish law, custom, tradition and usages for over a thousand years had been that pledges to a synagogue are moral obligations only and may not be legally enforceable contracts." [76] In support of their motions to amend to assert these defenses, the defendant members, seeking to avoid payment, annexed "the affidavit of a Rabbi Dr. Bernard D. Perlow, a rabbi for 25 years and a scholar." That affidavit states in part: [77]

That the religious customs, practices and laws binding on all Jews are codified in the work known as the Shulchan Aruch; that this code is generally regarded as binding as a matter of religious faith by both Orthodox and Conservative Jews; that there is no real distinction between the moral and ethical obligations of the Orthodox and Conservative Jews; that there is only a distinction in certain synagogue rituals; that although the synagogue now known as Congregation B'Nai Sholom is presently classified under the term Conservative, it is important to point out that such classification does not in any way lessen the binding obligation to obey Jewish religious laws as codified in the Shulchan Aruch in matters of conduct and social relations among Jews; that the term Conservative indicates the adoption of certain minor changes that are formalistic, such as mixed seating in the synagogue; the introduction of English in the liturgy and the like; that it is significant that the Orthodox practices and customs which are contained in the copy of the constitution of the synagogue, as submitted to this deponent, shows that numerous Orthodox customs and traditions are still embodied and are obligatory on B'Nai Sholom Synagogue, such as the requirement that the Torah shall not be taken out on Friday night or any other holiday night, with the exception of Simchos Torah and Yom Kippur; that the kitchen in the synagogue is to be maintained strictly kosher; that the wearing of the prayer shawls on Saturday and other holidays are mandatory; that no organ shall be installed in the synagogue proper and that any choir that is used shall be composed of persons of the Jewish faith; that these are clear indications that the said synagogue intended to be bound by Jewish custom, tradition and practices.

That in the opinion of this deponent, the Shulchan Aruch, as well as the custom and tradition for more than a thousand years, prohibits the bringing of a suit in the civil courts of any State by a synagogue against any of its members or vice versa and is contrary to Jewish law and is prohibited; that any such civil controversy must be first brought before the Jewish religious court known as the Beth Din (a Jewish rabbinical court); that under Jewish law, matters of charity to the synagogue go to the heart of the Jewish religion; that a charitable contribution to a synagogue is considered a religious matter by and between the synagogue and the member; that for a synagogue to file a suit against one of its members upon an alleged charitable contribution without submitting it to a Beth Din is what is known in Jewish law as a "Chillul Hashem" which is a profanation of God's name and such action is such a grave sin in Jewish law, that it warrants excommunication; that historically, pledges to a synagogue were always considered and are still considered as moral obligations and not the subject of a lawsuit; that since Jewish law does not even permit one Jewish member of a synagogue to sue another Jewish member on civil matters unless it is first submitted to a Beth Din, a fortiori, in case of a purely religious controversy that is involved in this case, it is even a greater violation of Jewish law; indeed it has been uniformly held that to take a case of this character involving Jewish charity, Jewish religion and the integrity of the synagogue and its members before a civil court is scandalous and disgraceful and subjects the moving party to excommunication (Responsa of Rabbi Jacob Tam [11th century], grandson of the famous Talmudic authority Rashi, Responsa of Rabbi Mayer of Ruttenberg [14th century] and all Rabbinic Responsa to Jewish history).

That it is expressly stated in Hyman E. Goldine's translation of Rabbi Solomon Ganzfried's "Code of Jewish Law, Kidzur Shulchan Aruch" published in New York City by the Hebrew Publishing Company in 1961, volume 4, page 67, that it is forbidden to bring a suit in the civil courts even if their decision would be in accordance with the law of Israel; that even if the two litigants are willing to try the case before such a court, it is forbidden; that even if they make an oral or a written agreement to that effect it is of no avail; that whoever takes a case against another Jew involving religious matters, is a Godless person and he has violated and defiled the law of Moses; that throughout the Shulchan Aruch, it is repeatedly stated that the Beth Din (Jewish rabbinical court) is the proper and only tribunal to hear controversies between a synagogue and its members; that it is especially and flagrantly contrary to Jewish law for a synagogue to sue in a civil court the chairman of its building committee who had apparently been one of the pillars of the synagogue for many years; that the whole concept of Jewish support for the synagogue, would be greatly endangered, if not destroyed, if a synagogue would be permitted to go to civil courts to enforce an obligation upon an alleged pledge by its members; that more is at stake than a contractual relationship between synagogue and its members in this litigation; that the integrity, the morality and the tradition of Jewish support of the synagogue predicated upon the moral law, is being attacked.

Therefore in the opinion of this deponent, the synagogue had no right under Jewish law, which is controlling and binding upon the parties, to institute this suit.

The court was persuaded. If its conclusion, "that the affidavit of Rabbi Dr. Bernard D. Perlow raised a question of fact as to Jewish custom which may be controlling upon the parties",[78] were the sole basis for its decision allowing the defendants to amend their answers, then the case would be the obverse of the New York *Kupperman* decision [79] in which the court by-passed Bet Din proceedings as having no impact on a civil contract litigation. However, the Michigan court stressed a distinction from other breach of contract cases. The pledge cards—the contracts in issue—were incomplete. Custom might be looked to for the purpose of filling the gap. Defendants should be allowed to prove, according to the court, that "the custom of their religion . . . requires disputes between the synagogue and its members over religious matters to be resolved according to Jewish law and to prove, if they can, that the . . . subscribers in signing their pledge cards contracted with reference to it." [80] Unlike the *Kupperman* opinion, the case was not judicially viewed as capable of separation into ecclesiastical and civil aspects, civil breach of contract being reserved for purely civil consideration. Instead, the court treated Bet Din deliberation as if it were at least an administrative procedure, exhaustion of which was a prerequisite to further civil appeal.[81]

While Jewish law may be an implied condition of contract as in the case of the Pennsylvania cantor, and evidence of Jewish law may be received, as is evidence of usage and custom, to complete an incomplete agreement, when contract interpretation is not in issue the courts must look to other guiding principles. Such is the case where changes in modes of worship are contested as violations of Jewish law by dissenting congregants.

An 1871 United States Supreme Court decision, *Watson v. Jones*,[82] has set the standard for state intervention where religious dissensions affect churches organized upon congregational principles, as Judaism is. A synagogue is "a religious congregation which, by the nature of its organization, is strictly independent of other ecclesiastical associations, and so far as church government is concerned, owes no fealty or obligation to any higher authority." [83] In such an organization, *Watson v. Jones* stands for the principal of majority rule.[84]

A 1961 Louisiana decision [85] quotes extensively from *Watson v. Jones* in turning back a minority effort to enjoin a congregation's officers from instituting mixed seating. Testimony from an expert rabbinic witness made the point "that the 1957 Edition of the Encyclopedia Britannica, Vol. 3, page 87(a) contains the following: 'There is no religious institution more democratic than a local Baptist Church, with the exception of a Jewish synagogue.' " [86] Majority rule was made even easier of application in the case by conflicting expert testimony on whether segregated seating was indeed a tenet of Orthodoxy. The congregation's own rabbi had testified it was not, and "the opinion of the Rabbi of the congregation is, in questions of doctrine, to be accorded great weight. . . ." [87]

The result of a similar minority challenge was directly contrary in a 1959 Michigan Supreme Court decision,[88] where, "because of defendants' calculated risk of not offering proofs, no dispute exists as to the teaching of Orthodox Judaism as to mixed seating," [89] that teaching being "that an Orthodox Jew could not worship in a synagogue where there is mixed seating." [90] The *Watson v. Jones* majority rule apparently gives way where the minority contends for a rule of undisputed sanctity, the violation of which would destroy the synagogue's basic identity. It would appear majority rule must be buttressed by at least some expert testimony that the proposed doctrinal departure does not constitute a fundamental religious deviation.

The earliest case found in state judicial reports reflecting an intrasynagogue doctrinal dispute is a 1909 Massachusetts case[91] which faithfully follows *Watson v. Jones* in imposing majority rule in a struggle over ritual changes. The precise nature of the changes protested by the minority is unclear but it was alleged "the defendants conspired together and 'prevented the plaintiffs from worshipping according to the form of service called Askinaz and have by force performed or caused to be performed in said synagogue divine services according to the doctrine of the Swards.' "[92] By the "doctrine of the Swards," possibly was meant the Sephardi ritual of Spanish and Portugese tradition as opposed to the Ashkanazi ritual of Central and Eastern European Jewry. More likely, considering the court's failure to mention any claim of major ritual changes, what may have been involved is the *nusakh sephard,* which many Orthodox synagogues follow, especially those whose members hail from southeastern Europe and Poland. A number of slight changes in the order of the prayers and their wording mark the *nusakh sephard,* which is also referred to as the *nusakh* of the Ari after innovations in the service attributed to Isaac Luria. He lived in Safed in the sixteenth century and was considered a saint by his disciples. At any rate majority rule prevailed in a case which may well have concerned minor ritual changes only.

The Massachusetts court held a congregational by-law provision requiring unanimity for ritual change invalid as "unreasonable and inconsistent with the legal right of control of the affairs of the corporation existing in its membership." [93] The majority of the members under *Watson v. Jones* had a right to make ritual changes and "the will of the majority having been lawfully expressed," the plaintiffs could not suppress it by civil remedy.

A 1929 Ohio case [94] turned on the court's refusal to regard the majority's proposed changes as fundamental. The minority petitioners had urged the court "to decide that a trust was imposed upon the church property; that the property should be used for the purposes of promoting the cause of traditional or orthodox Judaism." [95] The court took this charge as an unauthorized, unproductive and far too formidable undertaking for judicial discretion: [96]

> It is plain from the record that there is such a multitudinous variety of opinions in regard to orthodoxy and traditional doctrine that it would be impossible to grant any relief that would not be confusing and chaotic in its character, and thus is made apparent the impossibility of definitely defining a

course; and, especially, when an appeal is made to a judicial
instead of an ecclesiastical tribunal, does it appear inevitable
that to define a distinct course of conduct is beyond the bounds
of possibility and reason. . . . In the instant case we find the
complaints of plaintiffs are not of such a nature that they apply
to the fundamental and doctrinal belief. . . . There must be, in
order to grant the relief prayed for, such a perversion and
diversion of the original principles and purposes upon which
the church was founded as would either partially or totally
destroy the institution as a Jewish identity, and while all
points of orthodoxy and traditional Judaism may not be carried out according to a unanimity of opinion, yet, so long as
the primal elements of these doctrines remain undisturbed as
tenets and principles of the Jewish faith, a minority differing
upon this point is ineffectual. . . . Certainly this court could not
define Jewish orthodoxy and traditional Judaism except from
the testimony of experts, and it is an inevitable fact that such
an inquiry would result in multiplying dissension, instead of
eliminating it. We are content to follow the universal rule that,
where the remedy is within the church itself, a judicial tribunal
cannot interfere. . .

Watson v. Jones was relied upon in an 1879 Louisiana case [97]
to defeat a mandamus writ to compel congregational officers to
restore relator, "an Israelite," to synagogue membership from
which he had been expelled for "gross misconduct." The majority-
imposed expulsion was supported by the court despite a plea by the
relator that disabilities of more than spiritual consequence alone
flowed from his excommunication. Specifically, "the right to be
buried in its burying-ground will be, or is denied him." [98] The court's
response was "the relator has happily no present need of enforcing
his claim to burial anywhere, and *non constat* that before he does
need it, he will have his ban of excommunication removed, and be
restored to full fellowship in the congregation." [99] In the interim,
the court was content to allow Watson v. Jones decide the issue.
The Congregation's majority decision was not to be re-examined and
reversed by secular authority. The Congregation "is the tribunal
to which he submitted himself when he accepted membership of the
congregation, and its action is not examinable in a civil court." [100]

Watson v. Jones, as modified by subsequent decisions, has left the current state of the law governing intrasynagogue disputes firmly in the majority's favor, provided it can adduce expert testimony in support of its doctrinal stand. The courts, loath to enter upon ecclesiastical ground, delight to defer to a spirited spiritual majority present and voting, and will not, in the absence of overwhelming evidence, champion a minority's claim that revisions should be halted because they work a fundamental change.

NOTES TO CHAPTER 3

1. 43 *New York State Bar Journal,* 384. (Oct. 1971).

2. "Rabbinical Courts: Modern Day Solomons," 6 *Columbia Journal of Law and Social Problems,* 49 at 50 (Jan. 1970).

3. See People v. Gordon, 172 Misc. 543, 14 N.Y.S. 2d 333 (1939), revd. 258 App. Div. 421, 16 N.Y.S. 2d 833, affd. 283 N.Y. 705, 28 N.E. 2d 717 (1940).

4. 158 Misc. 358, 285 N.Y.S. 879 (1936). See Chapter 5, pp. 182-187.

5. See Chapter 5. The courts are tempted to react to differing rabbinic testimony in a manner predicted by an old English Lord Chancellor, who wrote that when "persons do hear of so many discordant and contrary opinions in religion; it doth avert them from the church, and maketh them to sit down in the chair of the scorners." Francis Bacon, "Of Unity in Religion," *The Harvard Classics: Bacon, Milton, Browne* (New York, 1937.)

6. Exodus 18:13.

7. Exodus 18:14. As many an overburdened judge has been warned, "Moses' father-in-law said unto him: 'The thing that thou doest is not good. Thou wilt surely wear away, both thou, and this people that is with thee; for the thing is too heavy for thee; thou art not able to perform it thyself alone.' " Exodus 18:17-18.

8. Exodus 18:25-26.

9. Deut. 16:18-20.

10. Solomon Zeitlin, *The Rise and Fall of the Judean State* (Phila., 1964) I, 204. Ch. 2 is devoted to the growth and development of the Bet Din.

11. Moshe Silberg, "Law and Morals in Jewish Jurisprudence," 75 *Harvard Law Review* 321 (1961).

12. Boaz Cohen, *Jewish and Roman Law* (New York, 1966) I, 68. See also Roscoe Pound, *Law and Morals* (1926) 27-29.

13. Leo Landman, *Jewish Law in the Diaspora* (Phila., 1968) 91; see George Horowitz, *The Spirit of Jewish Law* (New York, 1953) §343, 650; see affidavit quoted from Congregation B'Nai Shalom v. Martin, 382 Mich. 659, 173 N.W. 2d 504 (1969), *infra* at p. 136. "Inside the *aljamas* [Spanish ghettoes] great insistence was placed on the fact that no Jew could use the civil Christian legal system . . . The Jewish legal system was marked by a calm, painstaking feeling for justice and in many respects formed a contrast to the semi-barbaric practices which were general in the Middle Ages. It is characteristic that in the thousands of cases we know, we never find a Jewish judge accused of bribery. Normally it was the custom to include an entry called 'bribery and other expenses' when making out the accounts for a legal case." Poul Borchsenius, *The Three Rings* (London, 1963) 183.

14. "Rabbinical Courts: Modern Day Solomons," *op. cit.*, 53. Jewish antipathy toward patronizing non-Jewish courts goes back at least to talmudic times when a Jew's making use of local courts, notarial offices or archives

was frowned on. "Even the majority of Diaspora Jews doubtless shared Paul's sentiment of grieving over a brother going to law with a brother 'and that before the unbelievers.'" Salo W. Baron, *A Social and Religious History of the Jews*, 2nd ed. (New York, 1952) II, 265. See Gittin 88b and compare I Corinthians 6:1 where Christians are urged not to appeal to heathen courts. In the United States various ethnic groups have long followed their own means of legally resolving disputes. Local Chinese tongs in large cities such as New York, Chicago, Boston, Los Angeles and San Francisco, through voluntary submissions by the disputants, follow a means of resolving conflicts called "tiewo" in which Chinese concepts of justice are applied. Roger Grace, "Justice, Chinese Style," 75 *Case & Comment* 50 (Jan.-Feb. 1970). American Indian tribal courts retain jurisdiction over civil matters arising between Indians. Worcester v. Georgia, 6 Pet. 515 (1832). See J. Youngblood Henderson and Russel L. Barsh, "Oyate Kin hoye Keyuga u pe," *Harvard Law School Bulletin*, June, 1974, 10. Eskimo village councils are the principal forums for disputes in many Eskimo villages. The Indian Reorganization Act of 1934 has allowed such councils to make rules and enforce them upon village members. Stephen Conn and Arthur E. Hippler, "Conciliation and Arbitration in the Native Village and the Urban Ghetto," 58 *Judicature* 229 (Dec. 1974).

15. "Rabbinical Courts: Modern Day Solomons," *op. cit.*, 54.

16. *Ibid.*, 55. Bet Dins in other lands decreed the death penalty, but only in medieval Spain was it carried out. The severity of punishment meted out by Spanish Bet Dins for informing is described in Borchsenius, *The Three Rings, op. cit.*, and included "stoning to death at the most holy hour of the Day of Atonement or opening the criminal's arteries as he stood over his own grave." The author offers in mitigation "the state of emergency in which the Jews always lived. In such circumstances the *beth din* was really a court martial which made summary brutal judgments." A recent echo of past violence associated with informing sounded in 1972 in the U. S. Court of Appeals for the Second Circuit. A seventeen-year-old worker in Jewish Defense League headquarters refused to testify before a grand jury as to his knowledge of facts concerning the fatal fire bombing of the office of an impressario who brought Soviet artists to America. Smilow v. United States 465 F. 2d 802 (1972). He based his refusal on First Amendment religious grounds rather than any Fifth Amendment right to be protected against self-incrimination. He asserted that "as an observant and committed Jew" testifying would result in "Divine punishment and ostracism from the Jewish community" as an "informer." The Court denied the constitutional merits of his position. There are grounds in Jewish law as well for denying the claimed exemption. It only applies when unjust laws, laws aimed at Jewish persecution, have been violated. Otherwise there is a positive duty to inform. For example, Philo, two thousand years ago, observed: "If anyone knows that another has perjured himself and . . . fails to inform against him or bring him to justice, he must be liable to the same penalties as the perjurer." Boaz Cohen, *Jewish and Roman Law*, "Testimonial Compulsion in Jewish Law" (New York, 1966) II, 748. Similarly, the Midrash Tanhuma comments upon Leviticus Ch. 5, Verse 1, "Since he did not come and declare to the judge, so and so committed blasphemy; consequently, if he does not testify, he shall bear his sin."

17. Daniel J. Elazar and Stephen R. Goldstein, "The Legal Status of the American Jewish Community," *1972 American Jewish Year Book* (1972), Vol. 73, 82-83.

18. "Rabbinical Courts: Modern Day Solomons," *op. cit.*, 56; Elazar and Goldstein, *loc. cit.* There are also conciliation and arbitration bodies operating outside the rabbinical court system. The best known is the Jewish Conciliation Board of America, which began in 1921 as the Jewish Court of Arbitration. It is non-denominational and charges no fees for its aid and counselling, nor will it accept contributions from recent litigants. Parties appear before a three-person adjudicatory body consisting of a rabbi, a businessman and an attorney. A fascinating account of the variety of problems presented to such a panel are described in Ivan Schaeffer, *"Justice Justice Shalt Thou Follow,"* 79 *Case and Comment*, 37-41 (July-August 1974). See also Steven J. Levine, "Jewish-Style Conciliation" *N.Y. Law Journal*, Aug. 15, 1974, 1, col. 4.

19. Elazar and Goldstein, *op. cit.*, 84-85.

20. "Rabbinical Courts: Modern Day Solomons," *op. cit.*, 62.

21. See Chapter 5.

22. Friedman v. Swift & Co., 18 F. Supp. 596 (1937). The voluntary nature of Bet Din submission as a prerequisite for civil court recognition is illustrated in *Beck & Schachter Co. v. Kohn, N.Y.L.J.*, January 7, 1975, 2, col. 2, where withdrawal by a disputant from the proceeding effectively terminated it as far as the state court was concerned.

23. See note 5, Chapter 2 *supra*, with regard to ecclesiastical control over matrimonial law. The ecclesiastical courts in England at one period had exclusive cognizance of all suits relative to legacies. It was not until the late seventeenth century that the Court of Chancery, itself of religious origin, assumed concurrent jurisdiction. Deeks v. Strutt, 5 D. & E., 692; Atkins *et ux* v. Hill, Cowp. 284. Chancellor Kent discusses the matter at length in Ducasse v. Richaud, 1 Anthon's Nisi Prius 191, 193-194 (1813). Marriage and inheritance were regarded as having peculiarly religious ties in the ancient world as well. Through the influence of the Maccabees, in 161 B.C.E. all Jews within the Roman dominions obtained the status of *peregrini*, which allowed them to be judged by their own law, and to follow their own customs in such matters as marriage and inheritance. James Parkes, *The Conflict of the Church and the Synagogue* (New York, 1969) 8.

24. The rivalry between common law lawyers and judges and ecclesiastical authority has a long history. Blackstone writes of "the spleen with which the monastic writers speak of our municipal laws upon all occasions." Blackstone, *Commentaries on the Laws of England* (Phila. 1866) 19. Hargrave in his notes to the first volume of Blackstone presents a history of contests which have existed since early in the thirteenth century between the clergy and the common lawyers. Sharswood in his notes to Blackstone quotes Bishop Burnet who "seems to have thought that antipathy to the national church is an inseparable characteristic of the lawyers: . . . 'It has been everywhere observed that no host of men have made head against those things which have been called rights to the church with more zeal and indignation than lawyers and secular courts.' " Blackstone, *supra*.

25. *Mishneh Torah*, XXII, 4-6. Quoted in Horowitz, *op. cit.*, §344, 651.

26. Horowitz, *op. cit.*, §343, 651.

27. In the Matter of the Estate of Jacob J. Jacobovitz, 58 Misc. 2d 330 (1968).

28. *Ibid.*, 332, 334.

29. Article VI §12, subd. d.

30. Agur v. Agur, 32 App. Div. 2d 16, 298 N.Y.S. 2d 772.

31. *Ibid.*, 17.
32. *Ibid.*, 19.
33. Berk v. Berk, 8 Misc. 2d 732, 171 N.Y.S. 2d 592 (1957).
34. *Ibid.*, 733-734.
35. Cohen v. Eisenberg, 173 Misc. 1089, 19 N.Y.S. 2d 678 (1940), affd. 260 App. Div. 1014, 24 N.Y.S. 2d 1004 (1941); Cabinet v. Shapiro. 17 N.J. Super. 540, 86 A. 2d 314 (1952).
36. Berman *et al.* v. Shatnes Laboratory *et al.*, 43 App. Div. 736, 350 N.Y.S. 2d 703 (1973).
37. Deut. 22:11; Lev. 19:19.
38. Joseph A. Hertz, *Pentateuch and Haftorah*, 2nd ed. (London), 1965) 844. "The reason underlying the prohibition may possibly be the same as that against mixing seeds." Deut. 22:9. The explanation for that prohibition "is based on the idea that God has made distinctions in the natural world which it is wrong for man to obliterate by processes of intermixing." Hertz, *supra*, 843. The explanation is very close to a restatement of the prohibition.
   To a staunch defender of orthodoxy like the theologian, Samson Raphael Hirsch, *shatnes* exemplified a ritual law, a *chuk*, observance of which trains man's character so that he is able to perform broader social obligations, *mishpatim*. Hirsch's view is summarized by Isidor Grunfeld in his Introduction to Hirsch's *Horeb* (London 1962) lxiii and lxiv: "In his later writings, Hirsch repeatedly calls attention to the fact that *chukim* and *mishpatim* are usually mentioned together, and that *chukim* are mostly mentioned first. There is a deep reason for this order. The *chukim*, which deal with the character-training of man, are a pre-requisite to the *mishpatim*, the social laws, which are based on man's being able to control himself. 'the purer the body the clearer will the image of God in it come to be realized as long as the body submits itself to the spirit.' That the so-called ceremonial laws have the same aim as the moral laws is also evident from the fact that the most typical moral law—namely, the law 'Love thy neighbor as thyself' appears in the Pentateuch in juxtaposition with a typical 'ceremonial' law—namely, 'thou shalt not wear *shaatnez*' (wool and linen woven together.)"
   The cultural historian may see in *shatnes* the reflection of an age-old conflict between farmer and herder, the flaxgrower and the shepherd. Each pursues his separate ways, and to combine the products of their separate labors is contrary to nature. From earliest times, immiscibility of grower and stockman has marked human history. In America, Indians of the Southwest typify this phenomenon, the Pueblos being the confirmed agriculturists and their rivals, the wandering Navajo hunters, taking to sheepherding when the Spanish rancheros introduced flocks to that area in the eighteenth century. Matthew W. Stirling, *Indians of the Americas* (Washington, D.C., 1955) 106, 122. The early seventeenth-century Dutch jurist, Hugo Grotius, traces the conflict back to the world's first family, to Cain and Abel. In Book II, ch. 2, §11 of *De Jure Belli et Pacis*, he wrote, "Agriculture and pasturage seem to have been the most ancient pursuits, which characterized the first brothers. Some distribution of things would necessarily follow these different states; and we are informed by holy writ, that the rivalry thus created ended in murder."
39. 43 App. Div. 736, 350 N.Y.S. 2d 703 (1973).
40. See People v. Gordon, 172 Misc. 543, 14 N.Y.S. 2d 333 (1939), revd. 258 App. Div. 421, 16 N.Y.S. 2d 833, affd. 283 N.Y. 705, 28 N.E. 2d 717 (1940).
41. Berman *et al.* v. Shatnes Laboratory *et al.*, 43 App. Div. 736 at 737.

42. 64 Misc. 2d 109, 314 N.Y.S. 2d 439 (1970).

43. *Ibid.*, 443.

44. *Ibid.*, 446.

45. *Ibid.*, 449.

46. *Ibid.*, 445.

47. *Ibid.*

48. Hellman v. Wolbrom, 31 App. Div. 2d 477, 298 N.Y.S. 2d 540 (1969).

49. *Ibid.*, at 482.

50. *Ibid.*

51. Cooper v. Weissblatt, 154 Misc. 522, 277 N.Y.S. 709 (1935).

52. *Ibid.*, at 711.

53. *Ibid.*

54. *Ibid.*

55. *Time Magazine*, "The Black and the Jew: A Falling Out of Allies" (Jan. 31, 1969); *The Wall Street Journal* Sept. 9, 1968, 1, col. 4; Lindeman, "Urban Crisis and Jewish Law," *Hadassah Magazine* (March, 1969) 10; "Rabbinical Courts: Modern Day Solomons," *op. cit.*, 49; *The New York Times*, Feb. 6, 1973, 39.

56. *The Wall Street Journal, supra*, n. 55.

57. *Ibid.*

58. Schwartz v. Jacobs, 352 S.W. 2d 389.

59. *Ibid.*, at 392.

60. Kupperman v. Congregation Nusach Sfard of the Bronx, 240 N.Y.S. 2d 315 (1963).

61. *Ibid.*, at 317.

62. "Thus exhorts the Talmud: 'Let him who comes from a court that has taken from him his cloak [to satisfy a judgment] sing his song and go his way [since having been justly tried he had not been divested of property but rather had been relieved of an ill gotten object]." Introduction by Amihud I. Ben Porath to Silberg, *op. cit.*, 306, 307, citing Sanhedrin 7a (Rashi).

63. Kupperman v. Congregation Nusach Sfard of the Bronx, 240 N.Y.S. 2d 315, 317-318.

64. §25 of Article 2.

65. Kupperman v. Congregation Nusach Sfard of the Bronx, 240 N.Y.S. 2d 315, 318-319.

66. *Ibid.*, 319-320.

67. *Ibid.*, 322.

68. *Ibid.*

69. Fisher v. B'Nai Yitzhok, 177 Pa. Super. Ct. 359 (1955).

70. *Ibid.*, 362.

71. *Ibid.*, 359.

72. *Ibid.*, 362-363.

73. Congregation B'Nai Shalom v. Martin, 382 Mich. 659, 173 N.W. 2d 504 (1969).

74. *Ibid.*, 663.

75. *Ibid.*

76. *Ibid.*, 664.

77. *Ibid.*, 665. Despite the influence of Rabbi Perlow's affidavit on the outcome of the *B'Nai Shalom* case, neither his statement of Jewish law discountenancing a synagogue's resort to civil courts nor the decision in that case deterred another Conservative Michigan congregation from filing under Chapter XI of the Federal Bankruptcy Law. On June 5, 1975 Adat Shalom

Synagogue of Farmington Hills, "with great reluctance," sought protection from its creditors, particularly from its general contractor. Its bankruptcy petition listed $4.3 million in debts and over $10 million in assets, including real estate worth $8.5 million. It was the first synagogue bankruptcy "in the legal literature of the United States" according to the chairman of the Detroit Bar Association's bankruptcy committee. *The New York Times*, June 16, 1975, 52, col. 7.

78. Congregation B'Nai Shalom v. Martin, 382 Mich. 659, 668.

79. Kupperman v. Congregation Nusach Sfard of the Bronx, 240 N.Y.S. 2d 315 (1963), *supra*, pp. 132-133, notes 60-61.

80. Congregation B'Nai Shalom v. Martin, 382 Mich. 659, 669.

81. A defect in following such a course is that the parties may not, apart from other considerations, be remanded to a Bet Din which, except in certain divorce proceedings, can only act with the consent of the disputing parties. See Elazar and Goldstein, *op. cit.*, 67.

82. 13 Wall. 679, 20 L. Ed. 666.

83. Watson v. Jones, 13 Wall 679, 20 L. Ed. 666 as quoted in Katz v. Singerman, 241 La. 103, 118, 127 So. 2d 515 (1961).

84. The history of *Watson v. Jones, supra*, and its implications appears in Mark DeWolfe Howe, *The Garden and the Wilderness* (Chicago, 1965) 80 *et seq.* It is interesting to note that before the time of Hillel differences of opinion over issues of Jewish law were resolved by majority vote. Nahum N. Glatzer, *Hillel the Elder* (New York, 1956) 25.

85. Katz v. Singerman, 241 La. 103, 127 So. 2d 515 (1961).

86. Rabbi Jacob Agus' testimony as an expert witness in *Katz v. Singerman, supra*, at 117.

87. *Katz v. Singerman, supra*, at 117.

88. Davis v. Scher, 356 Mich. 291 (1959).

89. *Ibid.*, 304.

90. *Ibid.*, 297.

91. Saltman v. Nesson, 201 Mass. 534.

92. *Ibid.*, 536.

93. *Ibid.*, 542.

94. Katz v. Goldman, 33 Ohio App. 150.

95. *Ibid.*, 152-153.

96. *Ibid.*, 156, 162-163.

97. State *ex rel* Soares v. Hebrew Congregation Dispersed of Judah, 31 La. Ann. 205.

98. *Ibid.*, 208.

99. *Ibid.*, 209.

100. *Ibid.*

4·

SABBATH AND HOLIDAY OBSERVANCE

The people of Israel shall keep the Sabbath, observing the Sabbath throughout their generations, as a perpetual covenant.

Exodus 31:16

And Moses declared to the people of Israel the appointed feasts of the Lord.

Leviticus 23:44

I renounce the whole worship of the Hebrews, circumcision, all its legalisms, unleavened bread, Passover, the sacrificing of lambs, the feasts of Weeks, Jubilees, Trumpets, Atonement, Tabernacles, and all the other Hebrew feasts, their sacrifices, prayers, aspersions, purifications, expiations, fasts, Sabbaths, new moons, foods and drinks.

Profession of Faith, attached to the Clementine Recognitions, extracted from Jews on Baptism—Patrologia Graeco-Latina, I.

149

WHEN EMPEROR CONSTANTINE in 321 transferred the Christian Sabbath from Saturday to Sunday[1] he cast a far-flung net which has enmeshed Orthodox Jews as distant in place and time as the United States of the twentieth century. They are caught in the paradox of being Sabbath violators while being Sabbath observers even in American communities where they play a major role in trade and business, and in spite of constitutional religious protections.

To the Jew the Sabbath begins Friday at sundown and ends at sundown the following day.[2] "It is a sign between me and the children of Israel forever," the Bible has God say of the Sabbath.[3] It is the essence of the fourth of the Ten Commandments, and it is enjoined upon Jews as an occasion to remember the exodus from Egypt. On the Sabbath, "thou shalt not do any manner of work, thou, nor thy son, nor thy daughter, nor thy man-servant, nor thy maid-servant, nor thy cattle, nor the stranger that is within thy gates." [4]

The constitutional right to freedom of religion, according to the law texts,[5] permits individuals to practice the religious faith of their choice without interference: "No court, in the exercise of its judicial function, can or will assess any one creed against another. Each must be held to be *primus inter pares*. To take any other position would be a direct violation of the Constitution of our Nation and State." [6] However, the judicial interpretation, with respect to Sunday closing laws, which has gained currency as public policy enforceable with constitutional sanction is to see Sunday as "a day of community tranquillity . . . a day when the weekly laborer may best regenerate himself." [7] The "religiously oriented backgrounds" of the Sunday laws are acknowledged, but it is claimed that they have evolved so that today a Sunday law is no more than "a general law . . . to advance the State's secular goals [by providing] one day of the week apart from the others as a day of rest, repose, recreation and tranquillity . . ." [8] This is scant justification to the Jewish Sabbatarian whose religious scruples confine him to Saturday observance. Not only are Christian and Jewish Sabbaths on different days, but doctrinally the very rationale for a rest day stated by the United States Supreme Court is at odds with Jewish thinking. Viewing the Sabbath "as a day

when the weekly laborer may best regenerate himself" derives from
Aristotle. To the Jew,

> Labor is the means toward an end, and the Sabbath as a day
> of rest, as a day of abstaining from toil, is not for the purpose
> of recovering one's lost strength and becoming fit for the
> forthcoming labor. The Sabbath is a day for the sake of life.
> Man is not a beast of burden, and the Sabbath is not for the
> purpose of enhancing the efficiency of his work. "Last in
> creation, first in intention," the Sabbath is "the end of the
> creation of heaven and earth." The Sabbath is not for the sake
> of the weekdays; the weekdays are for the sake of the Sabbath.
> It is not an interlude but the climax of living.[9]

The effects of United States Supreme Court decisions on the
New York City Jewish corner grocer are depicted in the report of
criminal proceedings successfully prosecuted by *The People of the
State of New York against Hyman Finkelstein*,[10] for violation of
the New York Statute [11] then in effect which prohibited "all manner of public selling or offering for sale of any property upon
Sunday" with certain enumerated exceptions. To quote the majority
opinion convicting the defendant: [12]

> On the trial, the police officer testified and the defendant
> conceded, that on Sunday, November 4, 1962, at about 1:05
> P.M., he sold two quarts of milk, a loaf of bread, two bars of
> soap and some canned food to a customer; and that he sold
> milk, bread, corn flakes and crackers to another customer. The
> defendant further testified that he was a scrupulously religious
> man of the Hebrew Faith and that he keeps as his holy time, the
> period from sunset on Friday to darkness on Saturday, during
> which time he is restrained by the commandments of his re-
> ligion from performing any labor or work, which includes
> buying and selling. The defendant went on further to testify
> that he operates a one-man grocery store at 495 Atkins Avenue,
> Brooklyn, which is his sole source of income by which he sup-
> ports himself, his wife and three children. He is 43 years of
> age and has no capital for another business. He has no educa-
> tion nor training for some other vocation or profession. He tried

working at a factory for nine months in order to learn shirt-making, at which he received $28 or $29 per week. He then tried operating a chicken farm for seven years, but when that proved unprofitable he entered the grocery business which he presently operates and has operated for three years. This business supplies him with a bare existence, from which he nets approximately $85 per week. His Sunday business accounts for about $35 of his net income. There was other testimony in the case by the police officer to the effect that defendant's keeping his grocery store open on Sunday did not offend others in the community who practiced a different religious belief . . .

Under section 2147 of the Penal Law, it is not a defense that the defendant observes as a Sabbath, a day other than Sunday; nor that persons who observe Sunday, as their Sabbath, are not offended by the defendant's sales during prohibited hours on Sunday and such statute is constitutional.

The dissenting judge urged upon his brethren that they indeed have power to interpret the law in a manner favorable to the defendant and resorted to the words of Cardozo: [13]

We are told at times that change must be the work of statute, and that the function of the judicial powers is one of conservation merely. But this is historically untrue, and were it true, would be unfortunate. Violent breaks with the past must come, indeed, from legislation, but manifold are the occasions when advance or retrogression is within the competence of judges as their competence has been determined by practice and tradition.[14]

The dissenting judge pleaded: [15]

I close with acknowledgment of understanding of my learned brethren's decision and my respect for their judgment that a court may only adjudicate and not usurp the function of the Legislature. Of them I ask only, if the Legislature does not respond to what seems to be out of place in our way of life, must a court stand by impotently? Or should it, by decision jog its powers into appropriate action? I think the latter.

I conclude from the whole of the above discussion that the dignity of man deserves a better fate than that afforded him by the New York crazy-quilt legislation and the unpredictable court interpretations evolving from it.

Partially in response to the inequitable and insensitive treatment visited upon Hyman Finkelstein, the New York legislature enacted a statute in 1965 [16] granting cities with populations of over one million persons the local option to adopt ordinances which would ostensibly allow the proprietor of a trade or business who "uniformly keeps another day of the week as holy time" to raise his observance of such other "holy time" as a defense to prosecution for conducting business on Sunday. The Legislature subsequently dispensed with the local option character of the legislation and enacted it on a state-wide mandatory basis.[17]

However, this legislative attempt at "separate but equal" Sabbaths has not as yet reached a happy conclusion for the Orthodox Jew in New York. In 1968, the same Criminal Court judge who wrote the opinion of conviction in the case of Hyman Finkelstein held, in effect, that on the same set of facts, despite the new legislation, Finkelstein would still be guilty of violating the Sunday closing laws.[18] The legislation, purporting to provide Saturday observers with a defense, "is so ambiguous and vague as to preclude practical application. . . . Therefore, I must reluctantly hold that section 10 of the General Business Law affords no defense. . . ."[19]

Section 10 of the New York General Business Law, which deals with "conducting any trade or business or public selling or offering for sale of any property on Sunday," parallels section 6 of the same New York statute, which deals with "work or labor on the first day of the week." Both sections, as do corresponding sections of other state laws, aim at providing a defense against prosecution to defendants who keep another holy day should criminal proceedings be brought against them for working on Sunday. In 1961 Chief Justice Warren had indicated that such statutory exemptions for religious observers of holy days provide a preferred means of sheltering non-Sunday Sabbatarians: "A number of states provide such an exemption, and this may well be the wiser solution to the problem." [20]

But the fragility of such state-enacted protections is illustrated

by the hair-splitting analysis which led to the conclusion reached by
Hyman Finkelstein's judge, expressed in a later case,[21] that section
10 of the New York General Business Law "affords no defense to
the defendant herein." The judge's convoluted pilpul centers on
New York statutory definitions of the time period commonly known
as a "day": [22]

> The final paragraph of section 10 states: "The term 'day
> of the week' as used in this section shall mean and include the
> period of time of not less than twenty-four consecutive hours
> commencing at or before sundown on one day and terminating
> at or after sundown on the following day."
>
> In the light of section 19 of the General Construction Law,
> which provides: "A calendar day includes the time from mid-
> night to midnight. Sunday or any day of the week specifically
> mentioned means a calendar day," this court encounters diffi-
> culties in the initial portions of section 10 of the General
> Business Law which provide:
>
> "Notwithstanding any other provision of law, it shall
> be a sufficient defense to a prosecution pursuant to this article,
> for conducting any trade or business or public selling or offer-
> ing for sale of any property on Sunday, that the defendant
>
> "(1) as the proprietor of such business, uniformly keeps
> another day of the week as holy time and keeps his place
> of business closed on the seventh day of the week."
>
> Under section 19 of the General Construction Law, the
> specific mention of "Sunday" in the foregoing quotation means
> a calendar day and is the period from midnight Saturday to
> midnight Sunday. Because of the mandatory definition of the
> term "day of the week," as contained in section 10 of the Gen-
> eral Business Law, it becomes necessary for this court to as-
> certain what period of "twenty-four consecutive hours" is
> meant by the term "seventh day of the week" as used in such
> section. As Sunday is the first calendar day of a calendar week,
> we assume that the word "week" means a period of seven days,
> the first day of which commences on Sunday at or before sun-
> down and ends at or after sundown on Monday, and the
> "seventh day of the week" commences at or before sundown
> on Saturday and ends at or after sundown on Sunday. While

such interpretation is probably contrary to the actual intention of the Legislature, the language used must be strictly interpreted as such section is an exception to the public policy setting aside Sunday as a day of repose.

Other Sunday law pitfalls derive from seemingly arbitrary categorization of that which is permissible and that which is not.[23] Legislative efforts in New York to broaden or abolish Sunday restrictions have met with frustration.[24] Judicial declarations of constitutionality are being challenged increasingly. A 1972 Appellate Term reluctant concurrence in the indictment of a technical Sunday law violator is typical: [25]

There have been many judicial pronouncements in recent years to the effect that these Sabbath Laws, which now permit all sorts of activities on Sunday, merit reappraisal in light of present day realities.

These judicial calls for enlightened thinking are most compelling especially when we realize that the Sabbath Laws had their origin in this state over three hundred years ago in the Conditions of the Burgomaster of Amsterdam of 1658 which required that city to furnish the colonists with a schoolmaster to read the Holy Scriptures in public. This religious aspect of Sunday was carried over in the Duke of York's laws of April, 1664. When religious freedom was guaranteed to the colonists by the Charter of Liberties of October, 1683, the religious aspects of the then existing Sabbath Laws continued until the Act of October 22, 1695. That act contained provisions similar to article 192 of the Penal Law of 1909 from which our current Sabbath Laws are derived almost word for word.

We are now living with this set of laws which originated over 275 years ago. They have been amended repeatedly and during the last 50 years have been liberalized some eleven times. They present a crazy-quilt pattern which is arbitrary, capricious and unrealistic in this day and age. By permitting certain businesses to remain open, by permitting sale of certain items at specified times of the day and by generally using incongruous and contradictory standards and exceptions, the

statutes do not even logically further the supposed public
policy of the state.

Peculiarly enough, Canada, by statute [26] has reached the same
result with respect to Sunday law observance as have practically
all the states. Canadian Sunday legislation is federal, rather than
provincial, as a law affecting religion. Frankly religious in character, Sunday observance, it has been held, cannot be protested by
those who complain of its economic impact:

> The practical result of this law on those whose religion
> requires them to observe a day of rest other than Sunday, is
> a purely secular and financial one in that they are required
> to refrain from carrying on or conducting their business on
> Sunday as well as on their own day of rest. In some cases
> this is no doubt a business inconvenience, but it is neither
> an abrogation nor an abridgment nor an infringement of
> religious freedom, and the fact that it has been brought about
> by reason of the existence of a statute for the purpose of pre-
> serving the sanctity of Sunday, cannot, in my view, be con-
> strued as attaching some religious significance to an effect
> which is purely secular in so far as non-Christians are con-
> cerned.[27]

This rationale, paradoxically, is similar to Chief Justice Warren's opinion in the United States' Supreme Court Sunday Closing
Law Cases [28] that the challenged statutes imposed "only an indirect
burden on the exercise of religion," since they do "not make
unlawful the religious practice itself." [29]

Both Canada and the United States declare for the free exercise of religion. Sunday laws in both countries have been upheld
against claims by Jews, as expressed by Justice Potter Stewart,
that these laws compel the Orthodox "to choose between his religious faith and his economic survival," [30] or, in Justice William
Douglas' words, the states force them "to observe a second Sabbath,
not their own." [31] Failure has marked Jewish protests on both sides
of the border. Secular-economically grounded-remonstrance against
avowedly religious Sunday closing legislation failed in Canada,
as did religious protest against purportedly secular Sunday laws in
the United States.

The British solution appears as an acceptable compromise to Orthodox Jews. In England Jewish traders may remain open until 2 P.M. on Sunday, provided that they are closed all day Saturday and from sundown on Friday.[32] The British act requires the store-keeper to register with the appropriate authority, and to declare on registering that he "conscientiously objects on religious grounds to carrying on trade or business on the Jewish Sabbath." He appears not to be beset by the vagaries of interpretation that have often marked American Sunday closing law enforcement.

An ante-bellum California Supreme Court decision[33] comports most closely with the constitutional view of Sunday closing laws favored by the Orthodox. It occasioned the only high court majority opinion, state or federal, in the entire judicial history of the United States asserting the unconstitutionality of such a law. In the opinion of Chief Justice Terry and the dissent of Justice Field[34] are presaged the very arguments which little more than a century later would appear in the United States Supreme Court Sunday Closing Law cases, with the outcome reversed. Justice Field, in dissent, would have felt vindicated in his certainty that

> The rules of construction are settled . . . they are the same now that they were a century ago; they are the same now that they will be a century hence; and a concurrence upon their application of the highest tribunals of every state where a Sunday law exists . . . ought to inspire confidence in its soundness.[35]

His confidence was justified not long afterward when his dissent was judicially adopted in California and the earlier majority opinion from which he dissented overturned.[36]

The 1858 petitioner, one Newman, was

> an Israelite, engaged in the business of selling clothing, at Sacramento. The offense of which he was convicted was the sale of goods on Sunday. Upon his imprisonment [for 35 days], he petitioned this Court for a writ of *habeas corpus* . . . ,[37]

alleging the unconstitutionality of "An Act to provide for the better observance of the Sabbath"[38] pursuant to which he was undergoing enforced days of rest. The California State Constitution was Newman's bailsman, particularly the first section which declared "all men are by nature free and independent, and have certain inalienable rights, among which are those of . . . acquiring, possessing, and protecting property . . ." and the fourth section proclaiming "the free exercise and enjoyment of religious profession and worship, without discrimination or preference, shall forever be allowed in this State." [39]

The 1858 forensic battle between Chief Justice Terry and Justice Field was joined over the very issue which determined Chief Justice Warren's majority opinion 103 years later:

> "Does the act of the Legislature make a discrimination or preference favorable to one religious profession, or is it a mere civil rule of conduct?" [40]

Warren and Field found civil regulation merely; Terry saw "a law for the benefit of religion." [41]

Warren, Terry and Field all agree on the religious source of the Sabbath. In Terry's words ". . . this one day of rest is a purely religious idea. Derived from Sabbatical institutions of the ancient Hebrew, it has been adopted into all the creeds of succeeding religious sects throughout the civilized world. . . ." [42] In opposition, Warren and Field, in Field's words, argue: "If we admit that the law had its origin in the religious opinions of the members of the Legislature, we advance nothing in favor of its constitutionality, and concede nothing against it." [43]

But was the legislation civil and secular in character, merely coinciding with the Christian Sabbath, or was it discrimination in favor of one religion? To Chief Justice Terry, the answer of unconstitutionality was self-evident: [44]

> . . . the intention which pervades the whole Act is to enforce, as a religious institution, the observance of a day held sacred by the followers of one faith . . . the Act is expressive of an intention on the part of the Legislature to require a periodical cessation from ordinary pursuits, not as a civil duty, necessary for the repression of any existing evil, but in furtherance of the

interests, and in aid of the devotions of those who profess the Christian religion. . . .

In a community composed of persons of various religious denominations, having different days of worship, each considering his own as sacred from secular employment, all being equally considered and protected under the Constitution, a law is passed which in effect recognizes the sacred character of one of these days, by compelling all others to abstain from secular employment, which is precisely one of the modes in which its observance is manifested, and required by the creed of that sect to which it belongs as a Sabbath. Is not this a discrimination in favor of the one? Does it require more than an appeal to one's common sense to decide that this is a preference? And when the Jew or Seventh-Day Christian complains of this, is it any answer to say, your conscience is not constrained, you are not compelled to worship or to perform religious rites on that day, nor forbidden to keep holy the day which you esteem as a Sabbath? We think not, however high the authority which decides otherwise.

Warren and Field see an indirect interference with religion at most. "Concededly," wrote Warren,[45] "appellants and all other persons who wish to work on Sunday will be burdened economically by the State's day of rest mandate; and appellants point out that their religion requires them to refrain from work on Saturday as well . . . ," but while

legislative power over mere opinion is forbidden, it may reach people's actions when they are found to be in violation of important social duties or subversive of good order, even when the actions are demanded by one's religion . . . the Sunday law simply regulates a secular activity and, as applied to appellants, operates so as to make the practice of their religious beliefs more expensive.

Warren has echoed Field's presentation of a century before:[46]

The petitioner is an Israelite, engaged in the sale of clothing, and his complaint is, not that his religious profession or worship is interfered with, but that he is not permitted to dispose of his goods on Sunday; not that any religious observance is imposed upon him, but that his secular business is closed on a day on which he does not think proper to rest. In other words, the law as a civil regulation, . . . interrupts his acquisitions on a day which does not suit him. The law treats of business matters, not religious duties. In fixing a day of rest, it establishes only a rule of civil conduct.

Terry's perspective was broader,[47] "does our Constitution, when it forbids discrimination or preference in religion, mean merely to guaranty toleration?" His answer was a resounding "no": "What other nations call religious toleration, we call religious rights; they were not exercised in virtue of government indulgence, but as rights of which the government cannot deprive any portion of her citizens, however small." And such rights included religious observance without economic sanction.

However, as a later California opinion noted,[48] the aberrant decision in *Ex parte Newman* "was not permitted long to remain the law of the State." Chief Justice Terry's opinion was not only at variance with later California holdings but deviated from rulings of high courts elsewhere.[49] The 1881 California Supreme Court observed,[50]

the current of authority upon the subject is almost undisturbed by any conflicting decision . . . and the highest Court of this State, at an early day in our history returned to the well-beaten track of judicial authority on this interesting and frequently discussed question.

California was unique among the several states of the Union, and the Federal Government as well, for but a short-lived span which began with *Ex parte Newman* in 1858 and ended in the month of the Civil War's first battle, Bull Run, in July, 1861. When *Ex parte Andrews* became law that month, overruling *Ex parte Newman*, it marked an end to California's lonely secession on the issue of Sunday closing constitutionality.

Whatever the relative merits of constitutional claims advanced by advocates and opponents of Sunday closing laws, the motivating principles on either side were born, preponderantly, of lofty conviction until recent times. With the advent of the suburban shopping center and the highway discount store, particularly after World War II, a meretricious strain began to visibly color motivations. In the name of religion loins were girded for mercantile battle. Enforcement of dormant Sunday laws was a cudgel city merchants urged responsible officials to wield to curtail or prohibit booming Sunday sales at malls and on highways. In response, highway and shopping mall merchants pressed legislatures to broaden Sunday sale exemptions, and sought judicial declarations of unconstitutionality with hollow cries of state interference with religious free exercise.[51] The United States Supreme Court of 1961 was dealing with big retail business in religious garb; Chief Justice Terry in 1858 had responded sympathetically to the anguish of the Orthodox Jewish peddler.

The Newmans and Finkelsteins of America, seeking to survive economically while observing the ordinances of their faith, have been swept into the vortex of a maelstrom, and, while a time of tranquillity may be in the offing, the mists have not parted sufficiently to reveal whether that time includes twenty-four hours commencing at sundown on Friday.

OTHER ASPECTS OF SABBATH OBSERVANCE

Judicial Proceedings

In areas of Sabbath observance, other than Sunday laws, a growing responsiveness to Jewish sensitivities has developed over the years. In 1793 the Supreme Court of Pennsylvania matter-of-factly fined a Jewish witness who would not be sworn on Saturday. The complete report of the case is starkly revelatory:[52]

In this case (which was tried on Saturday, the 5th day of April) the defendant offered Jonas Phillips, a Jew, as a witness; but he refused to be sworn, because it was his Sabbath. The court, therefore, fined him £10; but the defendant, afterwards waiving the benefit of his testimony, he was discharged from the fine.

The reflex rejection of any concern for Jewish religious commitment is not repeated with the same dispatch in later cases. In 1857 a claim was preferred [53] against "a Jewish society, for services and disbursements in making passover bread, under a contract with them." [54] It was agreed unanimously by all the trustees and the unpaid baker that "it would be better to arbitrate the matter in difference." [55] The president of the society and two trustees were chosen as arbitrators "at the instance of one of their prominent ministers." [56] A hearing was held on a Sunday resulting in an award in favor of the baker. The society appealed, alleging as a fatal flaw, among other things, "that the arbitrators held their meeting upon Sunday." While the long established common law rule is expressed in the Latin phrase *Dies Dominicus non est dies juridicus,* judicial proceedings may not be held on the Lord's Day,[57] the appellate court [58] sympathetically found a way to uphold the arbitration:

> The parties and witnesses in this unpleasant controversy, which arose out of a claim of the plaintiff for baking the passover bread for this religious corporation, are all of the Jewish persuasion, and consequently observe the seventh day of the week as their Sabbath or day of rest. To them the Christian Sabbath is a secular day, but its universal observance as a day of rest, by the great mass of their fellow citizens, renders it a day upon which people of this persuasion are compelled more or less to abstain from their ordinary pursuits, and upon which they are necessarily less employed. It is very natural, therefore, that they should select, for a matter of this kind, a day when, from keeping Saturday as a Sabbath, they are privileged to engage in any labor that does not disturb the rest of their fellow-citizens.[59]

The appellate court seized on the arbitrators' delivery and publication of their award on a Monday as a technicality to avoid annullment of their Sunday deliberations.

Over a century later a Bet Din award following two Sunday hearings was denied confirmation by a New York court.[60] The 1857 matzoh case was distinguished as having dealt with religious concerns while the case in question involved a commercial dispute, seemingly a distinction without a difference. The case holds further interest in that the respondent, who successfully sought nullification of the arbitrators' award in a civil court because they had met on Sundays, also urged that the Bet Din had misapplied Jewish law. He argued,[61]

> the award cannot be held to be binding . . . according to the doctrines of Talmudic law, for the following reasons:
>
> (a) the tribunal refused to summon and question an essential witness to the controversy, although duly requested to do so by respondent;
>
> (b) the tribunal conferred privately with the petitioner without the presence of the respondent;
>
> (c) the tribunal refused to give respondent an opportunity to question the petitioner;
>
> (d) the tribunal refused to inquire into the question of possible illegal and criminal nature of the subject matter of the controversy which, if substantiated, would bar plaintiff from any relief in accordance with Talmudic law.

Furthermore, Jewish law had been ignored on the merits, argued the respondent. His adversary, who had claimed the right to be excused from his bargain because he had been robbed, had failed to cite Jewish law in support of that claim. "Under Talmudic law, if he was robbed, petitioner was required to sustain a portion of the loss. . . ."[62] This provision of substantive law should have been followed by the Bet Din, urged the respondent in his appeal.

The New York Supreme Court upset the Bet Din arbitration. With a gamut of alternative justifications to run, ranging from violation of the Christian Sabbath to misapplying Jewish law and embracing civil statutory infringements, the court found in favor of the party claiming breach of Jewish law on other available grounds.

Not every case illustrates sympathetic understanding. In 1896 the New York Supreme Court[63] rejected a certificate of incorporation submitted by a Synagogue which appointed "each and every second Sunday of January" as the date of its annual meeting. In rather intemperate language the court characterized the submission of the proposed charter as "an aggression upon the Christian Sabbath" and declared: [64]

> the legislation of the state against profanation of the Christian Sabbath is operative and imperative upon all classes of the community . . . sanctity of the Christian Sabbath is sanctioned and secured by repeated acts of legislation extending from the colonial period. . . . As justice of the Supreme Court, I may not approve that which the immemorial and uniform policy of the state condemns.

Mid-twentieth century opinions exude less parochialism and, at times, show a firmer grasp of scripture. Reversing the conviction of a New York defendant for washing his clothes in a laundromat on Sunday, the court observed,[65]

> Slovenliness is no part of any religion, nor is it conducive to rest. Scripture commends cleanliness. . . . "And the man shall wash his clothes, and shall be clean . . . and his clothes being washed he shall be clean." (Leviticus, ch. 13, pars. 6, 34.) [66]

Legislatively, Sunday laws are moving from penal to less pejorative classification. New York in 1967 moved its Sunday laws from the Penal Law into the General Business Law.[67] A case decided that year declared: [68]

> This move shows a trend . . . Sabbath laws are old laws. They had their origin in religion. They have survived only because the courts have twisted them into artificial atmospheres which rarely escape their truly secular labels given by dissenting Judges. . . . They are still here by sufferance. . . .

Jewish Sabbath and Holidays—Do They Count?

The same ambiguity which makes the validity or invalidity of Sunday proceedings unpredictable marks judicial treatment of the Jewish Sabbath and Holidays, insofar as inclusion for purposes of computing legal time periods is concerned. A 1961 New York

Appellate Division ruling [69] reversed the lower court and held the Jewish New Year could not be excluded in a determination of the last day to file a claim against the New York City Transit Authority.

The Jewish New Year was accorded greater respect in another New York decision of the same year.[70] A notice to renew or vacate given by a landlord to a tenant was held unreasonable when the eleven-day notice period included the two-day Jewish New Year. In 1933 a Jewish New York attorney was suspended from practice for a year in disciplinary proceedings [71] growing out of his service of papers on an adversary so timed that Yom Kippur would prevent his religiously observant opponent from making timely response.

As early as 1881 the malicious service of process on Saturday or setting a trial for that day was made criminal by the New York Legislature.[72] But the defendant has the burden of establishing malice on the part of the plaintiff or his process server, and that is not an easy burden to sustain.[73]

Civil Rights Act, Fair Employment Practices Acts and the Sabbath

The trend away from strict Sunday law enforcement has received impetus from federal and state legislation adopted since 1964. In that year President Johnson signed the Civil Rights Act [74] which made it unlawful for an employer to engage in practices tending "to deprive any individual of employment opportunities or otherwise adversely affect his status as an employee, because of such individual's . . . religion." In 1972 the Civil Rights Act was amended to provide:

> The term "religion" includes all aspects of religious observance and practice, as well as belief, unless an employer demonstrates that he is unable to reasonably accommodate to an employee's or prospective employee's religious observance or practice without undue hardship on the conduct of the employer's business.

The burden is on the employer to accommodate.

State Fair Employment Practices Acts also prohibit religious

166 JEWISH LAW IN AMERICAN TRIBUNALS

discrimination in employment, many using the same language as the 1964 Civil Rights Act.[75] However, state and local laws of this nature have not received the same liberal implementation by regulation and guideline as has the federal statute. State judicial construction of such laws has also not been expansive.[76]

The trend toward the breakdown of rigid Sunday law interpretation and enforcement appears to be accelerating. But inconsistent and unpredictable judicial decisions make tranquillity and repose on the Jewish Sabbath a tantalizing hope rather than a present reality.

NOTES TO CHAPTER 4

1. *Encyclopaedia Britannica* (Chicago, 1954) Vol. 21, 565. The extent of commitment to their respective Sabbaths by devout Jews and Christians has often been extreme. Josephus records in the first century that knowledge by enemy generals that the Jews would not fight on Saturday was often used to advantage by them. So, in a current version, in 1973, the Arab attack on Israel was launched on Yom Kippur, the Jewish "Sabbath of Sabbaths." Mark Twain was exasperated by some Sunday observers. In *The Innocents Abroad*, he writes of one unsmiling passenger, a candidate "for a vacancy in the Trinity," who asked the ship's captain if the ocean expedition would come to a halt on Sundays. Twain's flamboyant irreverence was fired by other instances of Sunday devotion by another companion. On a speaking tour with George Washington Cable, who attended church services and Bible classes on Sunday, Twain wrote, "He has taught me to abhor and detest the Sabbath day and hunt up new and troublesome ways to dishonor it." Justin Kaplan, *Mr. Clemens and Mark Twain* (New York, 1966) 41, 265-266.

2. Genesis 1:5 describes God's creation of Day: "And there was evening and there was morning, one day." Joseph H. Hertz, *Pentateuch and Haftorahs* (London, 1965) 2, concludes "The day, according to the Scriptural reckoning of time, begins with the preceding evening," and, as described in Lev. 23:32, runs "from even unto even." American law, in the absence of contrary statutory provisions designating a different period, describes Sunday as commencing at 12 o'clock midnight at the end of Saturday and terminating at 12 o'clock midnight at the beginning of Monday. Gillooley v. Vaughn, 92 Fla. 943, 110 So. 653 (1926); Walinski v. Gloucester, 25 N.J. Super. 122, 95 A. 2d 625 (1953); Muckenfuss v. State, 55 Tex. Crim. 229, 116 S.W. 51 (1909).

3. Exodus 31:17.

4. Exodus 20:10; Deut. 5:15. The devotion of the Hebrews to Sabbath observance and their scorn for the violator were well known among their neighbors. The Koran tells of a Biblical legend concerning Israelites who were changed into apes as punishment for breaking the Sabbath. Louis Ginzberg, *On Jewish Law and Lore* (New York, 1962) 71-72.

5. See 9 N.Y. Jurisprudence §207, 117.

6. Hehman v. Hehman, 13 Misc. 2d 318, 178 N.Y.S. 2d 328. Justice J. Irwin Shapiro in this case referred to an Official Referee for determination the wishes of a 13 year old. His father desired enforcement of a pre-nuptial agreement which provided that the boy be raised as a Lutheran while his siblings were to be raised as Catholics. In disregarding the agreement Judge Shapiro hearkened back to the Psalms for support. See Chapter 2, p. 58. "The Jewish prayer book contains the phrase 'Touch not mine anointed,' and the rabbis of old interpret the word 'anointed' in this phrase to mean the school

167

children." The best interests of the child only were to be the controlling consideration.

7. Braunfeld v. Brown, 366 U.S. 599, 6 L. Ed. 2d 563, 81 S. Ct. 1144 (1961) at 602, 607.

8. *Ibid.*, 607.

9. Abraham Joshua Heschel, *The Earth is the Lords and Sabbath* (New York, 1963) 14; the same thought is expressed by the humorist Sam Levenson in *Everything But Money* (New York, 1967) 71 in a serious reminiscence: "Friday night's dinner was a testimonial banquet to Papa. For that hour, at least, he was no longer the oppressed victim of the sweatshops, the harrassed, frightened and unsuccessful breadwinner, but the master to whom all heads bowed and upon whom all honor was bestowed. He was our father, our teacher, our wise man, our elder statesman, our tribal leader.

"I was aware even as a child that my parents through their traditions had the power to separate mundane time from sacred time, to declare one day out of seven above and beyond the slavish struggle for survival. What a sense of power for a man to be able to borrow a segment of time out of eternity to ask it into his home for twenty-four hours, to feel himself transfigured by it from man to Man."

The Biblical injunction to observe the Sabbath has given rise to a difference of opnion among scholars as to whether, by implication, the Jew is *commanded* to work during the balance of the week. Upon the lower court trial of Two Guys from Harrison—Allentown, Inc. v. McGinley, 366 U. S. 582 (1961), Dr. Solomon Grayzel was invited to testify to that effect and declined to do so. Dr. Sidney Hoenig of Yeshiva University, on the other hand, did testify that working six days is an obligation as much as rest on the seventh, in what Dr. Grayzel regards as a misconstruction of the fourth commandment. Cf. brief of Louis Gribetz, Esq., *supra* pp. 55-56.

10. 38 Misc. 2d. 791 (1963).

11. New York Penal Law § 2147.

12. 38 Misc. 2d 791-792.

13. Judge Milton Shalleck, at 38 Misc. 2d 794, *et seq.*

14. Cardozo, J., *The Paradoxes of Legal Science* (1928) 7.

15. 38 Misc. 2d 791, 811-812.

16. Laws 1965, ch. 1031, §45, eff. September 1, 1967.

17. New York General Business Law §10. The sweep of the law's protection is not broad enough to encompass a defendant who claimed Wednesday as his holy day. New York v. Smith, 75 Misc. 2d 554 (1973), aff'd 78 Misc. 2d 610 (1974).

18. People v. Bielecki, 56 Misc. 2d 730.

19. *Ibid.*, 733. The same reluctant application of Sunday "blue laws" remains. Late in 1974 a motion to dismiss a criminal prosecution for violation of such a law was denied by a judge who implored "the Legislature to once more review Article 2 of the General Business Law and, if it believes that it should be abolished in its entirety, it should do so," and, if not, "the statute be amended to provide for . . . clearer classifications of exceptions, if any . . . In any event this is a body of law that cries out for reform." People v. Wegman's Food Markets, Inc., 362 N.Y.S. 2d 902, 909.

20. Braunfeld v. Brown, 366 U. S. 599, 608.

21. People v. Bielecki, 56 Misc. 2d 730 (1968).

22. *Ibid.*, 732-733; cf. note 2, *supra*.

23. For example, in 1924 an indictment was sustained charging a store proprietor with violation of a North Carolina Sunday closing law because he sold a bottle of Coca-Cola in connection with a lunch ordered by a customer that day. The law prohibited the selling on Sunday of "goods, wares, *drinks* or merchandise of any kind or character, except in case of sickness or absolute necessity." State v. Weddington, 188 N.C. 643, 125 S.E. 257, 37 A.L.R. 573. See "Sunday Law-Discrimination," 57 *A.L.R.* 2d 997 *et seq.* Also see McGowan v. Maryland, 366 U.S. 420, 531 (1961).

24. In July, 1974 New York Governor Malcolm Wilson vetoed a measure revising New York's Sunday closing law which would have resulted in substantially increased protection for merchants who close their business on Saturday for religious reasons. It would have covered business enterprises regardless of size. The 1971 New York legislature also passed a measure, vetoed by Governor Rockefeller, which would have put Sunday closing laws on a county option basis. In his veto message, the Governor found the legislation, which was to be based on a referendum "fatally defective." For a report on the opportunities for graft which the present state of affairs provides, see *New York Post*, Dec. 22, 1971. Magazine Sec., 29.

25. People v. Stroup *et al* N.Y. Law Journal, August 4, 1972, 10, col. 1 (App. Term 9th and 10th Judicial Districts.) The early New England Sunday laws caught in their toils the first permanent Jewish resident of that area, one Sollomon, who was haled before the court in Ipswich, Massachusetts to account for his travel towards New Hampshire of a Sunday. Records of Quarterly Courts of Essex County, Massachusetts IV, 87. See Abram Goodman, *American Overture* (Phila. 1947) 16.

26. The Lord's Day Act, CAN. REV. STAT. c. 171 (1952). For a detailed comparison of Canadian with American Sabbath laws, see Jerome A. Barron, "Sunday in North America," 79 *Harvard Law Review* 42 (1965).

27. Robertson v. The Queen, Can. Sup. Ct. 651 (1964) at 657-658. 41 D.L.R. 2d 485 (1963) at 494.

28. Gallagher v. Crown Kosher Super Market, 366 U.S. 617 (1961); Braunfeld v. Brown, 366 U.S. 599 (1961); Two Guys from Harrison-Allentown, Inc. v. McGinley, 366 U.S. 582 (1961); McGowan v. Maryland 366 U.S. 420 (1961).

29. Braunfeld v. Brown, 366 U.S. 599, 606 (1961).

30. *Ibid.*, 366 U.S. 599, 616.

31. For Justice Douglas' dissent in the *Braunfeld* case, see *ibid.*, 366 U.S. at 561 *et seq.* From the early Middle Ages, a variety of church edicts ordered Jews to stay behind their ghetto walls on Sundays and Christian holidays. This meant no business could be transacted by Jews on such days. See also Salo Baron, *A Social and Religious History of the Jews.* (New York, 1965) IX, 43. As early as the year 589, the Church Council of Narbonne adopted the following decree in its canon 6: "No one, whether slave or free, Goth, Roman, Syrian, Greek, or Jew, shall do any work on Sunday, nor yoke his oxen, unless necessity imposes it upon him. If anyone dares do so, if a free man, he shall pay six solidi to the Court; if a slave, he shall receive a hundred stripes." Prohibitions against Jews working in public on Sunday or any Christian festival, where Christians could see them at work and presumably be insulted by the sight, appear in decrees of the Council of Avignon of 1209, the Council of Narbonne of 1227, the Council of Beziers of 1246, and the

Council of Albi of 1254. Solomon Grayzel, *The Church and The Jews in the 13th Century*. (Phila. 1933) 304-5, 316-17, 332-3, 336-7.

32. British Shops Act, 1950, §53, continuing in substance §7 of the Sunday Trading Restriction Act, 1936; 26 Geo. V and 1 Edw. VIII, c. 53. See Milton Konvitz, "Inter-Group Relations," in *The American Jew: A Reappraisal*, O. I. Janowsky, ed. (Phila., 1964) 88. In Connecticut, Sabbatarians may qualify under a similar exemption statute, Conn. Gen. Stat. Rev. §53-303, by filing a written notice of religious belief with the prosecuting attorney. Chief Justice Warren professed a concern that such exemption statutes "might make necessary a state-conducted inquiry into the sincerity of the individual's religious beliefs," which in itself might be unconstitutional. Braunfeld v. Brown, 366 U. S. 599, 609. Questioning exemption for the Saturday Sabbatarian is reminiscent of an 1882 New York case, Anonymous, 12 *Abbot's New Cases* 455, in which, in the course of upholding criminal penalties for "Hebrews, trading on Sunday," the court reflected that an interpretation "that it shall not apply to any person or persons doing business in this city who close up their places of business on Saturday and keep them closed during the whole day" would violate equal protection provisions of "the constitution and the law" since "before the constitution Jews and Gentiles are equal; by the law they must be treated alike." 12 *Abbot's N.C.* 455, 457 citing Shreveport v. Levy, 26 L. Am. 671, S.C. 21 Am. R. 553. Ergo, both must observe Sunday as Sabbath.

33. *Ex parte* Newman, 9 Cal. 502 (1858).

34. Stephen Johnson Field is a famous name in American law and a member of an illustrious family. His brother, Cyrus Field, promoted the first transatlantic cable. His brother, David Dudley Field, lawyer, jurist and congressman, drafted a code of civil procedure for New York, known as the Field Code, which was enacted in 1848 and became the model for similar legislation throughout the country. Stephen went to California with the Forty-niners, became a legislator and reorganized California's judicial code along the lines of his brother's New York code. He was appointed by Lincoln to the United States Supreme Court in 1863 and served longer than any other member of that bench until modern. times, almost thirty-five years. His staunch support of Sunday laws did not interfere with his offering an appointment as postmaster of San Francisco to that arch-enemy of piety, Mark Twain, in 1868. Kaplan, *op. cit.*, 60. A powerful politician, Stephen Field "even as an associate justice of the Supreme Court was still dispensing patronage." *Ibid.*

35. *Ex parte Newman*, 9 Cal. 502, 526-527. (1858). The consistent sustaining of Sunday laws after 1858 was nearly interrupted on July 10, 1975 when the New York Court of Appeals by a narrow margin reiterated its belief, expressed unanimously three years earlier, in the constitutionality of such legislation. In a 4-3 decision, the majority noted that provisions in the law for a "a day of rest . . . remain historically and constitutionally valid." *People v. Acme Markets, Inc. et al.* See *N.Y. Law Journal*, July 11, 1975, 1 col. 3. Dissenters Sol Wachtler, Jacob Fuchsberg and Hugh Jones saw an inevitable pattern of discrimination and manipulation emerging from a dormant state prodded to enforcement only at the instance of private complainants, a potential for mischief amounting to unconstitutionality.

36. *Ex parte* Andrews, 18 Cal. 685 (1861). Field was now in the majority. The judges who had constituted the majority in *Ex parte* Newman three years earlier were no longer on the bench.

37. *Ex parte* Newman, 9 Cal. 502, 504.

38. Otherwise known as the Act of April, 1858.

39. *Ex parte* Newman, 9 Cal. 502, 504.

40. *Ibid.*

41. *Ibid.*

42. *Ibid.*, 509.

43. *Ibid.*, 523.

44. *Ibid.*, 505-506.

45. Braunfeld v. Brown, 366 U. S. 599, 603, 605 (1961).

46. *Ex parte* Newman, 9 Cal. 502, 519.

47. *Ibid.*, 507.

48. *Ex parte* Burke, 59 Cal. 6, 19 (1881).

49. Field in his dissent in *Ex parte* Newman, 9 Cal. 502, had noted at 524-525; ". . . a Sunday law, resembling in its general features the one under consideration, has frequently been before the highest Courts of our sister States, the Constitutions of which embody provisions similar to those contained in the Constitution of this State, and in every instance without exception the constitutionality of the law has been affirmed."

50. *Ex parte* Burke, 59 Cal. 6, 19 (1881). The opinion goes off in a direction which would have exasperated Jefferson: "though Christianity is not the religion of the State, considered as a political corporation, it is nevertheless interwoven into the texture of our society, and is intimately connected with all our social habits and customs, and modes of life." An Arkansas case, Shover v. The State, 5 Eng. 259, is quoted: "the Christian religion is recognized as constituting a part of the common law; it's institutions are entitled to profound respect, and may well be protected by law. The Sabbath, properly called the 'Lord's Day,' is amongst the first and most sacred institutions of Christianity . . ." *Ibid.*, 14-15. Such views are not quaintly nineteenth century; a 1957 New York case, affirmed by the State's highest court, refers to Sunday as a day of rest by common law, and without the necessity of legislative action to establish it. People v. Polar Vent of America, Inc., 10 Misc. 2d 378, 174 N.Y.S. 2d 789, affd. 4 N.Y. 2d 954, 175 N.Y.S. 2d 825, 151 N.E. 2d 621. But cf. Merritt v. Earle, 29 N.Y. 115 (1864), which declares, "It must be remembered, that all prohibitions of ordinary business on Sunday, with us, come from statute. At the common law, judicial proceedings only were prohibited on Sunday." It is the sort of smug piety of *Ex parte Burke, supra,* which provoked Mark Twain to a celebrated quip. The occasion was the protest of twenty-two clergymen against Theodore Roosevelt's announced decision to abolish the motto "In God we Trust" from coins. The clergymen having reminded the President that the United States was a Christian country, Twain remarked to his friend, Andrew Carnegie, "Why, Carnegie, so is hell." Kaplan, *op. cit.*, 363-364. Nonetheless, Georgia's highest court could, ironically, summon the Ten Commandments in support of *Sunday* blue laws in 1939: "This is a Christian nation. The observance of Sunday is one of our established customs. It has come down to us from the same Decalogue that prohibited murder, adultery, perjury and theft. It is more ancient than our common law or our form of government. It is recognized by constitutions and legislative enactments, both State and Federal." Rogers v. State, 60 Ga. App. 722 at 724, 4 S.E. 2d 918.

51. See Konvitz, *op. cit.*, 84.

52. Stansbury v. Marks, 2 Dall. 213 1 L. Ed. 353. From the earliest Colonial days in New England, Jews were accepted as witnesses without challenge. Abram Goodman, *American Overture* (Phila. 1947) 20.

53. Isaacs v. Beth Hamedash Society, 1 Hilton (N.Y.) 469 (1857).

54. *Ibid.*

55. *Ibid.*, 471.

56. *Ibid.*, 473.

57. 1 Rev. Stat. 675 §70.

58. Court of Common Pleas.

59. Isaacs v. Beth Hamedash Society, 1 Hilton (N.Y.) 469, 472-473.

60. Katz v. Uvegi, 18 Misc. 2d 576, 187 N.Y.S. 2d 511, aff'd. 11 App. Div. 2d 773, 205 N.Y.S. 2d 972 (1959).

61. *Ibid.*, 18 Misc. 2d 576, 579-580.

62. *Ibid.*, 580-581.

63. Application of the Agudath Hakehiloth of New York, 18 Misc. 717.

64. *Ibid.*, 718.

65. People v. Aliprantes, 8 App. Div. 2d 276 (1959). The statute alleged to have been violated was New York Penal Law §2143.

66. Hillel in the first century before the current era, "proposed to care not only for the mind but also for the body—as a religious duty." Once his disciples asked, "Master, whither are you going?" He replied, "To do a pious deed." They said: "What may that be?" He replied: "To take a bath." They said: "Is that a pious deed?" He replied: "Yes; if the images of the King must be kept clean by the man to whom they have been entrusted, how much more is it a duty of man to care for the body, since man has been created in the divine image and likeness." Similarly, on another occasion, when going to take a bath, he remarked, "I am going to do a kindness to the guest in the house," the soul. Leviticus Rabbah 34:3. See Nahum N. Glatzer, *Hillel the Elder* (New York, 1956) ch. 3.

67. From former Article 192 of the Penal Law to Article 2 of the General Business Law.

68. People v. Spinelli, 54 Misc. 2d 485, 490 (1967).

69. Bloom v. New York City Transit Authority, 31 Misc. 2d 805, 220 N.Y.S. 2d 621, revd. 19 App. Div. 2d 521, 240 N.Y.S., 2d 124 (1961).

70. Unger v. Schwartz, 30 Misc. 2d 152, 213 N.Y.S. 2d 993 (1961). A New York State Supreme Court Justice in 1973 ordered the City Board of Elections to reschedule voter registration days to give voters observing Succoth more time to register. However, he also ruled that Saturday, having been mandated by the New York Secretary of State as a registration date, must stand as such thereby rejecting the plantiff's contention that the election laws constitutionally interfered with the Jewish Sabbath. *New York Times*, Aug. 31, 1973, 27, col. 1. The U. S. District Court for the Southern District of Florida did uphold, partially, a class action claim by teachers in Dade County "that in order for a teacher to observe holy days of worship . . . he must sustain a loss of sick leave and resulting diminution of terminal pay." Since Christian teachers celebrate Christmas and Good Friday, they will not sustain losses as a result of state establishment of school vacation periods to coincide with those holy days. Christmas was held "invulnerable from attack under the Establishment Clause," but the Court declared unconstitutional "the practice and custom of scheduling the Spring Recess to coincide with Good Friday." The policy of restricting religious leave with pay was also held unconstitutional. Speiller v. Whigham, U.S.D.C. S.D. Fla. No. 73-646 Civ. CA (1974).

71. In re Chaikin, 238 App. Div. 211, 264 N.Y.S. 221.

72. See Article 2, §13, General Business Law. A 1975 New York decision upholding the right of an observant Jewish attorney to adjourn a hearing date from Saturday to a weekday, contrasts the early 19th century attitude of American courts with their more recent accommodation of the Saturday Sabbatarian's beliefs:

"An early Pennsylvania case (May 1831), somewhat similar to the instant one, with one notable exception, it concerned the conscience of the party rather than his counsel, is of interest particularly considering the religious climate of the times. In those days it was held 'Christianity and conscience are parts of the common law of Pennsylvania, though the Jew is alike protected in his religious belief with the Christian' (*Updegraff v. The Commonwealth*, 11 S & R 408). In *Phillips v. Gratz*, 2 Penr. & W., 23 Am. Dec. 33, a Jewish plaintiff had been non-suited when the plaintiff refused to appear when his case came on for trial on a Saturday. Although the non-suit was reversed on other grounds, the case has been cited for the proposition that a man's moral or religious principles cannot be allowed to interfere with the administration of justice, so that a continuance for conscience sake will not be granted when a Jew has scruples in regard to appearing in court as a witness on Saturday. The reviewing Judge Gibson, S. J., did state (p. 416) 'The religious scruples of persons concerned with the administration of justice will receive all the indulgence that is compatible with the business of government, and had circumstances permitted it, this cause would not have been ordered for trial on the Jewish Sabbath. But when a continuance for conscience sake is claimed as a right, and at the expense of a term's delay, the matter assumes a difference aspect.'

"It seems that we have come a long way from a time when an observing Jew's conscience was referred to as 'Scruples.' " Justice McCarthy, In re Romeo, 368 N.Y.S. 2d 726, 731 (1975).

73. Martin v. Goldstein, 20 App. Div. 203, 46 N.Y.S. 961 (1897); Baldsin v. Winer, 216 N.Y.S. 2d 153 (1961).

74. 42 U.S.C. 2000 e-2 [9].

75. In 1974, forty-two states had adopted such acts, together with the District of Columbia, Puerto Rico, and the cities of New York, Philadelphia and Pittsburgh. See Daniel J. Elazar and Stephen R. Goldstein, "The Legal Status of the American Jewish Community," *American Jewish Year Book* 1972, vol. 73, 32-35.

76. The New Jersey Supreme Court has held that it was a discriminatory practice on the part of his employer to fail to charge time off for observance of the high holy days against a Jewish policeman's accumulated overtime. Ebler v. City of Newark, 54 N.J. 487, 256 A. 2d 44 (1969). The Connecticut Supreme Court has held that its state act does not require employers to make reasonable accommodations to the religious needs of their employees. Williams v. Commission on Civil Rights, State of Conn., 158 Conn. 622, 262 A. 2d 183 (1969). But cf. *Katz v. Howell Township*, a New Jersey Supreme Court 6-0 ruling which affirmed a plumbing inspector's entitlement to workmen's compensation for disability relating to a heart attack suffered after an "acrimonious dispute" with his superior over his failure to work on the second day of Rosh Hashanah (New Year). *New York Times*, March 19, 1975, 51, col. 3. Of course, the issue decided was not directly related to discriminatory practice.

5.

DIETARY LAWS OR KASHRUTH

I am the Lord your God, who have set you apart from the nations. Ye shall therefore separate between the clean beast and the unclean.

Leviticus 20:24-25

ERECTING A WALL between church and state is a constitutional ideal, but the difficulty of attaining that ideal is nowhere better illustrated than in cases which annotate those statutes aimed at enforcing the integrity of the professing kosher tradesman. On the one hand, the state has a legitimate interest in safeguarding consumers against false claims. On the other hand, when these claims relate to Orthodox ritual observance, the state invariably must trespass, however lightly, on the religious garden which lies on the other side of the wall of separation.[1] How to minimize this intrusion presents a continuing dilemma.[2]

Kashruth, or the doctrine held by Orthodox Jewry with regard to certain food restraints, relates both to food taboos[3] and to *shechitah,* the prescribed manner of animal slaughter, the violation of which renders the slaughtered animal unfit for consumption. Both aspects of Kashruth are the product of rabbinic interpreta-

175

tion and elaboration over the past fifteen hundred years. The Old
Testament never applies the term kosher to food, and the compilation of the Mishnah, the central core of the Talmud, while referring
"kosher" to food gives no hint of the elaborate ritual and regulation which Kashruth subsequently came to encompass.[4] Nonetheless,
Kashruth, with its demand for permanent daily observance, is
more the mark of the practicing Jew than any other explicit Biblical
injunction. Every time an observant Jew sits down to eat he is
compelled to identify historically and geographically, in time and
space, with his fellow Jews. Dining becomes an inescapable re-
minder, a bond among a people ancient and scattered, small in
number and large in achievements. Thrice daily, routine rooted
in physical need is made to stir remembrance. While commands
to the Jew to wear fringes on his garments[5] or not to round the
corners of the head[6] have been softened by rabbinic construction,
Kashruth observance has been expanded and made more rigorous.[7]

Justification of Kashruth has been found, with respect to a
number of its rules, in the Biblical conception of the animal as
a suffering beast to be treated with decency. The prohibitions
against eating any part of a living animal,[8] against killing the dam
and its young on the same day,[9] and against taking the fledgings
or eggs from a nest while the mother-bird is brooding[10] have all
been explained as violations of divine solicitude for nature's dumb
creatures.[11]

Roman and canon law have taken the opposite view of animal
nature. In Roman law the animal had absolutely no rights and
man was under no legal compulsion to show it any consideration
whatever. The owner had complete *jus utendi* and *jus abutendi*
over it. The Deuteronomic prohibition against muzzling the ox
"when he treadeth out the corn,"[12] the instruction that "A righteous
man regardeth the life of his beast"[13] and the compiling of an entire
set of laws teaching kindness to animals[14] were pecularly Jewish
concerns, contrary not only to contemporary attitudes but to theological and legal theories which have prevailed almost to our own
time. Paul asked scornfully, "doth God take care for oxen?"[15]
The Roman Catholic Church until recent times opposed the establishment of humane societies as grounded in theological error, animals lacking in reason, language, freedom, universal ideas and
bereft of an immortal soul. It is not surprising then, that only

among the Puritans of Massachusetts Bay, who borrowed a law code from the Jews, do we find Western world legislation protecting "bruite Creatures" from man's "Tiranny or Cruelties,"[16] until modern times.

In the field of Jewish dietary observance today, the New York legislature and courts (as well as other American jurisdictions)[17] have opened a chink in the wall of separation by legislating protection[18] for those who buy purportedly kosher meat. Once having poked through the breach and made the false claimant to Kashruth a violator of the law, the law's interpreters have hesitated and then retreated in confusion in the face of fierce internecine strife between "kosher" butcher and accusing Orthodox rabbi. Tracing the law's development reveals a shift from judicial acceptance of the rabbinate's competence in this field, and consequent reluctance to make secular incursions, to a declining confidence which favors the suspect tradesman.

Early Constitutional Tests

The early cases uphold the constitutionality of laws making it a crime to sell meat falsely labelled as "kosher." A 1916 case[19] considered constitutional challenges, among others, alleging in particular

> that the word "Kosher" is a foreign word; . . . that the law as framed assumes a knowledge in those addressed of the entire ecclesiastical history, law and literature of the hebrew race; that it is in fact the utterance of a speech strange to the community which it is intended to govern

and hence, the "statute is upon its face meaningless . . . impossible of interpretation" and "nugatory."[20] In constitutional terms, the statute was attacked as akin to a private or local bill creating a special privilege or immunity in contravention of the Fourteenth Amendment, and a violation of personal liberty in violation of the First.

In response, the court acknowledged its "task and duty . . . is to ascertain, if possible, by the means available, the application of the legislative description" and that "it may happen indeed, that the performance of this task may require large exploring in recondite fields of knowledge" but

> it is within the province and the duty of the Legislature, upon occasion, to deal with every element of human experience involved in the life of the community or of any class thereof . . . and the knowledge of the specialist must be available, both in framing and applying the law so evolved.[21]

The rabbinate's assistance was sought and relied upon and the constitutional challenge repelled. In a passing reference to the free exercise and establishment clauses, the court said:

> The statute is directed against a form of fraud, the victim of which is probably only a person belonging to a particular religious order; but such protection, instead of being contrary to constitutional provision which forbids the interference with the free exercise and enjoyment of religious profession and worship, is in distinct accord therewith. The legislature cannot enact a religious creed, but the Constitution enjoins religious freedom, and men of all creeds are entitled to the protection of the law of the land in undisturbed enjoyment of such freedom. Such protection is the evident aim of the statute which occasions this discussion.[22]

Constitutional anchor had been dropped and grounded, but the statute's enforcement in the case which gave rise to the constitutional test [23] resulted in acquittal of the defendant who, while advertising kosher meat for sale, sold both kosher and non-kosher products and, at the time of his arrest, had absolutely no stock of kosher provisions on hand. The majority view was that a penal statute must be strictly construed and "the evidence does not show that the defendant 'with intent to defraud, sold or exposed for sale any meat and falsely represented the same to be kosher.' "[24]

A 1918 case similarly upheld against constitutional assault the validity of a statute using the word "kosher." The term applies to "a product or products sanctioned by the orthodox Hebrew requirements" [26] states the majority opinion as opposed to a dissenter who wrote,

In the instant case, whether the act is violated depends entirely upon the meaning and interpretation given to it by those expert in the rules and prohibitions of the orthodox Hebrew religion. Therefore, the statute itself requiring such an interpretation is so indefinite and uncertain that it is void and should be so declared.[27]

To the dissenter's concern that equal protection had been subordinated to class legislation, the majority responded the law's purpose served Jew and non-Jew alike, since it afforded protection to all consumers whose concern was with cleanliness and who relied upon the tradition of care associated with kosher animal slaughter and preparation. There was no unconstitutional discrimination against meat dealers since the statutory purpose was to punish only those who acted with intent to defraud.

The Major Kashruth Case

The "major Kashruth case," as it has been denominated in a recent study,[28] was decided in New York in 1936.[29] A poultry dealer sued The Kashruth Association of Greater New York, Inc., a membership corporation formed under the auspices of the United Rabbinate, a loosely organized assembly of the rabbis of Greater New York, "a large number of orthodox rabbis, for the rescission of a contract and an injunction with incidental damages." The gravamen of the complaint was interference

> with plaintiff's contractual rights by procuring religious edicts prohibiting the faithful from buying and the plaintiff from selling, ritually slaughtered fowl without certain forms of supervision and means of identification not required by the Jewish law, notably the plumba or seal. The chief and most effective weapon specified as employed is a so-called issur or prohibitory decree [30]

promulgated by the rabbis.

The litigation arose against a backdrop of efforts begun nearly a century ago to prevent fraudulent and deceptive practices in the slaughter, distribution and sale of foods designated as kosher.

The first legislation aimed at this end was adopted in New York and Massachusetts in the 1880's and the movement swelled to a peak in the 1920's. There was a further expansion of legislative protection in the post-World War II decade, so that today eighteen states [31] and the District of Columbia have statutes in force to protect buyers of kosher food. Enforcement has been difficult,[32] however, and most states have relied on local rabbinic associations.[33] In New York in 1934 the mayor, at the urging of a committee of Orthodox rabbis, called several conferences to consider ways of dealing with alleged abuses in the slaughter and sale of kosher poultry. Attending were the mayor, the president of the Board of Aldermen, rabbis, prominent Jewish laymen, poultry farmers, kosher meat and poultry slaughterers (*schochtim*), and commission merchants. Mayor LaGuardia appointed Judge Otto Rosalsky to mediate disputes within the kosher poultry industry. After holding hearings he made his report to the mayor.[34]

The United Rabbinate then met to consider the report and approved in principle an *issur*, or decree, to control the kosher poultry business. A Bet Din of twenty-three Orthodox rabbis was appointed and after much deliberation issued the *issur*. The largest local rabbinical association approved it and it was formally adopted at a meeting of 219 members of the United Rabbinate. There followed a publicly announced meeting, attended by 300 rabbis and 200 laymen at the Norfolk Street Synagogue, the Beth Hamidrash Hagadol, which was illuminated by candlelight for the occasion. The Torahs were removed from the ark and the following was promulgated:[35]

> With the help of God, Monday, the 27th day of the month of Mar Cheschvan, 5695 (November 5, 1934).
>
> Whereas, in the City of New York, there is, as is generally known, chaos in the matter of slaughtering of poultry for Jewish consumption, and
>
> Whereas, in many poultry slaughtering establishments and markets there are manifold malpractices, in violation of the laws of the Torah, concerning "nevelah" and "trefah" (two classes of non-kosher food), and especially since investigations recently conducted have made it abundantly clear that the structure of Kashruth regarding poultry has collapsed,

as was demonstrated by the facts brought out in these many investigations, which show how far Kashruth in the slaughtering of poultry has been defective and imperfect, thus casting upon such slaughtered poultry the suspicion of their being forbidden under the Biblical dietary laws (a situation which we deeply deplore) and

WHEREAS, as rabbis, official guardians of our holy religion and the correct observance of its precepts, the laws of our sacred Torah place upon us specifically the responsibility of taking the necessary measures to keep our people from the consumption of forbidden food (and if at this juncture we should remain silent and inactive, we would be guilty of a serious breach of religious duty) ;

Therefore, in view of the situation here set forth and the duty devolving upon us, we have reached the following decisions:

(1) That the slaughter houses and the Schochtim must be placed under permanent and effective supervision, as approved by, and under the auspices of the rabbis of the City of Greater New York, who are united in the Kashruth Association.

(2) That each bird slaughtered as kosher must be marked with a "plumba" or a similar sign, such mark to be affixed by a person authorized by the rabbinate, . . . so that our coreligionists in New York City by purchasing only poultry which come from such slaughtering establishments as are under the proper supervision above described and which bear authorized tokens of Kashruth will be safeguarded from violation of the dietary laws.

(3) And, therefore, in accordance with the authority specifically vested in us by the holy Torah, for safeguarding the observance of its dietary laws, we herewith do, with the full strength and severity of the law, solemnly declare, pronounce, issue and publish an issur (religious prohibition), to go into effect forthwith on poultry not slaughtered in accordance with the above regulations or not bearing an authorized token, as above described, declaring that such poultry is forbidden to be consumed by Jews. . . .

(4) And every Schochet who, in contravention of these

regulations, will slaughter birds without supervision or without a token of Kashruth being affixed, as described above (unless the slaughtering is done in each case by express permission
of a qualified rabbi for the use of sick people), will lose his
status of reliability in regard to Kashruth, and as a violator
of the Jewish law will henceforth become disqualified to act
as Schochet.

We cherish confidence that no rabbi or scholar versed in
Jewish Law will attempt to diminish the force of this prohibition or rule to the contrary, and thus rebel against and separate
himself from the entire body of the Orthodox Rabbinate of
New York City in which case his ruling shall become null
and void as are the rulings of one who is a destroyer of the
fence of the law (nonconformist).

The plaintiff, a Bronx poultry dealer, not wishing to buy the
required *plumbas* or seals certifying the fowl as kosher, claimed in
its action that it was "faced with ruin through the conduct of
defendant" [36] acting in concert with the United Rabbinate and a
union of *schochtim* or ritual slaughterers.

The court reviewed the "Jewish system of laws (the Torah)"
and intoned,

One of the oldest enactments, pronounced by Moses himself
3400 years ago, relates to food. The dietary laws are mandatory
in form and traditionally regarded as a cornerstone of the
faith. What may be eaten is denominated "kosher," an adjec-
tive whose corresponding noun is Kashruth. From time immemorial the religious duty of every orthodox Jew, and pre-
eminently of the rabbi, has been to obey, enforce and safeguard
the principle of Kashruth.[37]

Needless to say, following such a prologue, the court found the
plaintiff's claims without merit and sustained the rabbinical court's
right to act as it did. Whether it acted properly in a religious sense
was not the concern of the secular tribunal.

Throughout Judge McCook's opinion, references to the United
Rabbinate and its decree, or *issur*, are made with the deference due
a court of equal dignity, if not coordinate jurisdiction, careful to

stay within its ecclesiastical confines even as Judge McCook, with equal care, patrols his secular beat. The Bet Din's authority is never questioned; its preemptive role within its own domain is buttressed by religious law citations [38] and its jurisdiction is as jealously guarded as Judge McCook ever tended his own secular garden.

Where objection is taken on the basis of New York law, the judge responds in kind. The plaintiff seeks rescission of its contract with the Kashruth Association. The court's response is "Since [plaintiff] does not here defend an action for breach of contract brought by the Kashruth Association, rescission may not avail...." [39] Procedurally, the plaintiff alleges inadequate notice of various meetings of the United Rabbinate leading to its prohibitory edict or *issur*. The court responds, "Applying criteria accepted in corresponding circumstances under our own law and rules, I find that adequate notice was given at each important stage to all concerned." [40]

Where religious objections are made, the court bows to its brother tribunal.

> We have heard the procedure characterized as a revolution in Jewish practice . . . ; the abandonment, at least for the occasion, of a congregational for a diocesan organization, and of an individualistic for a collective method of supervision and enforcement. Suffice it to say that this is the business of the orthodox Jews, not of the people of the State of New York.[41]

Where the objections raised by plaintiff approach the line between church and state, Judge McCook hangs back and calls on presumptions favoring the regularity of an orthodox body's procedures and rulings. Thus, to the plaintiff's claim "that this is the first issur promulgated [orally] within the memory of living man," [42] the court responds that though the "best view" is to reduce *issurim* to writing, this is a matter of proof "technically superfluous" under the instant circumstances. To other similar attacks on the extraordinarily broad nature of the disputed decree, the court answers in the spirit of orthodoxy:

> The answer in each instance is substantially the same—that

the duty of rabbis [is] to safeguard or hedge the faith, and
thus *schechita* [ritual slaughter] has never been questioned.[43]

When plaintiff attacks the use of a secular membership corporation
to implement religious policy, Judge McCook frames the issue:

Is it proper under the Jewish law to name such a secular
agent, and especially this non-religious corporation as the
arm of a religious body?,[44]

and finds the answer in plaintiff's failure to carry its burden of
proof.

The defendant's witnesses say yes, if justified by necessity, and
that this necessity has been established. The plaintiff has not
established the contrary and so fails on the point.[45]

To plaintiff's charge that defendant is engaged in perpetrat-
ing a monopoly, the court's reply rests on the New York Penal
Law [46] which cedes supervision in this regard to the rabbinate, and
thus makes the matter a distinctive exception to the usual rules of
monopoly.

Kosher poultry costs more than non-kosher. It would be inequitable to permit its sale by any one as kosher unless in truth
kosher. Whether it is so or not is a religious matter for the
rabbis to determine. An overwhelming majority of them support the issur. The plaintiff cannot obtain the advantages
of his business without assuming the disadvantages which
necessarily accompany it. In the very nature of things,
Kashruth must be a monopoly in the hands of those best qualified to administer it. By definition and tradition those persons
are the rabbis and their decree is final.[47]

Again,

The answer to plaintiff's complaint of injustice is that there is
no injustice. If plaintiff does not like the result of having
disagreed with the views of the orthodox Jews there remain

the plain alternatives of either once more complying or abandoning the field of kosher poultry sales.[48]

The school of American Legal Realism might make much of Judge McCook's Irish Catholic conditioning as influencing his decision favoring an organized orthodox religious authority. There is his willing perception of a sustainable distincton between the religious and the mundane,

> while the orthodox Jews, like other Jews, recognize, accept and obey the laws of the country in which they reside, they consider it their religious duty at all times to settle their differences according to their law.[49]

Again, plaintiff's criticism of the United Rabbinate's employment of New York State's Membership Corporation Law to organize in corporate form is brushed aside by Judge McCook:

> On the contrary, it shows a laudable purpose of separating the spiritual from the mundane, a laudable willingness to subject its business affairs to visitation by the state courts.[50]

There is a strong responsiveness to ceremony and a perception of dissenting conduct as faintly resembling heresy:

> Even plaintiff's chief expert witness actively participated in the ceremony of November fifth [promulgation of the issur]. Solemnly garbed for the purpose he convoked the assemblage in his own synagogue and offered opening prayer for the success of the venture.[51]

Further, the plaintiff

> has already taken the matter into its own hands and determined to proceed as it sees fit, discarding the issur and disregarding the United Rabbinate. [Plaintiff's] plan provides for an independent supervision, for which they have retained seven rabbis, of whom four testified for the plaintiff. This court is asked to overturn an issur, carefully prepared, duly

authorized and valid in substance and form, and give the stamp of approval to one of the very persons who organized what is at best their own method of accomplishing the same end.[52]

Judge McCook is obviously sympathetic to the religious significance of food taboos, citing Leviticus, 11:44-45, and the commentary of Sifra thereon.

"'I (saith the Lord) delivered you from the land of Egypt, in order that you might accept the yoke of these dietary laws.'"[53]

But whatever "the social-cultural matrix of inquiry"[54] of Judge McCook, his decision undoubtedly represents the highwater mark of judicial cognizance of Kashruth.

The Aftermath of the S.S.&B. Live Poultry Case

In the afterglow of the *S. S. & B. Live Poultry* case, the New York Supreme Court, in *Greenwald v. Noyes*,[55] supported the Commissioner of Agriculture and Markets against the efforts of the head of a butchers association to enjoin enforcement of the kosher food law against butchers. Enforcement had been sought not only for failure to comply with the quoted *issur*, but for offering as kosher meat products lacking the required *plumba* or tag. The missing *plumba* was "prima facie evidence of violation of the penal provision sufficient to warrant prosecution."[56] The court stated,

the question of what is or is not genuine kosher meat, and what is or is not a generally accepted indicia of its genuineness, must be left largely to the authorities of the religious faith under whose direction and rules the meat is prepared, and their determination must have substantial bearing, it seems to me, upon the question that arises under public policy of the state whether an intent to defraud is established in each case in which criminal prosecution is undertaken.[57]

The ebbing of legal protection began not three years after the *S. S. & B. Live Poultry case* and within months of *Greenwald v.*

Noyes. In *People v. Gordon,*[58] a retail kosher butcher was prosecuted for selling as kosher poultry that did not have the Kashruth Association's *plumba.* The defense was that defendant could not afford the cost of tags, but in all other respects his poultry was kosher. The trial court found defendant guilty since his poultry did not comply with the *issur.* It was not "sanctioned by Orthodox Hebrew religious requirements." On appeal, judgment was reversed for lack of proof

> that the so-called Rabbinate was a tribunal clothed with power to act and to decree that a fowl not slaughtered according to the regulation specified in the Issur and not bearing a token, as above described, is not kosher, and, therefore, forbidden to be consumed by Jews.[59]

In an understandable but crippling misconception of the scope of local rabbinic jurisdiction under Jewish law,[60] the Appellate Division continued:

> Furthermore, in view of the conceded fact that poultry slaughtered outside of the City of New York according to traditional ritual and brought into the city and sold without a "plumba" is considered kosher, a regulation adopted by a group of orthodox rabbis of the City of New York which forbids the consumption of poultry killed in the City of New York under traditional Hebrew rites, unless there be attached thereto a "plumba," authorized and issued by the Rabbinate, cannot be considered an orthodox Hebrew requirement. It is purely a local regulation which seeks to provide the evidence that a killing has been kosher.[61]

The Court of Appeals affirmed without opinion. A recent survey describes the consequences:

> As a result, there seem to have been no other attempts at prosecution for a kosher food law violation based on refusal to comply with a local rabbinical association's certification system. The issur remains in effect in Jewish law, but is essentially unenforceable as part of the state kosher food statutes.[62]

The eroding effects of the receding tide accelerated in a 1940 decision [63] upholding a slander verdict against a rabbi who proclaimed to plaintiff's customers that his kosher butcher shop was not kosher. Again, the Kashruth Association's *plumba* or tag was absent, but concededly other requirements to make poultry kosher had been complied with. The court stated:

> It appears that there are many rabbis in the city of New York who are not members of the association. This court is unwilling to hold that poultry which would otherwise meet every requirement to make it kosher—requirements that have been established for centuries—and which would be kosher if slaughtered and prepared in any place in the world except the City of New York, would become non-kosher solely because it was slaughtered and prepared in an establishment not maintained under the auspices of an incorporated organization by no means universally accepted as an arbiter by those of the Jewish faith. . . . The words spoken were actionable per se because they tended to injure plaintiffs in their business.[64]

The same theme was sounded in a 1952 New Jersey action for libel,[65] in which an Atlantic City Kashruth association and rabbi were sued for libel by a kosher butcher shop owner, about whose premises the defendants had distributed handbills reading: "Be cautious . . . Keep Your Home Kosher. The Chickens Sold at Ben's Poultry Market Atlantic and Congress Aves. Are Treifa." [66] The court declared:

> We feel that the principles involved in the complaint filed in this cause are not of a purely ecclesiastical nature. The civil and property rights of the plaintiffs are involved. The issur on which the defendants rely as a defense for their proclamation applies only to animals slaughtered within the City of Atlantic City. There is no allegation that the poultry of the plaintiffs did not meet all kosher requirements except that it was not killed under the supervision of Rabbi Mosheh Shapiro and did not bear the seal or plumba of the Vaad Ha' Kashress of Atlantic City. This court does not claim nor does it have the right, authority or jurisdiction, to declare

or to find what is kosher and what is non-kosher, but certainly poultry slaughtered and prepared according to the traditional Hebrew ritual, if kosher in one place of the world, must be kosher in each hamlet and community. We do have the right and the jurisdiction to determine a matter in violation of civil and property rights of a citizen even though such rights involve the fundamental concepts and dogma of the Hebrew religion and law. We concur with the holding of the court in the case of Cohen v. Eisenberg.[67] [supra].

The Supreme Judicial Court of Massachusetts saw the matter differently in a 1965 decision [68] in which it upheld a demurrer to an injunction sought by a kosher caterers association against the local Kashruth organization of Greater Boston to compel certification of its meat and poultry products as kosher once declared so by the caterer's rabbi of long standing. The court reviewed plaintiff's charges of "Restraint of Trade, elimination of a free market and the hindering and denying of free competition" and responded:

> It is settled by our decisions that courts will not interfere in a controversy which is exclusively or primarily of an ecclesiastical nature.
> In essence the plaintiff is asking that Associated and its allied groups be compelled to accept United's guaranty that products prepared under its auspices are authentically kosher. This we decline to do. Aside from constitutional freedoms involved, this court is not qualified to decide and therefor must refuse to consider an issue which is so exclusively one of religious practice and conscience. As was said by Rugg, C. J. in Moustakis v. Hellenic Orthodox Soc. of Salem & Peabody, 261 Mass. 462 at page 466, 159 N.E. 453 at page 455 "Such a course by the courts would in the end deprive the denominations themselves of interpretations of their own body of church polity, and would establish the courts as the final arbiter in every religious controversy. The evils attendant upon such a practice have been thought far to outweigh the incidental advantage that might flow from its adoption." [69]

The Massachusetts high court's restraint enabled it to avoid
the mistaken incredulity expressed in the New York and New
Jersey opinions at the notion that Kashruth standards may vary
locally. That such standards may indeed vary was the basis for
the action of the New York City Orthodox rabbinate originally
affirmed in the *S. S. & B. Live Poultry Corp.* decision.[70] Their
issur was intended to be

> binding on all Jews in the metropolitan area. They did so on
> the basis of traditional principles of Jewish communal or-
> ganization, which recognizes the ordained rabbinical authorities
> in each local community as constituting a body able to promul-
> gate ordinances under Jewish law.[71]

One consequence of an erroneous judicial view that Kashruth
is static, unvarying from locality to locality, is that the *plumba* or
seal affixed to poultry by Kashruth association *issur* becomes a
superfluous local idiosyncrasy. In New York in *People v. Gordon,*[72]
it was held that a group of local rabbis in New York City could not
decree that the affixing of a kosher tag was in and of itself
a religious requirement without which poultry would not be considered kosher. The New York legislature in 1942, in a compromise
response to *People v. Gordon,* enacted an amendment to its Agriculture and Markets Law that a *plumba* or other mark be employed
to indicate that a food product was kosher. In this way the legislature sought to sidestep the issue of "whether or not such marking
would be made an indispensable prerequisite for conformity to
religious requirements."[73] In subsequent prosecutions under the
statute for failure to affix a *plumba* or tag to poultry, a nominal
fine has been the punishment.

The constitutional implications of the legislatively mandated
plumba have never been litigated. However, the line of defense
which suggests itself against charges of secular entanglement, ad-
vancement of religion and non-secular purpose, is analogous to the
successfully asserted defenses in Sunday closing law and Humane
Slaughter Act cases.[74] The coinciding of secular and religious requirements is just that—a constitutionally permissible intersection.
Just as the State may direct a specific day of the week for rest
and a specific manner of slaughter as humane, both of which happen

to coincide with sectarian requirements, so it may require a tag on ritually prepared meat in the nature of a consumer protection against false claims even as that tag, perforce, coincides with fulfillment of a particular sect's ritual procedures.

Compared with New York, the California watering-down process of legal support for Kashruth enforcement is of tidal proportions. Appropriations for the use of a kosher-food law representative in the Department of Public Health for kosher-food law enforcement were eliminated in 1959. In 1965 the Department of Public Health proposed to Governor Reagan that the post of kosher-food law enforcement officer also be eliminated on the basis that the activity "does not make a major contribution to the purposes and objectives of the Department of Public Health." [75] In a letter dated May 7, 1971, the Chief of the Bureau of Food and Drugs, Department of Public Health of the State of California, wrote,

> since the employment of an Orthodox Rabbi was terminated in 1965 due to action of the legislative on funding, the annual expenditure has been minimal.[76]

A further impediment to enforcement, according to the Bureau Chief, has been the fact that

> actions have been clouded in many instances due to the interpretation of the term kosher. There is a wide divergence of opinion as to the meaning of this term among various factions of the Jewish Community.[77]

The doubts expressed in earlier constitutional assaults on the indefinite and uncertain nature of "Kashruth" for enforcement purposes have surged to certainties. No longer questionable on constitutional grounds, the same result of non-enforceability has been achieved through disputing the organized Orthodox rabbinate's competence as interpreters of Kashruth requirements. Judgments of community Bet Dins as a consequence have been accorded little attention or belittled for lack of universal application, and the issue of Kashruth compliance, excepting in Massachusetts,[78] is now justiciable by civil courts holding an erroneous view of the nature and extent of local community Bet Din jurisdiction over Kashruth definition.

The fervor of individual rabbis in denouncing violations of *issurim* has become the basis of defamation actions.[79] The courts have ignored the deep religious feeling of those rabbis, acting with prophetic passion, who publicly rebuke the offending butchers and have sustained the butchers' right to sue the denouncing rabbis. In so holding, the courts are more censurable for ignoring a relevant legal principle than for inattention to heartfelt motivations. The governing principle of law which the courts have ignored in the defamation cases and which, in the absence of malice, should protect the outspoken rabbis, is that of qualified privilege which attaches to

> a communication made bonafide upon any subject matter in which the party communicating has an interest, or in reference to which he has a duty . . . if made to a person having a corresponding interest or duty, although it contained criminating matter which, without this privilege, would be slanderous and actionable; and this though the duty be not a legal one, but only a moral or social duty of imperfect obligation.[80]

The earlier recognition of

> the religious duty of every orthodox Jew, and preeminently of the rabbi . . . from time immemorial . . . to obey, enforce and safeguard the principle of Kashruth [81]

had become a boomerang, and the rabbi exercising his religious and moral function of enforcing Orthodox compliance has been found civilly liable in damages to the religious offender.[82]

Those who would sunder state involvement with Kashruth have also turned, once again, to the country's basic legal document, the United States Constitution, for support. Why, following unsuccessful efforts in the early twentieth century, critics are emboldened to return to a constitutional attack in the 1970s is a subject worthy of analysis. It is a different constitutional route than was previously tried which has been found tempting, and the lure lies in recent decisional developments in the area of church-state relations.

The First Amendment and Challenges to
Kashruth Legislation

As we have observed, constitutional assaults on Kashruth legislation have been rebuffed when hinged on the Fourteenth Amendment's due process and equal protection clauses and on the Constitution's commerce clause.[83] The most menacing line of attack today lies through the Establishment and Free Exercise Clauses of the First Amendment as applied to federal legislation, and their incorporation in the Fourteenth where state action is concerned.

Changing styles of constitutional confrontation are evident in comparing litigation of a half-century ago with current resistance to Kashruth legislation on constitutional grounds. In 1924, potential defendants, apprehending criminal prosecution for violation of a New York statute prohibiting the sale of non-kosher meat as kosher, sought to enjoin the law's enforcement as unconstitutional.[84] Unconstitutionality was urged upon the popular "property right" principles of the day. One appellant, a purveyor of general provisions, alleged that the Kashruth statute imposed a direct burden on his shipments from Massachusetts to New York. Justice Sutherland, speaking for a unanimous court, with the exception of Justice Brandeis who "took no part in the consideration of this case," [85] saw only an incidental affect upon interstate commerce outweighed by the police power of the state. All appellants, in arguments reminiscent of the dissent in *People v. Atlas*,[86] relied heavily on the Fourteenth Amendment's due process and equal protection clauses, which they claimed were violated by reliance "upon a finding of fact by the jury of a body of law wholly foreign to the common law and our system of jurisprudence." [87] In addition, the criminal enactment was necessarily violative of due process, bottomed as it was on the vague, uncertain and indefinite "word 'kosher' and the phrase 'Orthodox Hebrew religious requirements' due to the sources, volume, and character of the foreign law which is the basis of the statute." [88] Equal protection was affronted by "an unreasonable classification" which denied equal treatment "to persons dealing in kosher and non-kosher meats."

Justice Sutherland, for the court, allowed "that a court of equity will interfere to prevent criminal prosecutions under an unconstitutional statute when that is necessary to effectually protect property rights."[89] However, since the statute required an intent to defraud and "the term 'kosher' has a meaning well enough defined to enable one engaged in the trade to correctly apply it"[90] there was no violation of due process or equal protection in the statute's prospective application to intentional transgressors.

Today, attention has veered from property rights to so-called human rights, and attacks on state involvement with religion focus on the First Amendment establishment and free exercise clauses, together referred to as "the Religion Clauses" by Justice Powell.[91] In *Jones v. Butz*[92] those sections of The Humane Slaughter Act which exempt ritual slaughter in accordance with the requirements of Kashruth were attacked as unconstitutional because the plaintiffs "believe that the exception unconstitutionally violates the Establishment and Free Exercise Clauses of the First Amendment."[93]

A series of United States Supreme Court cases decided in the 1970's define the elements of the Establishment clause by which statutory enactments are currently tested.

First, the statute must have a secular legislative purpose; second, its principal or primary effect must be one that neither advances nor inhibits religion . . . ; finally, the statute must not foster an excessive entanglement with religion.[94]

The "tests" of "purpose, effect, and entanglement" are recognized as being "no more than helpful signposts"[95] which means that judicial disagreement in "Religion Clause" cases follow a predictable pathway. Generally, legislative purpose is found to be primarily secular through expressions of temporal legislative intent often found in statutory preambles. But whether the "principal or primary effect" of a law is religiously neutral or whether a "particular entanglement with religion is excessive" are matters not as easily susceptible of objective evaluation.

The *Nyquist* case[96] reflects how agreement on the applicable tests of establishment in no wise insures unanimous agreement on whether a particular statute will pass or fail those tests. In that case a New York statute providing various forms of religious school financial assistance was struck down, unanimously in one aspect, but with bitter dissents as to others. Financial assistance for the repair and maintenance of religious school buildings was unani-

mously voided in the face of contention by state officials that
Everson v. Board of Education,[97] *Board of Education v. Allen,*[98]
and *Tilton v. Richardson* [99] all supported public aid in varying forms
to sectarian schools. Justice Powell distinguished each on the basis
that the "primary effect" was not to benefit religion. In *Everson*[100]
the program of reimbursement to parents of public as well as
parochial school children for bus fares paid in connection with
transportation to and from school was likened "to the provision
of services such as police and fire protection, sewage disposal, highways, and sidewalks for parochial schools." [101] Even so it approached
the "verge" of impermissible state aid and Justice Powell deprecat-
ingly refers to its diluted authority as "a five to four decision."
Allen is described as a case in which "the court upheld a New York
law authorizing the provision of *secular* textbooks for all children in
grades seven through twelve attending public and non-public
schools." [102] *Tilton* "upheld federal grants of funds for the construction of facilities to be used for *secular* purposes by public and non-
public institutions of higher learning." [103] The promotion of a
religious function was found to be incidental in each cited case, but
to be the primary effect in *Nyquist.*

Passing from subsidy of religious school maintenance and
repair to state aid in the form of tuition reimbursement and a pa-
rental income tax deduction for each child in a non-public school,
the issues of primary effect and legal entanglement fell from unanimity to discord. Justice Powell, speaking for the majority, found
an unconstitutional preferment of religion in both the tuition reimbursement and tax deduction plans. The dissenters, Justices
Burger, White and Rehnquist each wrote separate opinions, con-
curred in by the others, expressing the antithetical view that establishment was not threatened either by state reimbursement of
tuition or by a tax deduction to parents of non-public school children. The Chief Justice stressed the incidental religious impact of
plans which reimburse all parents of school-age children, citing
Everson,[104] *Allen* [105] and *Norwood v. Harrison,*[106]

> ... the balance between the policies of free exercise and estab-
> lishment of religion tips in favor of the former when the
> legislation moves away from direct aid to religious institutions

and takes on the character of general aid to individual families.[107]

Justice White emphasized in his dissent that laws which achieve preservation of "secular functions" as an "overriding consequence" are not unconstitutional because of "the resulting, but incidental, benefit to religion. . . ."[108]

Justice Rehnquist's dissent faults the majority's failure to honor a previously recognized distinction between an exemption for church related activity, an abstaining "from demanding that the church support the state," and its positive support of religion. He quotes from a 1970 opinion of Chief Justice Burger in which the Chief Justice had written, "There is no genuine nexus between tax exemption and establishment of religion . . ." and "The grant of a tax exemption is not sponsorship since the government does not transfer part of its revenue to churches. . . ."[109]

Justice Powell in *Hunt v. McNair*[110] had the delicate task of probing the limits of the third element in the tripartite establishment clause test: entanglement. This element had "surfaced" in 1970 in *Walz v. Tax Commission*[111] for the first time. In 1971 "excessive government entanglement with religion" proved the undoing of Pennsylvania and Rhode Island statutes[112] which provided for partial funding of costs incurred by private schools in furnishing secular education. The same objection failed when raised to a federal program offering direct grants for specified facilities at sectarian schools.[113] In *Hunt v. McNair*,[114] Justice Powell was confronted with a South Carolina statute[115] establishing an agency to assist construction and financing of state institutions of higher education, but excluding facilities for sectarian study or worship. Financing through issuance of revenue bonds was to be accompanied by conveyance of the project to the Authority which in turn would lease it back to the college and reconvey title when the bonds were paid in full. In the meantime the Authority's power extended

to determine the location and character of any project financed under the act; to construct, maintain, manage, operate, lease as lessor or lessee, and regulate the same; to enter into contracts for the management and operation of such project; to establish rules and regulations for the use of the project or any portion thereof; and to fix and revise from time to time rates, rents, fees and charges for the use of a project and for the services furnished or to be furnished by a project or any portion thereof.

It was the Authority's obligation to see that the project did not become entangled in the religious aspects of a sectarian institution financed under the legislation. Justice Powell upheld the South Carolina law, distinguishing it from *Nyquist*[116] and *Sloan v. Lemon*,[117] decided by him at the same time. In *Hunt v. McNair*,[118] Justice Powell argued, The Baptist College of South Carolina was no more sectarian in character, no "more an instrument of religious indoctrination than were the colleges and universities involved in *Tilton*,"[119] and in *Tilton* "inspection as to use did not threaten excessive entanglement." Furthermore, the sweeping powers granted the Authority were unlikely to "be exercised in their full detail," but were susceptible of "a narrow interpretation of the[ir] practical operation."[120]

"Excessive entanglement" is a test in process of being molded, let alone refined. However, certain "entanglements" appear constitutionally safe. Tax exemptions for religious institutions appear immune from assault, notwithstanding Justice Rehnquist's dissent in *Nyquist*[121] in which he characterized the majority opinion as making inroads on this principle. Not only does it have historical sanction in each of the fifty states,[122] but Justice Powell in *Nyquist* reaffirms the validity of the reason for the rule:

A proper respect for both the Free Exercise and the Establishment Clauses compels the State to pursue a course of "neutrality" toward religion. Yet governments have not always pursued such a course, and oppression has taken many forms, one of which has been taxation of religion. Thus if taxation was regarded as a form of "hostility" toward religion, exemption constituted a reasonable and balanced attempt to guard against those dangers.[123]

If exemption is exclusion of the Sovereign from an opportunity for religious oppression, inspection by the State to oversee separation of secular from religious involvement is a delicate middle

ground. Some cases uphold the constitutionality of a reserved
right of inspection as long as the institution inspected is not perme-
ated with a "substantial religious character." [124] Another factor
in inspection cases is whether there is a "comprehensive, discrimi-
nating, and continuing state surveillance." [125] As Justice Brennan
has characterized the saving aspect of tax exemption:

> Tax exemptions, accordingly, constitute mere passive state
> involvement with religion and not the affirmative involvement
> characteristic of outright governmental subsidy[126]

or other action. Similarly, inspection, to the extent that it is likely
to eventuate in active state involvement, risks constituting "excessive entanglement." Both factors: the "substantial religious
character" of the institution, and the nature and extent of the
surveillance required, are related. Religious institutions of monolithic and recondite doctrine invite insulation from proscribed entanglement, yet make state regulation of deceptive or fraudulent
practice upon the public easy to enforce by reference to church
authority. Cracks in doctrine make for active state involvement
and thereby threaten a constitutionally obnoxious entanglement in
religion. To legislate that marriage by a "clergyman" is valid, for
example, does not plunge the state into the mysteries of ordina-
tion if it can turn to clear religious authority for confirmation.[127]
Similarly, with respect to tax exemption cases where the creed
or sect seeking exemption meets standards of a recognized religion.
And the regulation of Kashruth toward the end of preventing
fraud or deception would likewise escape "excessive entanglement"
if Jewish ritual had as its acknowledged authority the local Bet
Din or other recognized religious authority to which the secular
courts could defer with aloof relief. Similarly, Jewish ritual slaughter, in accordance with time-honored practice, is more readily
granted asylum from state regulation when its religious integrity
is unquestioned.

The difference in result compelled on the "entanglement" issue
when the court confronts solid sectarian doctrine, as opposed to
schism or uncertain definition, is nowhere better illustrated than in
comparing the legal treatment which marks enforcement of disputes
over alleged false Kashruth claims with adjudications of the con-

stitutionality of kosher slaughter legislation. The latter is a procedure clearly defined by statute. Its descriptive instruction explicitly conforms with rabbinic injunction.

Religious integrity, through recognition of a clearly defined procedure consistent with ritual, incorporated in the Humane Slaughter Act, has resisted constitutional attack. In *Jones v. Butz*,[128] a Brooklyn Law School professor master-minded a gathering of First Amendment threads spun in recent U. S. Supreme Court litigation, and sought to weave a snare for ritual slaughter conducted under the shield of federal legislation. From *Lemon v. Kurzman*[129] he took the three independent desiderata for determining whether a statute violates the Establishment Clause of the First Amendment: (1) a secular legislative purpose, (2) a principal or primary effect which neither inhibits nor advances religion, and (3) no "excessive government entanglement with religion."

The plaintiffs represented by the professor claimed all three standards were violated by Sections 2(b), 5 and 6 of the Humane Slaughter Act. Section 2 declares as humane "slaughtering in accordance with the ritual requirements of the Jewish faith or any other religious faith that prescribes a method of slaughter whereby the animal suffers loss of consciousness by anemia of the brain caused by the simultaneous and instantaneous severance of the carotid arteries with a sharp instrument." The plaintiffs contended:

> that in failing to require that the animal be rendered insensible to pain before the handling process, and thus before it is shackled and hoisted, the provisions permitting ritual slaughter are offensive to and inconsistent with the humane purpose of the Act and have a special religious purpose in contravention of the First Amendment.[130]

They argued that the Act permitted non-ritual slaughter only under circumstances in which the animal is rendered insensible to pain before being shackled and hoisted, while "the Jewish slaughter method often involves the animal's being shackled and hoisted before the animal suffers loss of consciousness."[131] They concluded "that such legislative inconsistency can be explained only as so clear a piece of deference to the tenets of one religious group as to violate the First Amendment."[132] This statutory protection of a religious belief had no secular purpose, advanced a particular religion and fostered excessive government entanglement with religion and therefor violated the Establishment Clause.

The three-judge federal court considering the case first noted that Congress had prescribed alternative methods of humane slaughter, "and each one is supported by legislative history as a justifiable legislative determination that the stated method of slaughter is indeed humane." [133] With respect to *shechitah*, "Jewish ritual slaughter, as a fundamental aspect of Jewish religious practice, was historically related to considerations of humaneness in times when such concerns were practically non-existent." [134] Thus, the statute's secular purpose of requiring humane slaughter simply coincided with the historic practices of Jewish ritual slaughter, as Sunday closing laws coincide with the beliefs of Christianity.

If *shechitah* is viewed as an exemption from standard humane slaughter requirements, it is a constitutionally permissible exemption in the same category as exemption from military service for conscientious objectors on religious grounds, or the exemption from Sunday closing laws some states have legislated for the benefit of Sabbatarians observing another day of rest.

The courts are inclined to defer to clearly delineated religious practices and beliefs as exemptions from the general standard, particularly when such indulgence is importuned by a united religious community as opposed to squabbling schismatics. The latter invite state entanglement; the former grant a relieved government respite on an historically troubled front.

Resort by plaintiffs in *Jones v. Butz* to the First Amendment's Free Exercise Clause as an assault weapon against the Humane Slaughter Act was turned aside by the three-judge court, which noted plaintiff's failure "to demonstrate any coercive effect of the statute with respect to their religious practices . . . Assertion of ethical principles against eating meat resulting from ritual slaughter is not sufficient." [135]

Where Jewish law is not firm beyond peradventure, statutory doubts appear. Whereas most state humane slaughter statutes follow the Federal Act, Illinois,[136] Pennsylvania [137] and New Hampshire [138] pose for later resolution the issue of whether the shackling and hoisting of conscious animals preparatory to their killing may not be avoided by some otherwise ritually acceptable manner which would also not be economically prohibitive. If there is such a method, these state statutes call for its use. The New Hampshire statute, for example, defines *shechitah* as humane, "provided that the method used in bringing the animal into position for slaughter causes no injury or pain which can be avoided without interfering with the requirements of ritualistic slaughter or without imposing unreasonable economic hardships." [139]

CONCLUSION

"Kashruth" law challenges have been resisted through a path which is now coming nearly full circle. Success of Kashruth law defenders in current cases, as in the earliest cases, depends on a definition of the term "kosher" shared and enforced by each Jewish religious community.[140] Where the definition is murky and the community fragmented, a hopeless entanglement of church and state is bound to ensue upon judicial inquiry into the best intentioned protective legislation.

The earliest challengers bridled at the introduction of a foreign body of learning into a common law heritage, with all the potential for exotic infection such a suspect intruder carried.[141] In the early cases the courts were able to sustain the validity of state regulation only because they assumed a recognized, discrete body of Jewish authority to which they confidently referred and, by so doing, avoided detailed dissection of the subject. Thus the hedge between church and state remained inviolate or, on occasion, only gingerly trimmed.

Subsequent cases treat (1) state enforceability of Bet Din action involving Jewish adversaries, each pressing its version of Kashruth in accordance with state denominated "orthodox Hebrew requirements" and (2) defamation charges brought by accused butchers against rabbinic "defamers." The secular courts are reduced, respectively, to states of (1) nervous uncertainty and (2) sympathy for the economic victim at the expense of the moral guardian.

The attack on Kashruth laws most recently repelled proceeded from United States Supreme Court opinions which, since 1970, have begun to emphasize the perils of "an excessive entanglement" by the state in church matters. The constitutional microscope, when focused on a crumbling Jewish communal structure, magnifies fissures and leaves analysis, by default, to a nonplussed secular authority.

The experience of secular regulation of religion has left no doubt that the briar of entanglement is best avoided by united religious bodies with unquestioned definitional authority and beliefs. The same applies in the field of Kashruth. Cohesive structure and doctrine is an effective buffer, welcomed with relief by secular authority. Thus authoritative Jewish law makes for clarity and certainty of civil regulation. The state may then unhesitatingly exempt Kashruth from detailed interference as it has consistently insulated religious bodies from state taxation.

But the need for a coherent, authoritative body of Jewish law if it is to be readily recognized in American forums dramatizes the quandary in which Jewish law finds itself under the conditions imposed for its acknowledgment. Secular authority stands in awe of monolithic doctrine and infallible orthodoxy. Jewish law on the other hand has grown through the dynamic dialectic of argument and rebuttal, fragmented authority, community autonomy and the supremacy of scholarship, none of which factors are conducive to an impressive uniformity. As John Milton wrote, "Where there is much desire to learn, there of necessity will be much arguing, much writing, many opinions; for opinion in good men is but knowledge in the making." This manner of legal development requires a certain indulgence on the part of the inquirer. Jewish law has been, however, a legal development spanning the ages, expanding in scope, sophistication and subtlety, all the while obeying a throbbing, abiding ethical impulse.

Precedent for Jewish law's assistance in American trials and tribunals dates to New England's earliest archives. Despite this pedigree, its American experience has been that of the immigrant, an outsider on probation, searching for comfortable acceptance.

If American courts became more familiar with and sympathetically recognized the processes of Jewish law, its sacred texts, its machinery for enforcement, its basic humanizing bias and its past contributions, applied it judiciously, especially where parties stipulate for it, then the pursuit of justice within American constitutional and legal frameworks would be abetted by an extraordinary legal reservoir.

NOTES TO CHAPTER 5

1. Roger Williams in his writing entitled "Mr. Cotton's Letter Lately Printed, Examined and Answered" spoke of the garden and the wilderness. ". . . The Faithful labors of many witnesses of Jesus Christ, extant to the world, abundantly proving that the church of the Jews under the Old Testament in the type, and the church of the Christians under the New Testament in the antitype, were both separate from the world; and that when they have opened a gap in the hedge or wall of separation between the garden of the church and the wilderness of the world, God hath ever broke down the wall itself, removed the candlestick, and made His garden a wilderness, as at this day. And that therefor, if He will ever please to restore His garden and paradise again, it must of necessity be walled in peculiarly unto Himself from the world; and that all that shall be saved out of the world are to be transplanted out of the wilderness of the world, and added unto his church or garden." Quoted in Perry Miller, *Roger Williams: His Contribution to the American Tradition* (1953) 89, 98. See Mark DeWolfe Howe, *The Garden and the Wilderness* (University of Chicago Press, 1965) ch. I.

2. Justice Powell of the United States Supreme Court, wrote in 1973 in Committee for Public Education v. Nyquist, 37 L. Ed. 948, 956, ". . . this Nation's history has not been one of entirely sanitized separation between Church and State. It has never been thought either possible or desirable to enforce a regime of total separation, and as a consequence cases arising under these clauses have presented some of the most perplexing questions to come before this Court."

3. Food taboos are among the most common in all social history. Restrictions against meat-eating are imposed upon the Hindus. The Jains sweep the ground in walking so as not to step on living things and then wear a veil to prevent the accidental breathing in of an insect. See Frazer, *The Golden Bough*, one-volume abridgment (New York, 1951) 24, 277. A vestigial "Kashruth" remained with the medieval Church. For example, it forbade eating meat of an animal, such as the horse, which "does not divide the hoof nor chew the cud." *The Horizon Book of the Middle Ages* (New York, 1968) 238. Protestantism, too, is not lacking in traces of Kashruth. The Glasites or Sandemanians, an offshoot of The Church of Scotland, abstain from all animal food which has not been drained of blood in accord with Deut. 12:23-25. The same prohibition is mentioned in Lev. 18:11, 14; 19:26 and Gen. 9:4. Seventh Day Adventists, as well as other religious groups in America, when shopping, look for the insignia of the letter "K" inside a circle indicating kosher food certification by the Committee for the Furtherance of Torah Observance, or the letter "U" inside a circle of the Union of Orthodox Jewish Congregations of America. Seventh Day Adventists "believe in certain aspects of the Jewish

dietary laws." *New York Times,* May 18, 1975. F 3, col. 1. Followers of Islam, of course, do not eat pork or imbibe alcohol.

4. Erich Isaac, "Jews and Forbidden Foods," *Commentary* magazine (January, 1966) 36. The word "Kosher" appears in the Bible only three times (Esth. 8:5; Eccles. 10:10; 11:6) and then not in connection with food. *Encyc. Jud.,* vol. 6, 26.

5. Deut. 22:12.

6. Lev. 19:27.

7. "It is almost as if the rabbis seized upon the thing most central to everyday living, and created in the elaborate structure of Kashruth, with its demand for permanent daily observance, the method for holding the Jews together as a separate group." Isaac, *op. cit.,* 36.

8. Lev. 22:8. In the absence of refrigeration, many peoples native to tropical regions take blood and limbs from living animals as a means of preserving fresh meat for as long as possible. The Masai tribe of east Africa to this day engage in this practice. See Louis B. Leakey, *Animals of East Africa* (Washington, 1969) 183.

9. Lev. 22:28.

10. Deut. 22:6, 7.

11. Isaac, *op. cit.,* 39. The prohibition of cruelty to animals is one of the Laws of the Sons of Noah (B. Sanhedrin 56 a—60 a; Tosefta, Abodah Zarah 8:4-8), deriving from the apocryphal Book of Jubilees. These Noachide Laws antedate the Talmud. The compilers "could not conceive of untold generations of men before Moses living without divine revelation." Robert Gordis, *The Root and The Branch* (Chicago, 1962) 46. The Book of Jubilees attributes to Noah, who was not a Hebrew, a code of conduct binding on all men which includes a prohibition against cruelty to animals by eating the limb of a living creature. See note 8, *supra.* The New Testament may harken back to the Noachide Laws in Acts 15:20, 29 where abstention from "things, strangled, and from blood" are adjured. Old Testament references relating to animal treatment include Exodus 23:12, Leviticus 22:26-33, Deuteronomy 22:6-10 and 25:4. A concern for nature extends to trees which may not be axed when laying siege to a city. Deuteronomy 20:19. Interestingly enough, arboreal concern has heightened and spread in recent years as environmentalists have raised the issue of the legal standing of natural objects to sue. See C.E. Downey, "He Speaks for the Trees," *Juris Doctor,* April 1975, 50 ff.; Alexandra D. Dawson, "Tongues in Trees," 26 *Harvard Law School Bulletin* 14 (Spring, 1975); Christopher D. Stone, "Should Trees Have Standing?—Toward Legal Rights for Natural Objects," 45 *Southern California Law Review* 450 (1972). Justice Douglas in *Sierra Club v. Morton,* 405 U.S. 727 (1972), has stated, "Contemporary public concern for protecting nature's ecological equilibrium should lead to the conferral of standing upon environmental objects to sue for their own preservation. . ." This is a far cry from Gilbert and Sullivan's Victorian spoof of peerage and Chancery, "Iolanthe," in which the attribution of legal standing to natural objects provoked fantastical hilarity— a swain, who calls upon Nature as witness to his love, before the Lord Chancellor, is rebuffed with the Chancellor's chill response, "Now an affidavit from a thunderstorm, or a few words on oath from a heavy shower, would meet with all the attention they deserve." The current stirrings of solicitude for natural objects augurs a trend to vegetarianism, the ideal kosher diet. Chulin 84a; P'sachim 49b. See Samuel H. Dresner and Seymour Siegel, *The Jewish Dietary Laws* (New York, 1959) 21-27.

12. Deut. 25:4.

13. Prov. 12:10.

14. See Joseph H. Hertz, *Pentateuch and Haftorahs*, 2nd ed. (London, 1964) 854.

15. I Corinthians 9:9.

16. See Chapter 1, note 24. In a 1975 prosecution of a Central Park hansom cab driver for persistently driving a lame horse after being warned against it, a violation of New York's Agriculture and Markets Law (§ 353), the Criminal Court justice in his opinion convicting the defendant first noted that "History prior to the middle of the 19th century is devoid of any laws as to cruelty to animals." But to support the wrongful nature of such conduct from time immemorial he quotes Proverbs 12:10: "A righteous man regardeth the life of his beast." He also cites Deuteronomy 22:4, commenting, "The Bible also states that if you see an animal hurt or overburdened, one should not look away but help it." People v. O'Rourke *et ano.*, 369 N.Y.S. 2d 335.

17. See note 31, *infra*. In 1928 the Governor of California vetoed a "Kosher Bill" because he considered it "designed to aid the observances or ordinances" of Judaism.

18. Originally enacted in 1915 as Penal Law §435, subd. 4 (Laws of 1915 c. 233). State protection of the kosher meat consumer does not extend to an obligation to furnish the Orthodox Jew with kosher food as a matter of right in public assistance programs. Such a claim was rejected in Stark v. Wyman, Sup. Ct., Kings Co. Sp. Term Part I, N.Y.L.J. April 24, 1969. The petitioner's claim for an increased allowance from the Department of Social Services for kosher food was denied. Petitioner argued "denial of such a grant is a violation of her guarantee of freedom of religion and the equal protection of the laws under the Federal and State Constitutions." Nor does state consumer protection extend to an obligation to serve kosher food to inmates of state prisons, although that service has been urged as a state duty. See *The Jewish News* (N.J.), Feb. 17, 1972, 4, col. 3 quoting a New York City councilman who called on the City's Department of Corrections Commissioners to "respect the dietary laws of Orthodox Jews." In response to the argument that very few Orthodox Jews are prisoners, the councilman said, "But even if only one, he is entitled to observe his religious beliefs," implying First Amendment imperatives. See W. Leeke, *The Emerging Rights of the Confined* (1972). Most cases discourage a sympathetic view of prisoners' constitutional rights. Howard v. Warden Petersburg Reformatory, 348 F. Supp. 1204, aff'd. 474 F. 2d 1341 (1973); Ralls v. Wolfe, 448 F. 2d 779 (1971); Blake v. Pryse, 444 F. 2d 218 (1971); Brooks v. Wainwright, 428 F. 2d 652 (1970); Brown v. Wainwright, 419 F. 2d 1376 (1970).

The same Jeffrey H. Smilow who lost his First Amendment plea to remain silent on pain of being ostracized as an informer (see note 16, Chapter 3), also lost his application to the Federal District Court of the Southern District of New York for the right to have kosher food served to him during his detention for contempt as a silent witness. U. S. v. Smilow, 73 Cr.—Mis. 24 (1975). See also U.S. v. Huss, 73-cr-25 (1975). The delicate constitutional balance between First Amendment religious free exercise and establishment was highlighted when, in the same week that the *Smilow* and *Huss* decisions were rendered in Manhattan, the federal court across the river in Brooklyn ruled that to deprive Rabbi Meir Kahane, an "observant Orthodox Jewish rabbi . . . of opportunities to observe basic religious practices in light of his particular beliefs" was tantamount to cruel and unusual punishment forbidden by the Eighth Amendment. The Allenwood, Pennsylvania prison to which he had been remanded as a parole violator was ordered to serve kosher food to Rabbi Kahane. U. S. v. Kahane, 71—Cr.—479 (1975). So Jeffrey Smilow who kept his mouth closed in Court was provided with no incentive to open it in captivity; while Meir Kahane, who operated under no similar restraint while at large, was permitted uninterrupted oral gratification in kosher confinement. See *N.Y. Law Journal*, May 8, 1975, 1, col. 3. Judge Jack B. Weinstein's closely reasoned constitutional analysis in the *Kahane* case combines a profound understanding of the importance of Kashruth to the observant with a balanced effort at accommodating the demands of penal administration. The opinion appears in the Bulletin of the International Ass'n of Jewish Lawyers and Jurists, No. 11 (July, 1975). Undoubtedly the issues in conflict await resolution at the appellate level. See addendum page 214.

19. People v. Goldberger, 163 N.Y.S. 663.

20. *Ibid.*, 665.

21. *Ibid.*, 665-6.

22. *Ibid.*, 666.

23. People v. Goldberger, 168 N.Y.S. 578 (1916).

24. *Ibid.*, 578.

25. People v. Atlas, 183 App. Div. 595 170 N.Y.S. 834, aff'd 230 N.Y. 629, 130 N.E. 921; see also Hygrade Provision Co. v. Sherman 266 U.S. 497 (1924) in which the New York statute was upheld by the United States Supreme Court against a charge of unconstitutional vagueness.

26. People v. Atlas, 183 App. Div. 595, 597.

27. *Ibid.*, 603.

28. "Rabbinical Courts: Modern Day Solomons," 6 *Columbia Journal of Law and Social Problems*, 72 (Jan. 1970).

29. S.S.&B Live Poultry Corp. v. Kashrut Ass'n of Greater New York, 158 Misc. 358, 285 N.Y.S. 879 (1936).

30. *Ibid.*, 359.

31. Arizona, Arkansas, California, Connecticut, Illinois, Kentucky, Maryland, Massachusetts, Michigan, Minnesota, New Jersey, New York, Ohio, Pennsylvania, Rhode Island, Tennessee, Virginia and Wisconsin. These states are inhabited by ninety per cent of the approximately six million Jews in the United States.

32. The problems of Kashruth enforcement in the United States, historically, have been staggering. "According to one estimate made in 1917, a million Jews, two-thirds of the total Jewish population of New York City consumed 156 million pounds of Kosher meat annually . . . One investigation in 1915, conducted under the aegis of the Kehillah, [the Jewish community organization] estimated that only 40 percent of the retail butchers claiming to sell kosher meat were in fact doing so. Most of the rabbinical supervisors and schochtim [slaughterers] were in the direct employ of the slaughterhouses (a religious prohibition since it compromised the independence of the religious functionary) . . . According to one estimate made in 1915, there were 5,000 retail butcher stores and over 1,000 schochtim . . . The poultry sector suffered from a mutitude of small processing units, cutthroat competition, and depressed wages. Hundreds of middlemen, the so-called 'speculators,' provided credit for the small retailers and connived frequently in selling non-kosher meat." Arthur A. Goren, *New York Jews and the Quest for Community* (Columbia University Press, 1970) 78-9. A 1936 lawsuit found a court-ap-

pointed expert estimating the number of kosher poultry consumers in the Greater New York City area at 1.25 to 1.5 million annually. See Elazar and Goldstein, "The Legal Status of the American Jewish Community," *American Jewish Year Book 1972* (Philadelphia, 1972) 42. See also Harold Gastwirt, *Fraud, Corruption and Holiness* (Port Washington, N.Y., 1974) ch. 1, 3 and 6. For the background of the *S.S.&B. Live Poultry* case, see ch. 11.

33. In New York, the most heavily Jewish populated American city and state, community organization is directly traceable to Eastern European roots. From the Middle Ages forward, reaching a peak in seventeenth-century Poland, Jewish community organization has been marked by strong internal leadership and initiative, principally in rabbinic hands. "Rulers interested in the Jews for fiscal and financial reasons permitted them a measure of authority in arranging their communal life; governments thereby held the community accountable for the obligations of the individual. They granted Jews the right to self-taxation, limited juridical autonomy, and a free hand in the internal administration of the community. The leadership—lay and rabbinical—used this secular power to reinforce a body of religious precepts which, in its own right, claimed authority over the private and public life of the Jew." Goren, *op. cit.*, 6. From this tradition, the Jewish community, *(Kehillah)*, of New York City drew its strength. Efforts were made in the early twentieth century to form a communal organization to regulate certain Jewish practices. Dr. H. Pereira Mendes, senior rabbi of the Spanish and Portugese Synagogue and chairman of the New York Kehillah's religious committee, in 1909 proposed a large rabbinical commission of Orthodox rabbis "whose ordinances would be respected" to control Kashruth supervision. Eventually such a rabbinical commission known as the United Rabbinate was formed. The decline of organized community regulation of Kashruth in New York City is described in Gastwirt, *Fraud, Corruption and Holiness, op. cit.*, ch. 10, 11 and 12.

34. Elazar and Goldstein, *op. cit.*, 40-41. Gastwirt, *Fraud Corruption and Holiness, op. cit.* ch. 11.

35. Quoted in *S.S.&B Live Poultry Corp. v. Kashrut Ass'n of Greater New York, supra*, note 29.

36. *Ibid.*, 359.

37. *Ibid.*, 360.

38. Cited are the Rambam (Maimonides), *Pirke Avoth*, the *Shulchan Aruch, Choshen Mishpat* and other Jewish law authorities.

39. *S.S. & B. Live Poultry Corp. v. Kashrut Ass'n of Greater New York, supra*, 367.

40. *Ibid.*, 362. Overruling objections made to admissibility of hearsay testimony before the Bet Din, and to the testimony of rabbis as witnesses who also must act as judges, the court saw no objection "under the Jewish authorities."

41. *Ibid.*, 367.

42. *Ibid.*, 364.

43. *Ibid.*

44. *Ibid.*, 364-365.

45. *Ibid.*, 365.

46. §§435, 435-a, 435-b.

47. *S.S.&B Live Poultry Corp. v. Kashrut Ass'n of Greater New York, supra*, 365.

48. *Ibid.*, 367.

49. *Ibid.*, 360, citing "Code of Rambam (Maimonides) Laws of Sanhedrin, ch. 26, last section."

50. *Ibid.*, 366.

51. *Ibid.*, 365.

52. *Ibid.*, 367.

53. *Ibid.*, footnote 6.

54. Patterson, *Jurisprudence*, (New York, 1953) 542; Dewey, *Logic* (New York, 1938).

55. 172 Misc. 780, 17 N.Y.S. 2d 707 (1939).

56. *Ibid.*, 708.

57. *Ibid.*, 709.

58. 172 Misc. 543, 14 N.Y.S. 2d 333 (1939), rev'd 258 App. Div. 421, 16 N.Y.S. 2d 833 (2nd Dept. 1940), aff'd 283 N.Y. 705, 28 N.E. 2d 717 (1940).

59. 258 App. Div. 421 at 422, 16 N.Y.S. 2d at 834.

60. "Halachah (Jewish Law) guarantees the right of a Jewish Community to appoint specific schochtim (ritual slaughterers) and to declare non-Kosher the meat of those who disregard its orders." I.N. Tuchman, *Jewish Law and Custom and the Courts of New York State*, a Master's Project Submitted to the Faculty of the Bernard Revel Graduate School of Yeshiva University (1971) 44. Haim Cohn, *Jewish Law in Ancient and Modern Israel* (New York, 1971) XVI, "communal customs having been absorbed into the law as it was known and practised in a given community, the various communal laws have become different and been allowed to develop differently with the result that what is permitted (Kasher) to a Jew of one community, may be prohibited to a Jew of another community, and vice versa." See note 71, infra.

61. People v. Gordon, 16 N.Y.S. 2d 833 at 834-5.

62. Elazar and Goldstein, *op. cit.*, 43.

63. Cohen v. Eisenberg, 173 Misc. 1089, 19 N.Y.S. 2d 678 (1940), aff'd 260 App. Div. 1014, 24 N.Y.S. 2d (1941).

64. *Ibid.*, 1092.

65. Cabinet *et ux* v. Shapiro *et al.*, 17 N.J. Super. 540, 86 A. 2d. 314.

66. *Ibid.*, 316.

67. *Ibid.*, 318.

68. United Kosher Butchers Association v. Associated Synagogues of Greater Boston, Inc. *et al.*, 211 N.E. 2d 332.

69. *Ibid.*, 334.

70. 158 Misc. 358; 285 N.Y.S. 879 (1936). See note 71, *infra.*

71. Elazar and Goldstein, *op cit.*, 42. Judicial failure to comprehend community autonomy in prescribing Kashruth standards proceeds either from a misconception or ignorance of the dual aspect of Kashruth. Understanding would bring with it recognition that local community regulation is unavoidable. The Kashruth laws not only forbid certain foods but prescribe the manner in which slaughter shall be conducted. The provisions regulating slaughter, *shechitah*, are set down in the first segment of the "Yoreh Deah" volume of Joseph Caro's sixteenth century *Shulchan Aruch* (Code of Jewish Law). The role played by the *shochet*, the ritual slaughterer, is critical. His credibility and reliability, in addition to his physical dexterity, must be unquestioned. See note 189, Ch. 2. He must stand as a witness that the ritual of *shechitah* has been correctly and successfully completed. For example, the incision required must be made in one swift motion. A pause for even a fraction of a second makes the slaughtered animal ritually unfit. "Yoreh Deah," ch. 23.

Only the *shochet* can verify that his hand has not faltered. It is this desideratum of integrity which led Rabbi Asher in a fourteenth century responsum to emphasize the role of the local community in Kashruth enforcement:

> A locality which imposed an interdiction which provided that no man might slaughter except the butcher designated by the congregation; and someone violated the interdiction and slaughtered. [What is the law?]
>
> It would appear that it is prohibited to eat from his slaughtering for the congregation disqualified everyone's slaughter except the slaughter of the [designated] butcher, in order to prevent everyone, particularly non-experts, from slaughtering. And the community is authorized to stipulate a condition and to aid their decision by monetary sanction; and such [a monetary sanction] will not involve a larcenous taking. And similarly, to prohibit that which is permissible in order to "construct a fence"; and that which is prohibited is prohibited to all the city's inhabitants.
>
> And a *fortiori* he who has ignored the *cherem* and slaughtered deserves to be compared to a non-believer with respect to the laws of ritual slaughter because he ignored the *cherem* by slaughtering, and even though he may not be suspected of eating a prohibited food, nevertheless his actions are repulsive and he deserves to be penalized that others should not eat of his slaughter. Rabbi Asher, *Responsa*, Section 7 (Grossman Edition, New York 1960). (translation of Stewart Wahrsager, Esq.)

The *ratio decidendi* of the responsum advances upon two lines. First, the author concludes that the edict prohibiting *shechitah* by anyone save the designated butcher is a reasonable exercise of rabbinic authority since it "builds a fence around the law" by preventing unqualified persons from slaughtering for the community. Second, Rabbi Asher reasons that one who rebelliously overrides this interdiction is likened to a "non-believer with respect to the laws of ritual slaughter" and such a party's ritual slaughter may not be eaten. There is nothing novel in Rabbi Asher's affirmation of rabbinic authority to prohibit qualified but undesignated *shochets* from serving the community; plenary jurisdiction for publication of such an interdiction or *cherem* is inherent in every rabbinic court. Yet such a ban does not go to the substantive Kashruth of the food. What was unprecedented about the decision is that Rabbi Asher placed violators of the *cherem* on the same footing as "non-believers with respect to the law of ritual slaughter." The Talmud makes it clear in several instances that the *shechitah* of such "non-believers" is intrinsically unkosher—as opposed to merely prohibited—inasmuch as such persons lack capacity to bear witness and therefore cannot supply the essential verification that *shechitah* was successfully completed. Thus, it would appear that in Rabbi Asher's view, slaughter, in all other respects in accord with Kashruth, fails if performed by a non-designated, though qualified, *shochet*, and the slaughtered meat becomes *nevailah*, or substantively unkosher.

Subsequent rabbinic scholars, while basically accepting Rabbi Asher's view, have moderated the severity of his decision by engrafting various *caveats* upon it. The Shach, observing that the dispositive factor in Rabbi Asher's position is the *shochet's* willful disregard of an authoritative rabbinic edict, contended in his commentary to the *Schulchan Aruch* that the meat of an animal slaughtered by one unaware of the ban would be kosher. (Shach, Commentary upon "Yoreh Deah," ch. 1, §11.) Rabbi Ezekiel Landau, in the early nineteenth century, in his responsum [Responsa, Nodeh Beyehudah,

"Yoreh Deah," Responsa 1 (first collection) (Grossman, New York)] dis-
tinguishes between *cherems* promulgated with respect to the slaughtering
process itself and those published in connection with all post-slaughter
procedures. It is the latter which lead to local variation. Conceding to Rabbi
Asher that the meat of animals slaughtered in contravention of *cherems* of
the former type is substantively non-kosher, Rabbi Landau points out that
meats marketed in violation of the latter type of *cherem*, while they too may
not be eaten in the community where the *cherem* has been pronounced, are
not viewed as substantively non-kosher. Rabbi Landau bases his distinction
upon the observation that only violations of the slaughter-type *cherem* effect
a legal change in the status of the transgressing *shochet*, i.e. render him a
"non-believer with respect to the laws of ritual slaughter," and thus disqualify him from bearing witness. Rabbi Landau also points out the practical
effect of what otherwise would be a purely theoretical distinction: in instances
where a post-slaughter type of violation is involved, e.g. where otherwise
kosher meat is sold without a *plumba*, or seal, where the authorities in the
community have determined that a *plumba* is required, although the consequence is to make such meat non-kosher to Jews in that community, if the
rabbinate in a neighboring community determines that such meat is in fact
substantively kosher, they may set aside the prohibiting community's ban
with respect to inhabitants of their community.

The community system, in turn, created its own regulatory responsibilities
and demands. For example, a rabbinic interdiction might prohibit the
beef of a particular slaughterhouse upon a determination that its business practices adversely affected the community's economic well being. See
Schulchan Aruch, "Choshen Mishpat," ch. 242 §28. Of course, with responsibility and autonomy go the opportunity for abuse and corruption. See Harold
Gastwirt, *Fraud, Corruption and Holiness* (Port Washington, N.Y. 1974).

72. *People v. Gordon, supra.*

73. New York v. Johnson Kosher Meat Products, Inc. 42 Misc. 2d. 534
(1964) at 536.

74. The Constitutional clause against establishment of religion by law
"does not ban federal or state regulation of conduct whose reason or effect
merely happens to coincide or harmonize with the tenets of some or all
religions." McGowan v. Maryland, 366 U.S. 420, 442 (1961).

75. Glasner v. Dept. of Public Health, 61 Cal. Reptr. 415-16 (1967).

76. Letter to Elazar and Goldstein dated May 7, 1971, from R. Kenneth
Buell, Chief, Bureau of Food and Drugs, Dept. of Public Health, California
quoted in "The Legal Status of the American Jewish Community," *op. cit.*, 40.

77. *Ibid.*

78. See p. 189. A 1931 Massachusetts case, Cohen v. Silver, 178 N.E.
508, also supports the judgment of a communal rabbinical association. Certification had been denied a wholesale kosher butcher who had been accused
of being a Sabbath violator and who had refused a summons to appear before
a Jewish tribunal or Bet Din. The court, while acknowledging the mortal
impact of the rabbinic association's decision on the butcher's business, recognized as binding upon a man so engaged in a trade subject to Jewish law
those Jewish law provisions forbidding a kosher butcher from being a Sabbath
law violator (or one suspected of this transgression) or a Talmud non-believer,
or a consumer of non-kosher food, or a non-responder to a Bet Din summons.
These were religious matters with which it declined to interfere. From Colonial

days to John Adams to the mid-twentieth century Massachusetts has displayed an indulgent sympathy toward Hebrew laws and practices. See Abram Goodman, *American Overture* (Phila., 1947) ch. 2.

79. Cohen v. Eisenberg, 173 Misc. 1089, 19 N.Y.S. 2d 678 (1940), aff'd 260 App. Div. 1014, 24 N.Y.S. 2d. 10004 (1941); Cabinet v. Shapiro, 17 N.J. Super. 540, 86 A. 2d 314 (1952). See also *Erlich v. Etner, 36 Cal. Reptr.* 256 (1964) in which the defendant rabbi was charged with conspiring to expose and publicize a kosher food violation. Recovery in the trial court was reversed on appeal on the ground that plaintiff failed to prove loss of net profits. A kosher meat dealer, on the other hand, had his libel complaint sustained, against Armour & Co., which had listed the dealer together with non-kosher meat dealers in an advertisement stating: "These progressive dealers listed here sell Armour's Star Bacon in the new window top carton." Braun v. Armour & Co., 254 N.Y. 514. In Friedman v. Swift & Co. 18 Fed. Supp. 596 (1937) the District Court in a negligence action by a kosher meat dealer against a meat packer, struck the packer's defense that rabbinical authority had "exonerated the defendant" with respect to the particular meat deliveries which were the subject of the action. The court, however, did allow the packer to re-plead its defense which, the court instructed "must be elaborated so as to show the binding effect of the rabinical decree upon the parties to the present controversy. Defendant should plead the nature of the rabbinical authority, by virtue of what mandate it operates, the nature of the proceeding before it, the parties thereto, and the judgment upon the matter in controversy."

80. Byam v. Collins, 111 N.Y. 143, 150, 19 N.E. 75, 2 L.R.A. 129; see, also, Shapiro v. Health Ins. Plan of Greater N.Y., 7 N.Y. 2d 56, 163 N.E. 2d 333, 194 N.Y.S. 2d 509, 512-513 (1959); Stillman v. Ford, 122 N.Y. 2d 48, 238 N.E. 2d 304, 209 N.Y.S. 2d 893, 897 (1969); Trim-A-Way Figure Contouring v. National Better Business Bureau, 37 App. Div. 2d 43, 322 N.Y.S. 2d 154 (1971); Kirschner v. Peerless Importers, Inc. 354 N.Y.S. 2d 955 (1974).

81. *S.S.&B. Live Poultry Corp. v. Kashrut Ass'n of Greater New York, supra,* 360.

82. See *Cohen v. Eisenberg, supra; Cabinet v. Shapiro, supra;* and *Erlich v. Etner, supra,* for New York, New Jersey and California decisions respectively.

83. People v. Goldberger, 163 N.Y.S. 663 (1916); People v. Atlas, 183 App. Div. 595; Hygrade Provision Co. v. Sherman, 266 U.S. 497 (1924).

84. *Hygrade Provision Co. v. Sherman, supra,* note 25.

85. *Ibid.,* 503.

86. 183 App. Div. (New York) 595, 603. See *supra,* note 26.

87. *Hygrade Provision Co. v. Sherman, supra,* 497.

88. *Ibid.*

89. *Ibid.,* 500.

90. *Ibid.,* 501.

91. Committee for Public Education v. Nyquist, 37 L. Ed. 2d 948, 956.

92. 374 F. Supp. 1284 (1947), certiorari denied by the U.S. Supreme Court, October 15, 1974.

93. Paragraph 27 of Plaintiffs' complaint.

94. Lemon v. Kurtzman, 403 U.S. 602, 612-613, 91 S. Ct. 2105, 2111 (1971).

95. Hunt v. McNair, 37 L. Ed. 2d 923 at 930. Chief Justice Burger in Tilton v. Richardson, 403 U.S. 672, 677-678 views the criteria "as guidelines."

96. Committee for Public Education v. Nyquist, 37 L. Ed. 2d 948 (1973).

97. 330 U.S. 1 (1947).

98. 392 U.S. 236 (1968).

99. 403 U.S. 672 (1971).

100. 330 U.S. at 17-18.

101. Committee for Public Education v. Nyquist, 37 L. Ed. 2d 948, at 964.

102. *Ibid.*

103. *Ibid.*

104. 330 U.S. 1 (1947).

105. 392 U.S. 236 (1968).

106. 413 U.S., 37 L. Ed. 2d 723 (1973).

107. Dissent of Chief Justice Burger, Committee for Public Education v. Nyquist, 37 L. Ed. 2d 948 at 980.

108. Dissent of Justice White, 37 L. Ed. 2d 948 at 987.

109. Dissent of Justice Rehnquist, 37 L. Ed. 2d 948 at 988, quoting in part from Walz v. Tax Commission, 397 U.S. 664 at 675.

110. 37 L. Ed. 2d 923 (1973).

111. 397 U.S. 664, 25 L. Ed. 2d 697, 90 S. Ct. 1409.

112. Lemon v. Kurtzman, 403 U.S. 602, 29 L. Ed. 2d 745, 91 S. Ct. 2105 (1971) (Lemon I) ; Earley v. DiCenso, 403 U.S. 613 (1971).

113. Tilton v. Richardson, 403 U.S. 672 (1971).

114. 37 L. Ed. 923.

115. *Ibid.*, 935-936, referring to South Carolina Code Ann. § 22-41. (Cum. Supp. 1971).

116. Committee for Public Education v. Nyquist, 37 L. Ed. 2d 948.

117. Sloan v. Lemon, 37 L. Ed. 2d 939 (1973).

118. 37 L. Ed. 2d 923.

119. 403 U.S. 672.

120. 37 L. Ed. 923 at 934.

121. 37 L. Ed. 2d 988.

122. 37 L. Ed. 2d 974.

123. *Ibid.*

124. Lemon v. Kurtzman, 403 U.S. 602 at 616, 29 L. Ed. 2d 745, 91 S. Ct. 2105 (1971).

125. *Ibid.*, at 619.

126. 397 U.S. 680, 690-691, 25 L. Ed. 2d 697 (1970).

127. See Chapter 2, p. 69.

128. Jones v. Butz, 374 F. Supp. 1284 (1974), certiorari denied by the U.S. Supreme Court, October 15, 1974.

129. 403 U.S. 602 (1971).

130. Jones v. Butz, 374 F. Supp. 1284 at 1289-1290. The claim is not unique. Several European countries, notably Switzerland (1893), Norway (1930), Sweden (1937), Nazi Germany and Fascist Italy have banned *shehita* on "humanitarian" grounds. *Encyclopedia Judaica*, Vol. 14, 1340-1341 (1971). See I. Lewin, *Religious Freedom: The Right to Practice Shehita* (New York, 1966).

131. Jones v. Butz, 374 F. Supp. 1284, at 1290.

132. *Ibid.*

133. *Ibid.*, at 1291.

134. *Ibid.*

135. *Ibid.*, at 1294.

136. Ill. Stat. Ann., Tit. 8 § 229.54.

137. 3 Purd. Pa. Stat. 451.52.

138. N.H. Rev. Stat. Ann. 575-A: 1 III [6].

139. Jewish concern with animal suffering in the shackling and hoisting procedure preparatory to the throat cut in *shechitah* is reflected in rabbinic efforts to develop special pens which restrain livestock in a more humane fashion. Rabbi Israel Klavan describes such efforts in an interview reported in *The New York Times*, Jan. 4, 1972, 67. In Jones v. Butz, 374 F. Supp. 1284 at 1290 the court records a statement of counsel for a Jewish organization appearing as an intervenor in the action: "In Israel, and indeed, in the old traditional Jewish method, the animal would be laying on its side, and the throat would be cut on the floor." Department of Agriculture regulations rule out this procedure for sanitary reasons and shackling and hoisting have been substituted to position the animal for slaughter.

140. Harold Gastwirt, in the preparation of his book, *Fraud, Corruption and Holiness* (Port Washington, N.Y., 1974), had access to the records of the kosher law enforcement squad of the New York City Department of Markets. In one prosecution *People v. Ideal Cake Company, Inc.* (1943), involving issues of whether pastry baked on the Sabbath could be kosher and whether a rabbi named as a conspirator was validly ordained, one of the Justices lamented in anguish, ". . . one rabbi disagrees with the other on one of the most important points in the whole case, with reference to the Conspiracy charge against the defendant Rabinowitz, and if they disagree on that, I am sure if we went into it further, I am sure they will disagree further and further—that has been our experience in these cases, you never get two to talk alike when you ask any of them questions regarding what is kosher and what is nonkosher." *Fraud, Corruption and Holiness*, ch. 8, 138-139. The accused conspirator was acquitted.

141. Reference to Jewish law still is attended with a certain defensiveness. Unlike their Puritan predecessors, today's American judges at times feel constrained to elaborately justify resort to it. In October, 1975, in Matter of Juan R., *N.Y. Law Journal*, October 28, 1975, 9, col. 5, a Kings County, New York, Family Court judge employed a principle of talmudic law in formulating his opinion. To forestall anticipated outcries against such sinister insinuation of Jewish law into the common law family, Judge Stanley Gartenstein takes pains to demonstrate Jewish law's legitimacy—and that by rights of parentage. Jewish law is the source of certain early common law practices and principles (see Chapter 1, pp. 2-3). For example: (1) The twenty-three grand jurors at common law may well derive from the twenty-three veniremen called for by the Talmud (Sanhedrin 2a and b); (2) "The equitable concept of construing a nominal deed of conveyance as a security of equitable interest and not absolutely in accordance with its written terms (see Leviticus 25, 13-16) is directly traceable to the Biblical injunction surrounding the Jubilee year that all conveyed property revert to its original owner, thus leading to the legal doctrine of considering deeds as leases until the Jubilee year and assessing a pro-rated purchase price accordingly." (3) The origin of filing and rcording, first practiced in furtherance of Hillel's *prosbol* device (see Chapter 1, p. 21), was precedent for "the Recording Act, centuries prior to the Domesday Book dating from the Norman Conquest of 1066 (see M. Gittin IV, 3; Shevi'it X 3)." (4) The common law real property doctrine "of incorporeal easements against the will of the record owner of real or personal property in furtherance of the public good" is foreshadowed in Tur H.M. 292; 20 Darke Moshe, "the ten conditions of Joshua in dividing

land." Baba Kamma 80B. On the basis of such "absorptions of Talmudic Law into the Common Law in its most formative stages," Judge Gartenstein found it "not unreasonable to assume that the very 'Rosetta Stone' of Talmudic exegesis wherein law was derived from text, history, custom and usage via thirteen principles of construction, played a major part in the development of classic rules of construction in the Common Law. These thirteen principles enunciated by Rabbi Ishmael in Sifra I are inclusive of any subsequent refinement and/or adoption in whole or in part thereof by the Common Law. The very first of them, the kal v'chomer holds that where a principle of law holds true of a major category, it most certainly applies to every minor category included therein." Applying this principle, Judge Gartenstein held the Family Court had a right, *a fortiori*, to entertain a petition by a putative father solely seeking child visitation rights where the Court had an unquestioned right to adjudicate and award the broader right of custody.

Addendum to note 18

On Thanksgiving eve, 1975, the Second Circuit Court of Appeals in Kahane v. Carlson, 75-2088, affirmed District Court Judge Weinstein's decision, modifying it to allow the Bureau of Prisons to supply the prisoner from its existing store of "fruit, vegetables, eggs, cheese, tinned fish and other regular prison supplies." *The New York Times*, Nov. 27, 1975, 66, col. 3. Rabbi Kahane had demanded special kosher TV dinners and fresh meat as a matter of right. The court held: "The dietary laws are an important, integral part of the covenant between the Jewish people and the God of Israel". As a matter of practical administration, the Court of Appeals found difficulties reduced by "the small number of practising Orthodox Jews in federal prisons (which the evidence indicated would not exceed approximately twelve) . . ." On Thanksgiving day Rabbi Kahane digested the appellate opinion and little else. He turned the Pilgrims' feast day to a personal fast day. The next day he relented and decided to eat again, according to *The New York Times* of November 29, 1975, when prison "officials arranged for separate pots, pans and other utensils and a special kosher nook in the prison kitchen."

INDEX

BIBLICAL

SUBJECT

A

Abel—145 n.38
Abiather—13
Abraham—41, 103 n.2; 106 n.21
Adams, John—36 n.83; 53, 211 n.78
additional ketubah—111 n.105
Adonijah—12
adoption—45, 46, 49, 50
adultery—4, 12, 13, 62, 63, 71, 84, 93, 94, 171 n.50
Agus, Jacob—147 n.86
Ahab—4, 30 n.13; 53
Akiba, Rabbi—47, 55
Aland, (Fortescue) Sir John—25
Alfasi, Isaac—117 n.232
Alfred, King—3, 26, 27
algebra—55
aljamas—142 n.13
Amish—56, 109 n.71
anatomy—55
Ancona—35 n.73
Anglican Church—27, 78
Anglo-Saxon law—82
animals—9, 32 n.24; 56, 176, 177, 188, 199, 200, 204 notes 8, 11; 205 n.16; 208 n.71; 213 n.139
annulment—65, 66, 67
antenuptial agreement—45, 65-68, 76, 78
Antiochus—40, 41, 121
Aragon—35 n.73
Aramaic—55
Arbella—ix
arbitration—48, 49, 120, 124-126, 143 n.14
Ari—139
Aristotle—151
Arizona—206 n.31
Arkansas—206 n.31
Asher, Rabbi—209 n.71
Asherah—30 n.13
Ashkanazi—139

B

astronomy—54, 55
atheism—107 n.36
Australian divorce law—112 n.120
Austria—69, 89

Baal Melcarth—30 n.13
Babylonia—122
Bacon, Francis—2, 142 n.5
bailment—27
bankruptcy—147 n.77
Baptism—41, 109 n.71
Baptist Church—138
Bar Kochba—41
bar mitzvah—40, 109 n.71
Bathsheba—13
Ben Porath, Amihud I.—146 n.62
Berman, Ronald—31 n.19
Bet Din (rabbinical court)—23, 71, 73-84, 108 n.59; 113 n.121; 115 n.175; 119-137; 143 n.16; 144 n.22; 163, 180, 191, 192, 198, 201, 207 n.40; 210 n.78
bigamist—95
Blackstone—34 n.53; 117 n.232; 144 n.24
blasphemy—ix, 9, 27, 28, 46, 143 n.16
Board of Regents—51-53, 60
Body of Liberties—8-10, 13, 14, 16, 17, 23, 32 n.24
Bolingbroke—36 n.83
Booth, A.—3
Borchsenius, Poul—103 n.2
Boston—123, 130-131, 143 n.14
Boston Club—108 n.59
Bracton—34-35 n.53
Brandeis, Justice Louis D.—193
Brazil, divorce law—112 n.120
bribery—142 n.13
Brindisium—116 n.191
Britain, divorce law—112 n.120
British Shops Act—157, 170 n.32

218

CASE

A

Agur v. Agur, 32 App.Div. 2d 16, 298 N.Y.S. 2d 772 (1969)—48, 108 n.48-52, 125-126, 144-145 n.30-32

Albeg v. Albeg, 259 App. Div. 744, 18 N.Y.S. 2d 719 (1940)—86, 115 n.179

Anonymous, 12 Abbot's New Cases 455 (1882)—170 n.32

Application of the Agudath Hakehiloth of New York, 18 Misc. 717 (1896)—163-164, 172 n.63-64

Atkins et ux v. Hill, Cowp 284—144 n.23

Auster v. Weberman, 278 App. Div. 656, 102 N.Y.S. 2d 418, affd 302 N.Y. 855, 100 N.E. 2d 47, 342 U.S. 844, 72 S.Ct. 178, 96 L. Ed. 663—61, 110 n.84

B

Baldwin v Winer, 216 N.Y.S.2d 153 (1961)—173 n.73

Battalla v. State of New York, 10 N.Y. 2d 237 (1961)—106 n.20, 107 n.28

Beck & Schachter Co. v. Kohn, N.Y. Law Journal, Jan. 7, 1975, 2, col. 2—144 n.22

Beller v. City of New York, 269 App. Div. 642—106 n.27

Berk v. Berk, 8 Misc. 2d 732, 171 N.Y.S. 2d 592 (1957)—126, 145 n.33-34

Berman et al v. Shatnes Laboratory et al, 43 App. Div. 736, 350 N.Y.S. 2d 703 (1973)—127, 145 n.36, 146 n.41

Blair v. Union Free School District #6, Hauppauge, 324 N.Y.S. 2d 222 (1971)—43, 106 n.18, 107 n.31, 32

Blake v. Pryse, 44 F.2d 218 (1971)—205 n.18

Application of Bleistift, 193 App. Div. 477 (1920)—102, 118 n.244

Bloom v. New York City Transit Authority, 31 Misc. 2d 805, 220 N.Y.S. 2d 621, revd 19 App. Div. 2d 521, 240 N.Y.S. 2d 124 (1961)—164-165, 172 n.69

Board of Education v. Allen, 392 U.S. 236 (1968)—195, 212 n.98, 212 n.105

Braun v. Armour & Co., 254 N.Y. 514—211 n.79

Braunfeld v. Brown, 366 U.S. 599, 81 S.Ct. 1144, 6 L. Ed. 2d 563 (1961)—168 n.20, 169 n.28-31, 170 n.32, 45

Brett v. Brett, 1 W.L.R. 487 (1969)—79, 114 n.140

Brooks v. Wainwright, 428 F.2d 652 (1970)—205 n.18

Brown v. Wainwright, 419 F.2d 1276 (1970)—205 n.18

Ex parte Burke, 59 Cal. 6, 19 (1881)—171 n.48

Burtis v. Burtis, 1 Hopkins 557 (N.Y. 1825)—104 n.5

Byam v. Collins, 111 N.Y. 143, 19 N.E. 75, 2 L.R.A. 129—211 n.80

C

Cabinet v. Shapiro, 17 N.J. Super. 540, 86 A.2d 314 (1952)—127, 145 n.35, 188-189, 192, 208 n.65-67, 210 n.78, 211 n.82

In re Cassin's Estate, 126 N.Y.S. 2d 363 (1953)—69, 111 n.84

In re Chaikin, 238 App. Div. 211, 264 N.Y.S. 221 (1933)—165, 172 n.71

Chaplinsky v. State of New Hampshire, 315 U.S. 568, 62 S.Ct. 766, 86 L.Ed. 1031—61, 109 n.82

Chapman v. Chapman, 269 Mo. 663, 192 S.W. 448 (1917)—104 n.5

Chertok v. Chertok, 208 App. Div. 161, 203 N.Y.S. 163 (1924)—86, 115 n.177

227